The Call of the Wild

The American Culture

NEIL HARRIS—General Editor

I   **REMARKABLE PROVIDENCES: 1600–1760**
John Demos, Brandeis University

II   **THE RISING GLORY: 1760–1820**
Gordon S. Wood, Brown University

III   **NOTIONS OF THE AMERICANS: 1820–1860**
David Grimsted, University of Maryland

IV   **DEMOCRATIC VISTAS: 1860–1880**
Alan Trachtenberg, Pennsylvania State University

V   **THE LAND OF CONTRASTS: 1880–1901**
Neil Harris, University of Chicago

VI   **THE CALL OF THE WILD: 1900–1916**
Roderick Nash, University of California

VII   **THE PLASTIC AGE: 1917–1930**
Robert Sklar, University of Michigan

VIII   **CULTURE AND COMMITMENT: 1929–1945**
Warren Susman, Rutgers University

THE CALL OF THE WILD

(1900–1916)

Edited,
with Introduction and Notes by

Roderick Nash

George Braziller   New York

Standard Book Number: 0–8076–0552–2, cloth; 0–8076–0551–4, paper
Library of Congress Catalog Card Number: 74–104699
Designed by Jennie Bush   7-/1-77
FIRST PRINTING
Printed in the United States of America

Acknowledgments

The editor and publisher wish to thank the following for permission to reprint certain materials in this book:

Mrs. Samuel Crowther—for a selection from *My Life and Work,* by Henry Ford and Samuel Crowther.

Holt, Rinehart & Winston, Inc.—for "Chicago," by Carl Sandburg.

Mr. Nicholas C. Lindsay—for selections from *The Art of the Moving Picture,* by Vachel Lindsay.

The Macmillan Company: Free Press of Glencoe—for "General William Booth Enters Into Heaven," by Vachel Lindsay.

The New Republic—for *Ragtime,* by Hiram K. Moderwell.

Penguin Books Ltd.—for a selection from *The Penguin Book of American Folk Songs,* edited by Alan Lomax.

Sources of the visual materials used in this book are acknowledged in the contents (illustrations), and the editor and publisher wish to thank the various individuals, museums, and publishers indicated for permission to use these materials.

070757

Preface

"Do not tell me only of the magnitude of your industry and commerce," wrote Matthew Arnold during his visit to the United States in the 1890's; "of the beneficence of your institutions, your freedom, your equality: of the great and growing number of your churches and schools, libraries and newspapers; tell me also if your civilization—which is the grand name you give to all this development—tell me if your civilization is *interesting*."

The various volumes that comprise THE AMERICAN CULTURE series attempt to answer Matthew Arnold's demand. The term "culture," of course, is a critical modern concept. For many historians, as for many laymen, the word has held a limited meaning: the high arts of painting, sculpture, literature, music, architecture; their expression, patronage, and consumption. But in America, where physical mobility and ethnic diversity have been so crucial, this conception of culture is restricting. The "interesting" in our civilization is omitted if we confine ourselves to the formal arts.

The editors of THE AMERICAN CULTURE, therefore, have cast a wider net. They have searched for fresh materials to reconstruct the color and variety of our cultural heritage, spanning a period of more than three hundred years. Forgotten institutions, buried artifacts, and outgrown experiences are included in these books, along with some of the sights and sounds that reflected the changing character of American life.

The raw data alone, however fascinating, are not sufficient for the task of cultural reconstruction. Each editor has organized his material around definitions and assumptions which he explores in the volume introductions. These introductions are essays in their own right; they can be read along with the documents, or they can stand as independent explorations into social history. No one editor presents the same kind of approach; commitments and emphases vary from volume to volume. Together, however, these volumes represent a unified effort to restore to historical study the texture of life as it was lived, without sacrificing theoretical rigor or informed scholarship.

NEIL HARRIS

Contents

PREFACE/vii

INTRODUCTION–*Roderick Nash*/1

I ENVIRONMENT

1. The Birth of the Boy Scouts/19
   Boy Scouts of America—Ernest Thompson Seton/19

2. The Dilemma of Urban Growth/26
   The Drift to the Cities—G. S. Dickerman/26
   Advantages—Mark Jefferson/30

3. Rejuvenation Through Conservation/36
   Conservation of Natural Resources—Theodore Roosevelt/36

4. The Virtues of Nature/46
   The Need of Conserving the Beauty and Freedom of Nature in
   —Charles W. Eliot/46

5. Environmental Tastes/53
   Illustrations/54

6. Rural Uplift and Nature Education/60
   Country Life—Liberty Hyde Bailey/60
   Nature Study—Liberty Hyde Bailey/65

7. Responses to the Vanishing Frontier/69
   The Frontier Gone at Last—Frank Norris/69
   The Wilderness—George S. Evans/75

8. Fundamental Frontier Virtues/79
   The Strenuous Life—Theodore Roosevelt/79

9. Use *Versus* Beauty/85
   The Hetch Hetchy Dam Site—U. S. Congress/86

II ARTS

10. Styles of Decoration and Design/99
    Illustrations/100

11. Wealth Against Taste/106
    The Poor Taste of the Rich—Anonymous/106

12. Conflicting Philosophies of Architecture/115
    The Ministry of Art—Ralph Adams Cram/115
    In the Cause of Architecture—Frank Lloyd Wright/119

13. Buildings and Values/123
    Illustrations/124

14. Literary Rebellion/132
    Mush for the Multitude—Henry L. Mencken/132

15. Rebellion in Music/137
    Ragtime—Hiram K. Moderwell/137

16. Rebellion in Poetry/141
    Two Editorials—Harriet Monroe/141
    General William Booth Enters Into Heaven—Vachel Lindsay/145
    Chicago—Carl Sandburg/147

17. An Art Is Born/149
    Motion Pictures (Stills)/150

18. The Potential of Motion Pictures/158
    The Art of the Moving Picture—Vachel Lindsay/158

19. The Response to "Modern" Art/171
  The "Modern" Spirit in Art—Kenyon Cox/171
  The Post-Impressionist Illusion—Royal Cortissoz/175
  The International Exhibition of Modern Art—W. D. MacColl/179
  A Layman's View of an Art Exhibition—Theodore Roosevelt/184

20. Rebellion in Painting/189
  Illustrations/190

III WORK AND PLAY

21. The New Humor/203
  The German Senator—Aaron Hoffman/203
  The American Sense of Humor—Katherine Roof/209

22. Comic Strips and Cartoon Art/215
  Illustrations/216

23. The Searchlight of Satire/222
  Gullible's Travels—Ring Lardner/222

24. Heroes of Popular Fiction/240
  The Virginian—Owen Wister/241
  Frank Merriwell at Yale—Burt L. Standish/244
  Tarzan of the Apes—Edgar Rice Burroughs/250

25. The Showgirl/256
  Picking Out Pretty Girls for the Stage—Florenz Ziegfeld, Jr./256

26. Motor Sports/266
  Up Mount Hamilton on a Motor Cycle—Walter H. Burr/266

27. The Sport of Scandal/272
  Thaw-White Murder—The New York Times/272

28. Refinements in Advertising Technique/286
  Illustrations/287

29. Why They Play Ball/294
  Baseball and the National Life—Addington H. Bruce/294

30. The Gospel of Production/301
     My Life and Work—Henry Ford/301

31. Patterns of Work and Play/314
     Illustrations/315

32. Men and Machines/320
     John Henry/321
     Casey Jones/324
     Paul Bunyan and His Big Blue Ox/325

SELECTED BIBLIOGRAPHY/330

Illustrations

ENVIRONMENTAL TASTES/53

1. Transforming the Landscape: Sluicing down Seattle's hills in 1907. *Library of Congress.*

2. The Synthetic Skyline: Pittsburgh, 1909. Photograph by Lewis W. Hine. *George Eastman House Collection.*

3. People in Cities: Slum backyard about 1910. Photograph by Lewis W. Hine. *George Eastman House Collection.*

4. Green Belts: Park system proposed for Washington, D.C., 1901. George F. Chadwick, *The Park and the Town (New York, F. A. Praeger, 1966).*

5. Beautification: Landscaped railroad station, St. David's, Pennsylvania. *Nineteenth Annual Report of the American Scenic and Historic Preservation Society (Albany, State of New York, 1914).*

6. The Visible Past: Pioneer cabin, Letchworth Park, New York. *Nineteenth Annual Report of the American Scenic and Historic Preservation Society (Albany, State of New York, 1914).*

7. Historical Landmarks and Patriotism: Restored barracks, Fort Ticonderoga, New York. *Eighteenth Annual Report of the American Scenic and Historic Preservation Society (Albany, State of New York, 1913).*

8. Nature as History: 225-year-old Inwood tulip tree, Spuyten Duyvil Creek near the Hudson River, New York. *Eighteenth Annual Report of the American Scenic and Historic Preservation Society (Albany, State of New York, 1913).*

STYLES OF DECORATION AND DESIGN/99

1. The Ornate: Lewis C. Tiffany, hand mirror, about 1900. William Harvey Pierson, Jr., and Martha Davidson, eds., *Arts of the United States (New York, McGraw-Hill, 1960).*

2. The Functional: Eastwood Manufacturing Company, valve handle, about 1900. *New York Public Library photograph.*

3. The Ostentatious I: Second landing of the Grand Staircase, "Biltmore," Ashville, North Carolina. *Biltmore House and Gardens (Ashville, N.C., The Biltmore Co., 1965).*

4. The Ostentatious II: Library, "Biltmore," Ashville, North Carolina. *Biltmore House and Gardens (Ashville, N.C., The Biltmore Co., 1965).*

5. The Ostentatious III: Banquet Hall, "Biltmore," Ashville, North Carolina. *Biltmore House and Gardens (Ashville, N.C., The Biltmore Co., 1965).*

6. Survival: Slum kitchen about 1910. Photograph by Lewis W. Hine. *George Eastman House Collection.*

7. The Clean Line: Living room, Avery Coonley residence by Frank Lloyd Wright, Riverside, Illinois. *Chicago Architectural Photographing Company.*

8. The Deliberately Primitive: Living room, Frank Lloyd Wright's Taliesin I, Spring Green, Wisconsin. *Chicago Architectural Photographing Company.*

BUILDINGS AND VALUES/123

1. Palaces for the Very Rich: "Biltmore," Ashville, North Carolina, 1895, by Richard Morris Hunt. Wayne Andrews, *Architecture in America (New York, Atheneum, 1960).*

2. Gothic Imitation: Graduate College, Princeton, New Jersey, 1911–1913, by Ralph Adams Cram. *University Prints, Boston.*

3. Greek Imitation: Lincoln Memorial, Washington, D.C., 1917, by Henry Bacon. *University Prints, Boston.*

4. The Baroque: Clark Mansion, New York City, 1901–1903. *University Prints, Boston.*

5. Toward Functionalism: Carson Pirie Scott Store, Chicago, 1904, by Louis Sullivan; detail of doorway ornament. Wayne Andrews, *Architecture in America (New York, Atheneum, 1960).*

6. Functionalism: Larkin Building, Buffalo, New York, 1903, by Frank Lloyd Wright. *University Prints, Boston.*

7. F. C. Robie Residence, Chicago, Illinois, 1909, by Frank Lloyd Wright. *Chicago Architectural Photographing Company.*

8. Blending with the Landscape: Taliesin I, Spring Green, Wisconsin, 1911–1914, by Frank Lloyd Wright. *Chicago Architectural Photographing Company.*

9. Naturalness: Exterior detail, Taliesin I, Spring Green, Wisconsin, 1911–1914, by Frank Lloyd Wright. *Chicago Architectural Photographing Company.*

AN ART IS BORN: MOTION PICTURES/149

1. The Potential of the Camera: "The Steerage, 1907" by Alfred Stieglitz. Beaumont Newhall, *The History of Photography* (*New York, Museum of Modern Art, 1949*).
2. Primitive Melodrama: "The Great Train Robbery" (1903). *Museum of Modern Art Film Stills Archive, New York City.*
3. "Perils of Pauline" (1914). *Larry Edmunds Bookshop, Hollywood, California.*
4. The Director as Artist: "Birth of a Nation" (1915) directed by David Wark Griffith. *Larry Edmunds Bookshop, Hollywood, California.*
5. The Hollywood Treatment: "Intolerance" (1916) directed by David Wark Griffith. *Larry Edmunds Bookshop, Hollywood, California.*
6. The Little Guy: Charlie Chaplin in "The Tramp" (1915). *Museum of Modern Art Film Stills Archive, New York City.*
7. The Comic Art: Charlie Chaplin throttles a thug in "Easy Street" (1917). *Larry Edmunds Bookshop, Hollywood, California.*
8. Cowboy as Hero: Tom Mix in a publicity still. *Larry Edmunds Bookshop, Hollywood, California.*
9. Primitivism: Elmo Lincoln, the first movie Tarzan, in "Tarzan of the Apes" (1918). *Larry Edmunds Bookshop, Hollywood, California.*
10. The Spectrum of Heroines: Mary Pickford and Theda Bara. *Larry Edmunds Bookshop, Hollywood, California.*

REBELLION IN PAINTING/189

1. The Traditional: John Singer Sargent, "Mrs. William Crowninshield Endicott" (1901). *National Gallery of Art, Washington, D.C.*
2. William Merritt Chase, "Blue Kimono" (1902). *Berkeley, Regents of the University of California, 1964.*
3. Saloons in Art: John Sloan, "McSorley's Bar" (1912). *Detroit Institute of Arts.*
4. The City Scene: John Sloan, "Backyards, Greenwich Village" (1914). *Whitney Museum of American Art, New York City.*
5. Raw Power: George Bellows, "Stag at Sharkey's" (1909). *The Hinman B. Hurlbut Collection, Cleveland Museum of Art.*
6. Ash Can Realism: George Bellows, "The Steaming Streets" (1908). *Preston Morton Collection, Santa Barbara Museum of Art.*
7. Cubism: Marcel Duchamp, "Nude Descending a Staircase" (1912). *Philadelphia Museum of Art.*

8. Abstraction: Max Weber, "Chinese Restaurant" (1915).

9. Arthur G. Dove, "Plant Forms" (1915). *Whitney Museum of American Art, New York City.*

10. Advanced Expressionism: John Marin, "Movement, Fifth Avenue" (1912). *Alfred Stieglitz Collection, Art Institute of Chicago.*

11. The Discovery of Order and Beauty in Modern Civilization: Joseph Stella, "Battle of Lights, Coney Island" (1913). *Yale University Art Gallery, Gift of the Société Anonyme.*

12. Stella, "Brooklyn Bridge" (1917–1918). *Wright Ludington Collection, Santa Barbara, California.*

13. Stella, "New York Interpreted—The Bridge" (1922). *Newark Museum.*

COMIC STRIPS AND CARTOON ART/215

1. A Reversal of Roles and a Moral: Richard F. Outcault, "Buster Brown." Editors of Time-Life Books, *This Fabulous Century: Sixty Years of American Life, Vol. I, 1900–1910 (New York, Time-Life Books, 1969).*

2. A Fantasy World: George Herriman, "Krazy Kat." George Herriman, *Krazy Kat (New York, Henry Holt and Co., 1946).*

3. The Eternal Optimist: George Herriman, "Krazy Kat." Pierre Couperie and Maurice C. Horn, *A History of the Comic Strip (New York, Crown Publishers, 1968).*

4. Cartoons and Social Issues: W. O. Wilson in *Judge* (1904) and Robert Minor in *The Masses* (1915). Thomas Craven, ed., *Cartoon Cavalcade (Chicago, Consolidated Book Publishers, 1945).*

5. The Gibson Girl: Charles Dana Gibson in *Collier's* (1903). Thomas Craven, ed., *Cartoon Cavalcade (Chicago, Consolidated Book Publishers, 1945).*

REFINEMENTS IN ADVERTISING TECHNIQUE/286

1. Simply Performance: "The Oldsmobile 'Goes,'" *Life, 42 (Nov. 5 1903).*

2. The Suburban Routine: "Maxwell 'Mascotte,'" *Life, 59 (March 21, 1912).*

3. The Cost of Respectability: "Lozier," *Life, 59 (May 23, 1912).*

4. Beauty as Function: "The Evolution of the Peerless," *Life, 61 (June 5, 1913).*

5. Self-expression Through Consumption: "The owner of a Pierce-Arrow," *Life, 62 (August 7, 1913).*

6. Practicality: "The New Studebaker," *Life, 67 (Jan. 27, 1916).*

7. Auto as Art: "Simplex," *Life, 67 (Feb. 3, 1916).*

PATTERNS OF WORK AND PLAY/314

1. The Assembly Line: The Ford Motor Company plant at Highland Park, Michigan, 1914. John B. Rae, *The Early American Automobile: A Brief History (Chicago, University of Chicago Press, 1965).*

2. On the Line: Magneto "feeder" assembly line, Ford Motor Company, Highland Park, Michigan, 1914. Allan Nevins and Frank Ernest Hill, *Ford: The Times, the Man, the Company (New York, Charles Scribner's Sons, 1954).*

3. The Sweatshop: New York garment factory, about 1912. Photograph by Lewis W. Hine. *George Eastman House Collection.*

4. The Modern Pioneer: Theodore Roosevelt in the Dakotas. Hermann Hagedorn, *Roosevelt in the Bad Lands (Boston, Houghton Mifflin Co., 1921).*

5. A New Woman: Eleanora Sears belts a forehand. *Wide World Photos.*

6. Wilderness Recreation: The Sierra Club's Tenth Annual Outing on the trail. *Sierra Club Bulletin, 8 (Jan., 1911).*

7. Nature and Civilization: Cars outside the National Park Inn at Mt. Rainier about 1916. Department of the Interior, *National Parks Portfolio (Washington, D.C., Government Printing Office, c. 1917).*

Introduction

RODERICK NASH

Jack London's *The Call of the Wild* was published in 1903. It was an immediate best seller and thirty years later it still ranked as the seventh most widely read American novel of the time.

London wrote of a huge dog, part St. Bernard and part shepherd, who was stolen from his master's lush California ranch and sold to the Klondike to haul sleds. The reader's first reaction is anger and pity, but it is short-lived. Exposed to the primitive conditions of the Far North, Buck gradually sheds his domesticated habits and becomes a superdog. His muscles grow tough under the discipline of the long trail; his repressive "moral" nature withers away. The ancient instinct of self-preservation springs alive to bring Buck through a variety of crises. The fierce joy of "sheer surging life" returns. Gradually California is forgotten, and "the dominant primordial beast" emerges. At the end of the book one is compelled to join the author in a paean to Buck, now reverted to the wolf, "running at the head of the pack through the pale moonlight or glimmering borealis, leaping gigantic above his fellows, his great throat a-bellow as he sings a song of the younger world." There is no doubt that Jack London felt it was also a *better* world. Indeed by exchanging civilization for wilderness, Buck had attained the "summit of life."

The popularity of a book like *The Call of the Wild* is one of the windows through which the cultural historian peers at the past. He sees a complex montage. No aspect of the human experience is irrelevant to his task of delineating the shared patterns of thought and behavior that characterize a slice of time. But if the historian of culture is blessed with abundant evidence, he is also confronted with a mind-boggling task of selection, interpretation, and generalization. The meaning of a document must be determined, and this often entails understanding the ambivalence, if not the outright contradictions, it reflects. One must also decide what level of the culture under consideration is being expressed.

This involves distinguishing the official, established form from the work of rebellious, innovative minds, and then distinguishing both from popular or folk culture. Frequently this three-way tension becomes the battleground for the backward and forward-looking parts of the national mind. Problems of regional, vocational, and ethnic variation also demand attention. The question of representativeness—how many Americans *really* shared a particular attitude—haunts the cultural historian. Finally, after taking the pattern apart, he must put it all back together again; after establishing the significance of the various components, he must hazard a guess about the whole. The result, ideally, is insight into what made an era tick—a portrait of its hopes and fears, likes and dislikes, values and traditions.

In the case of *The Call of the Wild* the significance is comparatively clear. The book is an allegory; it deals with dogs but pertains to men. In describing Buck's progress from tameness to wildness, the author passed judgment on his contemporaries. They too, he implied, suffered from overcivilization, and in the early 1900's the idea struck a sympathetic chord. For many the growth and change of the United States over the previous hundred years seemed to have brought not the millennium once expected but rather a state of confusion, corruption, and debilitating abundance. For such people, Buck's simple, vigorous, unrestrained life in the North was very appealing. As the twentieth century dawned, the nation found itself drawn toward virility, toward novelty, toward nature. Significantly, London's *White Fang* (1906), in which a wolf became a family dog, never enjoyed the popularity of *The Call of the Wild*.

The enthusiasm of many Americans for Buck's reversion to the primitive points the way to a general interpretation of American culture in the early twentieth century. A middle-aged mood prevailed; the nation, after all, was no longer young. It had passed through its heyday of continent-striding growth and was, as Van Wyck Brooks wrote in 1915, "coming of age." The upshot was both outward confidence and inward uneasiness. Even in the midst of celebrations of progress, moral absolutism, and Anglo-Saxon cultural superiority (Henry May's "nineteenth century credo"), the feeling could not be downed that the American culture had seen its greatest moments. The biological metaphor of middle age was apt. Could not the curving pattern of rise and decline in individual lives, also apply to the life of the nation? Did not decline and decay inevitably follow a flowering?

This realization, or rather this mood, influenced many aspects of turn-of-the-century thought and behavior. The frontier, or wilderness, had been the preeminent symbol of the youth and potential of the new nation. People did not have to study Frederick Jackson Turner to realize that frontier conditions were on the wane. With its wild country largely developed, American civilization was no longer becoming; it had become. Unprepared to accept the implications of change, people grew critical of the urban environment, nostalgic for a return to nature. If the Klondike, or big game hunting in Africa, was beyond the reach of most, there were the suburbs or summer camping or even country clubs. Popular aspirations tended toward nature in proportion to its decreasing role in American life.

In scholarship and the arts, the first two decades of the present century witnessed a search for newer, "wilder" forms—a "revolt against formalism" in Morton White's words, the "end of American innocence" in Henry May's. Norms long considered as fixed were closely scrutinized and often discarded. Impatient with cultural middle age, many artists and writers pursued the untraditional. The resulting clash with the proponents of older styles and values became one of the period's major intellectual dialogues.

Another symptom of change was the growth of the American economy to the point where it was viewed as a threat to the effectiveness of the individual. Machines displaced men, and the mass undermined the importance of the singular, as did the increasingly complex forms of economic organization and urban living that accompanied industrialization. Work, on the assembly line, assumed quite a different significance than it had on a farm or at an artisan's bench. Their individuality challenged, people sought ways of reasserting themselves in their leisure-time activities and, vicariously, in their choice of heroes. Sports offered a chance for individual glory. If one could not participate effectively himself, he could pay to watch others enact a ritualistic celebration of the major components of the national faith. Alternatively, the beleaguered "little man" could identify and commiserate with pathetic characters like the cartoon protagonist, Krazy Kat, or Charlie Chaplin's tramp.

The reform enthusiasm of the Progressives was also symptomatic of American middle age. Uplift and efficiency, bywords of the movement, seem today not so much the expression of confidence as the admission of concern. The new expanding nation had no thought of conservation, but it became a household word in the Progressive era.

Good, fat, and cocksure as the years between 1900 and 1916 were, the rosy glow could not entirely obscure a deep, almost subconscious anxiety which revealed itself in the compulsive urge to prove the national vitality and to heed the multi-faceted call of the wild. Undoubtedly this observation would have been heatedly denied at the time, but the denial only supports the diagnosis.

Consider the American culture in, say, 1913:

August 4; Spencer Lake, Maine: A group of men crouching in an open boat lower their heads into a cold drizzle. After landing on the far shore, one begins to shed his clothes. Stark naked at last, he nonchalantly shakes hands with the others, lights a last cigarette and, with a final wave, disappears into the wilderness.

Joe Knowles proposed to live off the land, in complete isolation, for sixty days. Whether he did so in fact or not, the report of his saga made headlines throughout the East and as far away as Kansas City. Delighted Americans learned by way of birchbark letters (written in charcoal and left under a prearranged stump) of his success in catching trout, dispatching deer, and even killing a bear. He also found time to philosophize on birchbark. "According to my opinion," one letter declared, "the way the world is living at present is entirely wrong. Civilization has carried us along to a point where . . . we are accepting an artificial life rather than a natural one. Commercialism and the mad desire to make money have blotted out everything else, and as a result we are not living, but merely existing."

On October 4, a disheveled but healthy Joe Knowles emerged from the Maine woods extolling the values of his primitive way of life. Immediately, a wave of public acclaim engulfed him. A huge crowd jammed Boston's North Station to mark the return of "the modern primitive man." Clad in a bearskin, he was driven through the cheering throng to Boston Common where an estimated 20,000 persons waited. His speech was disappointingly brief, but the audience thrilled, according to one newspaper account, at the way he leaped onto the podium with "the quick, graceful movements of a tiger."

In the next few days Joe Knowles even upstaged an exciting World Series. At Harvard, physicians reported on the excellence of his physical condition, and there were numerous interviews—one with the governor of Massachusetts—and banquets. "There is too much refinement," one toastmaster exclaimed. "It leads to degeneration. My friend Knowles has taught us how to live on nothing. It is better than living on too much. We should all get down to nature."

Publishers besieged "the modern primitive" for the rights to a book about his experience. Entitled *Alone In the Wilderness,* it sold some

300,000 copies, and he toured the vaudeville circuit with top billing. The Boston *Post* published full page color reproductions of his paintings of wild animals, pointing out that they were suitable for framing and "just the thing to hang in your den." When a rival newspaper presented evidence that Knowles was a fraud whose wilderness adventure actually occurred in a secret, snug cabin, a vociferous denial arose in reply.

Obviously Americans wanted to believe in the authenticity of the "Nature Man." The important question is "Why?," and the answer lies in the mood that prevailed in 1913.

On the one hand there was a feeling of confidence, of pride in the progress of the previous century that had transformed wilderness into civilization. But there was also widespread uneasiness. Progress had brought not only comfort, power, and affluence but also a host of frustrating problems. A flood of immigrants seemed to be diluting the American strain and weakening native traditions. Business values and urban conditions appeared to be undermining character, taste, and morality. Many wondered, with Turner, if democratic ideals had gathered enough momentum during the frontier period "to sustain themselves under conditions so radically unlike those in the days of their origin." Beneath the optimism, then, the sobering belief persisted that the growth and change of the past century had not been entirely for the better.

In this context Joe Knowles' feat had several significances. He reminded his contemporaries that they still lived in a country young and new enough to have considerable wilderness, and that they could survive by brain and brawn, the way their forefathers did. He had relied on no machines whatsoever, not even a knife or a match. His fellow Americans could forget their anxieties. Members of a sophisticated civilization they might be, but instincts and abilities still lived in them. In applauding Knowles, people paid tribute to what they hoped was true of themselves. If they had to, they could still survive in the wilderness alone. Such knowledge was of no small importance to a society worried about becoming overcivilized.

Knowles, a kind of real life Buck, had not only survived but flourished in the wilderness. According to his own belief and the widely-publicized reports of physicians, the two months in the woods had actually improved his health. He returned tanned, confident, and carefree. It seemed to his urban observers as if he had found the much-discussed and much-coveted simple life. In returning to nature, moreover, he claimed he had drawn closer to God. His primitivism, in sum, represented prescription as well as protest for his generation.

February 17, 1913; New York City: Looking up for a moment at the enthusiastic activity that was transforming the somber Sixty-ninth Regiment Armory into an art gallery, Arthur B. Davies could smile in satisfaction. Only six years before, the genteel National Academy of Design, self-styled arbiter of American art, had refused to exhibit the radical young painters he most admired. Indignantly Davies arranged a small show for eight of the outcasts at the Macbeth Gallery in New York. And now, from the partitioned floor of the massive Armory, he prepared to launch a further assault on the unbending cultural establishment. With the opening that night, Davies mused, rebellion would shake American art to its foundations.

The aim of the insurgent Association of American Painters and Sculptors, over which Davies presided, was to champion "modern" art. It was not an easy task. At the turn of the century the country's artistic apparatus—galleries, academies, patronage, commissions—was firmly in the hands of the conservatives. Doting on European models and disparaging anything native as well as anything new, the artists and critics associated with the National Academy cultivated a quiet, refined offshoot of French Impressionism. Subject matter was strictly "polite" and the feelings of the artist something to be kept out of the painting. The insipid and overpolished art that resulted was the essence of pale, genteel aestheticism.

Bleak as the future looked in 1900 for artistic innovation in the United States, the next decade and a half saw the momentum swing its way. Indeed the intellectual life of the nation as a whole began to simmer and boil as writers and artists sought to shake off the stuffy respectability of cultural middle age. Innovation in art received considerable support from the rebellious spirit in other fields. The poetry renaissance, naturalism in the novel, experimental theater and dance, jazz, functional architecture, the daring "little" magazines even the politics of the Progressive era served iconoclasm. The call of the wild and the ensuing passion for freedom moved a large part of the nation's intellectual community.

One of the first results, so far as painting was concerned, and a milestone on the road to the Armory Show, was the 1905 opening of the Little Gallery of the Photo-Secession by Alfred Stieglitz at 291 Fifth Avenue, New York City. "291," as it was known among the initiates, quickly gained a reputation as a purveyor of the new "pictorial" photography—the work of men who put film and cameras to artistic purposes. In 1908 Stieglitz began to exhibit the works of radical European painters such as Rodin and Matisse. The gallery also gave a semblance of institutional support to

American artists who dared to be different. Any participant in or sympa-thizer with the rebellion from traditional aesthetics and ideas could count on finding kindred spirits at "291." Stieglitz declared his rooms open to any medium providing it had "honesty of aim, honesty of self-expression, honesty of revolt against the autocracy of convention." He particularly favored the trend away from objective realism and toward deliberate distortion of natural forms and colors. The aim was a more accurate portrayal of the emotions and values of the individual artist. This was expressionism, an essential element in the modernist movement.

Another criterion for modernism was a willingness to paint subject matter that the establishment would have considered beyond the pale. The American avant-garde included a group of Philadelphia newspaper illustrators turned artists. John Sloan, George Luks, Everett Shinn, Wil-liam Glackens and their unofficial mentor, Robert Henri, had all kept the wolf from the door with hack journalism drawing. In this capacity they were accustomed to sketching the commonplace. When they changed from pen and ink to brush and paint, they saw no reason to alter their subject. If there was beauty in the lives of ordinary people living in cities, they would capture it; if there was ugliness they would portray it honestly.

Prizefighters and chorus girls, bars, bedrooms, and back alleys appeared so often in the work of these painters they were given the label "Ash Can School." Hostile critics called them "the black revolutionary gang" or "the apostles of ugliness." But the insurgents were not easily discouraged. Some shared the sustaining faith of the socialists and regarded their canvasses as contributions to the cause. For others it was enough to tweak the beard of the custodians of official culture. "Art, my slats!," roared the flamboyant Luks: "Guts! Guts! Life! Life! That's *my* technique!"

The Armory Show gave the Ash Can School and the "291" group their day in the sun. Of the 1600 pieces of sculpture, paintings, drawings, and prints exhibited, America furnished three-quarters. This itself was news in a nation accustomed to assume the posture of a gawky schoolboy in relation to European art. The European art exhibited in the Armory was startlingly different from what Americans were used to seeing. They got their first concentrated dose of Picasso, Matisse, Van Gogh, and Gaugin and other breakers with tradition.

The public interest the show aroused was also striking. An estimated half million persons, lowbrows as well as highbrows, saw it in New York and, later in 1913, in Chicago and Boston. The effect was to enlarge the American culture and clear the way for the acceptance of Max Weber, Charles Demuth, Arthur G. Dove, and other exponents of advanced cubism, futurism, and similar nonrepresentational (abstract) styles. Arthur Davies could well be proud of the wildness he had injected into American art.

December 9, 1913; Asuncion, Paraguay: The small river steamer tied to the wharf creaked and groaned as it took on equipment for a major expedition to the unmapped headwaters of the Amazon. Finally all was loaded and the leader of the expedition, Theodore Roosevelt, stepped aboard. Ahead were five months in totally unexplored country including a forty-seven day voyage down a stream the explorers aptly named the River of Doubt. There would be boat-smashing rapids, malaria, hostile Indians, and starvation. For a large part of the river run, Roosevelt lay weak and feverish urging the others to go on without him. At last the explorers reached the outposts of civilization on the upper Amazon.

"I am pleased . . . ," an aging Roosevelt remarked in retrospect, "that I was able to take the South American trip. I knew it would be my last thing of the kind." But he still had sufficient energy to write *Through the Brazilian Wilderness,* volunteer with the utmost seriousness for military duty in World War I, and receive tribute as the "greatest living American" in a poll of public opinion.

Theodore Roosevelt had a special significance for Americans of the early twentieth century, and being President was only a minor facet—a result rather than a cause of his popularity. The key to his appeal was sheer gusto. He symbolized virile manliness, the kind that clutched big sticks and dared the world. A product of the genteel tradition, he freed it from sterility. He reassured his contemporaries that Americans were still capable of the strenuous life.

Personally and politically Roosevelt succeeded in balancing the forward and backward-looking tendencies of the American mind. He was both gentleman—complete with a Harvard degree—and cowboy. He owned a tuxedo and a buckskin hunting suit. He could write books and lead the charge of the Rough Riders up San Juan Hill. East and West, city and country, the machine and the garden—in Roosevelt they existed in delicate balance. Conservation, which the Roosevelt administrations championed, is a case in point. It brought science to the service of nature. Technologists and engineers worked on behalf of farms, forests, and rivers. In a real sense the conservation movement assumed the role of the recently-vanished frontier. It attempted to keep the nation vigorous, prosperous, democratic, replete with opportunity for the individual, and, because of its relation to nature, wholesome and moral. These had once been the frontier's functions. For Americans of the time, conservation was welcome tonic—for the minds of people as well as for their land.

Roosevelt, indisputably, was *the* hero of the years 1900 to 1919. If one single subject had to be selected on which to base generalizations about the culture of the period, the most logical choice would be TR. Yet the real reason for the Roosevelt cult was not the man but the needs and dreams of his culture.

September 20, 1913; Memphis, Tennessee: W. C. Handy was incensed. The letter he had just opened told him that the New York music publishing house to which he had unwisely sold complete rights to his piano piece "The Memphis Blues" for fifty dollars was making a killing. Fifty thousand copies had been distributed, and the supply could not keep up with the demand. The letter condescendingly praised Handy, a Black, as "the greatest ragtime writer of the day" and hoped he would write more hit songs soon.

Despite his frustration with "The Memphis Blues," Handy could take satisfaction from playing a leading role in revolutionizing American music. The new, insurgent force was jazz—a Black folk music that in 1913 was on the verge of stampeding the musical taste of the entire nation. The origins of jazz are buried in work songs, "shouts," and rhythms that go back to the African seedbeds of the race. As a musical idiom, jazz was the antipode of formal, symphonic composition. Its essence was spontaneous improvisation. Handy, to be sure, had to write down "The Memphis Blues" in order to publish the piece, but for the most part classical jazz exists only in the head of the musician at the moment he plays. There is no score; indeed most jazzmen (especially the pioneers) could not read musical notation. Like the expressionists in art, they communicated their feelings in a highly personalized style. As a consequence, jazz is filled with disjointed counterpoints, antiphonal melody, dissonances, deviations in pitch, and breaks from the melodic line which gave the player free rein to improvise. The result, uncontrolled music. Clearly the call of the wild could be heard in jazz.

The rise of jazz (and the rags and blues that presaged it) is one of the best examples in the American experience of an unrefined, vernacular product of popular culture becoming accepted art. Because of its "low" associations (such as those in New Orleans' legendary Storyville), and its complete break with European music, jazz had to overcome more obstacles in the path to cultural respectability than usual. But the music was vital; it responded to the joys and hurts of people in general with such force as to transcend the limits of its early audience; it benefited from the prevailing cult of the primitive. Its unrepressed naturalness, its sensuality and wildness, touched a sympathetic chord in the early twentieth century. By 1917 jazz had come out of the Mississippi Valley to Chicago and New York and won general acceptance.

Rereading the letter he had received from the New York music publishing house, Handy bitterly recalled how every major musical publisher had once rejected his songs because their twelve-bar, blues strains were not in accord with the sixteen-bar convention. But now the tide was in his favor even if he had not immediately shared its benefits. Handy determined to write a new song from which *he* would benefit. He rented a room on Beale Street in the heart of Memphis' tenderloin and set to work. Recalling his skid row days in St. Louis, he began to write: "I hate to see de evenin' sun go down." With that line the most recorded and arranged composition in the entire history of American music was born: "The St. Louis Blues."

October 7, 1913; Highland Park, Michigan: As Henry Ford and his executives watched tensely, a rope attached to a Model T's chassis tightened and inched it across a 250 foot track on the factory floor. Workmen kept pace, adding part after part. Five hours and fifty minutes later a finished car rolled off the line under its own power. The Ford men were pleased. Their previous production record had been halved.

A few months later, after the completion of careful time, motion, and efficiency studies, the Highland Park plant produced 600 cars in a single working day. Soon the average time-per-car fell to ninety-three minutes. The unbelievable day of a car-a-minute was just ahead.

In the eyes of his contemporaries Henry Ford was a god of only slightly less stature than Theodore Roosevelt; his religion, the gospel of efficiency. Ford seemed to express the culmination of an American characteristic first developed in the Yankee tinkerer. For generations the practical crafts had been considered as something of an inferior order, something to be put away in the woodshed when company arrived. By the twentieth century, however, the national inferiority complex in this regard was on the wane. Perhaps, some conceded, business was indeed the business of America, an authentic expression of its cultural energies and a subject for national pride. Perhaps engineering and technology should be viewed as the American way of art rather than its enemy. By 1913, at any rate, it was increasingly possible to speak of the "art" of production and to regard the Model T with the enthusiasm other cultures reserved for plays and paintings. The possession of a car, especially an expensive one, became an indication of taste, like the possession of an art collection.

While there was much to celebrate in the success of Ford and his colleagues in the automobile industry, the liabilities of the new industrial order could not be denied. On the assembly line work became mindless drudgery. The old-time craftsman had been entirely responsible for a finished product; he could take pride in his work. But the man whose labor consisted of tightening several nuts on a moving chassis in no sense "made" a car. He was a machine, and if possible was replaced with one. Even the five dollar minimum wage Ford promised for a day's work could not sweeten the pill. The individual was lost in a maturing economic order no longer dependent upon his special skill.

Men responded to their growing obsolescence in several ways. Some expressed their feelings by perpetuating the memory of folk heroes like John Henry, the steel driving man, who competed with the steam drill only to die with his hammer in his hand. The train wreck that killed Casey Jones in 1900 afforded an opportunity to celebrate a man who showed class and courage while operating a machine. Between 1910 and 1920 Paul Bunyan stories were set down in print for the first time. The giant lumberman was just plain fun, but he was also a response to mechanization—a triumphant colossus, born of wish fulfillment, whose prowess was such that he needed no machine assistance.

The vogue of sports, both participatory and spectator, was another response to the Age of Ford. On the playing field the individual *mattered*. Competition was direct and easily understood. Victory, people assumed, went to superior ability and determination. Previously pioneering had offered this opportunity for glory. But with the frontier gone and the individual increasingly eclipsed by the size and complexity of civilization, sports assumed importance as a moral equivalent of pioneering. Indeed the rise of organized athletics in the United States coincided almost precisely with the disappearance of the frontier and the advent of industrialization.

For Americans after 1900, at any rate, sports were no idle matter. College football and professional baseball led the parade of spectator sports. They elicited fierce loyalties and equally strong antipathies. It was cowboys *versus* Indians or bears *versus* giants as in days of old except that now the names of sponsoring cities were prefixed. For the participant, especially if he was of the social elite, there was the appeal of tennis and golf, of hiking, camping, and bicycling. And thanks to Henry Ford almost everyone would join in a new sport—motoring. The skill and resourcefulness demanded by the early cars and old roads made every highway a new frontier.

February 1, 1913; New York City: The house of Macmillan announced the publication of a new book by an associate professor of politics at Columbia University named Charles A. Beard. In its own way *An Economic Interpretation of the Constitution* was also a response to the call of the wild. Beard made bold to challenge tradition. Indeed he took on one of the most sacred of all American cows: the Constitution of 1787. Asserting that the document was not a divinely-inspired and unquestionable stroke of altruistic genius, he discussed it as the work of ordinary men motivated by ordinary economic considerations.

An Economic Interpretation elicited howls of protest, but for many intellectuals of Beard's time it was a welcome contribution to the revolt against outworn and frozen creeds. Men of this mind had become impatient with the conception of truth as an absolute, especially in regard to human (as opposed to scientific) problems. They preferred to think of truth as relative and malleable—something made by men and shaped to the needs of the present by a constant process of testing and evaluation. The effects of this way of thinking on law, education, economics, philosophy, and, in Beard's case, political science was extraordinary. Everything was open to question. Experience, not logic, became the basis of acceptance. In regard to the Constitution, Beard called for recognition that a particular context produced the document. By 1913 the context had changed drastically. In the interest of the best possible government, Beard called for changing the Constitution (or at least its meaning) to suit new conditions.

December 6, 1913; Washington, D.C.: For the fifth consecutive working day the Senate of the United States labored late into the night on the Hetch Hetchy question. At issue was an undeveloped valley in the northern section of Yosemite National Park. The city of San Francisco wanted permission to build a dam at its mouth for the purpose of obtaining a municipal water supply and a hydropower-generating facility. The opposition was concerned about the further loss of an increasingly rare commodity—wilderness.

For five years prior to the climactic Senate debate, the Hetch Hetchy controversy had raged in the press and through several sets of Congressional hearings. Frequently its swirling passage bared some basic tensions in American culture. One was the clash between utility and aesthetics.

The dam builders argued that Hetch Hetchy's highest possible use was serving man's material needs for water and power. In this opinion they were joined by conservationists of the Gifford Pinchot school for whom "conserve" meant to develop wisely and efficiently; keeping a portion of the environment wild, even when it was in a national park, was unprogressive.

Others had a different definition of "progress." For them conservation meant preservation. The value of the environment, they believed, should be determined by aesthetic and spiritual criteria rather than in terms of dollars and cents. Robert Underwood Johnson, poet, genteel author, and self-styled upholder of America's "standards," was typical of those who defended national parks in general and Hetch Hetchy in particular. The bookish Johnson had little actual contact with the wilderness nor did he desire any. It was, instead, the *idea* of wilderness embattled against what he conceived to be crass and ruthless exploitation that aroused his wrath. In Johnson's eyes wild country was like fine art or *belles lettres*—a fragile yet priceless commodity that needed defense against the insensitivity of his countrymen.

Writing in *Century* in 1908 Johnson lashed out at the would-be dam builders, calling them people who had not advanced beyond the "pseudo-'practical' stage." Their presence in the nation, he added, "is one of the retarding influences of American civilization and brings us back to the materialistic declaration that 'Good is only good to eat.'" Elsewhere Johnson explained that he was defending wilderness "in the name of all lovers of beauty . . . against the materialistic idea that there must be something wrong about a man who finds one of the highest uses of nature in the fact that it is made to be looked at." Such an argument, of course, was designed to embarrass San Francisco as much as to defend Hetch Hetchy. Paradoxically, according to Johnson, appreciation of the primitive was a mark of superior cultivation.

Others took up Johnson's theme with even more pointed reference to the nation's shortcomings. One man, who had camped in Hetch Hetchy, angrily demanded of the House of Representatives' Committee on the Public Lands: "Is it never ceasing; is there nothing to be held sacred by this nation; is it to be dollars only; are we to be cramped in soul and mind by the lust after filthy lucre only; shall we be left some of the more glorious places?" Another letter of protest concluded: "may we live down our national reputation for commercialism." At the Senate hearings in 1909 Henry E. Gregory of the American Scenic and Historic Preservation Society appeared in person and spoke of the need to counteract "business and utilitarian motives." He pointed out that a wilderness like Hetch Hetchy had more than monetary value "as an educator of the people and as a restorer and liberator of the spirit enslaved by Mammon."

Another tactic of the preservationists emphasized the spiritual significance of wilderness and the tendency of money-minded America to ignore religion. John Muir, the president of the Sierra Club, for instance, believed so passionately in the divinity of wild nature that he saw the defense of Hetch Hetchy as an opportunity to serve the Lord. He took his crusade for wilderness to be part of the broader campaign to resist the influence of "these mad, God-forgetting progressive days." At one point Muir referred to San Francisco as "the Prince of the powers of Darkness"; at another as "Satan and Co." In a widely-publicized outburst of 1912 he cried: "These temple destroyers, devotees of ravaging commercialism, seem to have a perfect contempt for Nature, and, instead of lifting their eyes to the God of the mountains, lift them to the Almighty Dollar." The innumerable puns about "damning" Hetch Hetchy were only partly in jest.

Fired by rhetoric of this sort, the Hetch Hetchy issue was white hot when it came to Congress for final decision in 1913. Applying the time-honored utilitarian yardstick to the environment, Representative John E. Raker asserted that the "old barren rocks" of the valley had a "cash value" of less than $300,000 whereas a reservoir would be worth millions. "I am not for reservations and parks," flatly declared Martin Dies of Texas. But many proponents of the dam in Congress were ambivalent. The claims of civilization and the claims of wilderness both pulled strongly. "Mr. Chairman," Finly H. Gray of Indiana declared, "much as I admire the beauties of nature and deplore the desecration of God's creation, yet when these two considerations come in conflict the conservation of nature should yield to the conservation of human welfare." Men of this opinion eased their consciences with the thought that San Francisco's dam would create a lovely mountain lake and actually enhance the beauty of the valley. Answering this logic was Halvor Steenerson of Minnesota who charged that it was nonsense to claim that an artificial reservoir would add to Hetch Hetchy. "You may as well improve upon the lily of the field by handpainting it," he said, adding that all the city offered was a "dirty, muddy pond" and a power plant making a "devilish hissing noise." Despite such statements and the thousands of pieces of protest literature mailed by the Sierra Club, the Senate passed the dam bill at three minutes before midnight December 6, 1913. Forty-three favored the bill, twenty-five opposed it, and twenty-nine could not make up their minds. Later in the month it became law, and, soon after, construction crews moved into the valley.

Near the close of the Senate debate on Hetch Hetchy, James A. Reed of Missouri arose to confess his incredulity at the entire affair. How could it be, he wondered, that over the future of a piece of wilderness "the Senate goes into profound debate, the country is thrown into a condition of hysteria." Observing, accurately, that the intensity of resistance to the dam increased with the distance from its site, he remarked that "when we get as far east as New England the opposition has become a frenzy." In Senator Reed's opinion this was clearly "much ado about little." But the point, as he himself suggested, was that a great many of his contemporaries did regard wilderness as worth getting excited about.

The most significant aspect of the Hetch Hetchy controversy was that it occurred at all. One hundred or even fifty years earlier a similar proposal to dam a wild river would not have occasioned the slightest ripple of public protest. Traditional assumptions about the use of undeveloped country did not include reserving it in national parks. The emphasis was all the other way—on developing it in the name of progress and prosperity. This conquering posture was grounded on the belief that American civilization was good, its extension desirable. By 1913, however, many Americans were no longer so sure.

The foregoing six windows into the American culture in 1913 could be multiplied many times. Yet one senses that the revealed image would be changed only in size, not in substance. Joe Knowles, the Armory Show, Theodore Roosevelt, "The Memphis Blues," Ford's assembly line, *An Economic Interpretation of the Constitution,* and the Hetch Hetchy controversy all suggest that reaction against cultural middle age was the main dynamic of the two decades after 1900. The wild, in its several senses, called strongly to Americans in these years of growing uneasiness.

Culture has many layers. Some of the documents which follow describe "official" culture and illustrate the traditional standards of elegance accepted by the establishment. Others reflect the taste and values of insurgent writers and artists who regarded tradition as a drag on creativity. Still others reveal popular hopes and fears. The composite is the American culture, illusive, ambivalent but always exciting to explore and occasionally productive of some of the most profound insights into the nature of the American experience.

PART ONE

ENVIRONMENT

1. The Birth of the Boy Scouts

The frontier no longer existed but nostalgia for the frontier remained. One of the expressions of that nostalgia was the Boy Scout movement. Although the English hero of the Boer War, Sir Robert S. S. Baden-Powell, was its official founder in 1907, his ideas were anticipated in the United States. As early as 1886 the popular nature writer, Ernest Thompson Seton, began to promote outdoor-oriented clubs for boys. In 1902 he described an organization called Woodcraft Indians in the *Ladies Home Journal*. Two years later Seton met with Baden-Powell and discussed the potential of scouting. The Englishman also had the example of the Sons of Daniel Boone and the Boy Pioneers which Daniel S. Beard launched in America in 1903. The Boy Scout movement succeeded immediately in the United States, quickly becoming the nation's largest youth organization. Uniformed, always "prepared" Scouts doing their daily "good deed" and building fires without matches became a familiar part of American culture. In the organization's first *Handbook,* Seton set forth the ends and means of the Boy Scouts of America and offered instruction in woodcraft and citizenship. In the thirty years following its publication in 1910, the *Handbook,* in various editions, sold an estimated seven million copies.

Boy Scouts of America
ERNEST THOMPSON SETON

Every American boy, a hundred years ago, lived either on a farm or in such close touch with farm life that he reaped its benefits. He had all the

Ernest Thompson Seton, *Boy Scouts of America: A Handbook of Wood-craft, Scouting, and Life-craft* (New York, Doubleday, Page & Co., 1910), xi, xii, 1–4, 34–38.

practical knowledge that comes from country surroundings; that is, he could ride, shoot, skate, run, swim; he was handy with tools; he knew the woods; he was physically strong, self-reliant, resourceful, well-developed in body and brain. In addition to which, he had a good moral training at home. He was respectful to his superiors, obedient to his parents, and altogether the best material of which a nation could be made.

We have lived to see an unfortunate change. Partly through the growth of immense cities, with the consequent specialization of industry, so that each individual has been required to do one small specialty and shut his eyes to everything else, with the resultant perpetual narrowing of the mental horizon.

Partly through the decay of small farming, which would have offset this condition, for each farm was a college of handicraft.

And partly through the stereotyped forms of religion losing their hold, we see a very different type of youth in the country to-day.

It is the exception when we see a boy respectful to his superiors and obedient to his parents. It is the rare exception, now, when we see a boy that is handy with tools and capable of taking care of himself under all circumstances. It is the very, very rare exception when we see a boy whose life is absolutely governed by the safe old moral standards.

The personal interest in athletics has been largely superseded by an interest in spectacular games, which, unfortunately, tend to divide the nation into two groups—the few overworked champions in the arena, and the great crowd, content to do nothing but sit on the benches and look on, while indulging their tastes for tobacco and alcohol.

It is this last that is turning so many thoughtful ones against baseball, football, etc. This, it will be seen, is a reproduction of the condition that ended in the fall of Rome. In her days of growth, every man was a soldier; in the end, a few great gladiators were in the arena, to be watched and applauded by the millions who personally knew nothing at all of fighting or heroism.

Degeneracy is the word.

To combat the system that has turned such a large proportion of our robust, manly, self-reliant boyhood into a lot of flat-chested cigarette-smokers, with shaky nerves and doubtful vitality, I began the Woodcraft movement in America. Without saying as much, it aimed to counteract the evils attendant on arena baseball, football, and racing, by substituting the better, cleaner, saner pursuits of Woodcraft and Scouting. Its methods were fairly successful; at least 100,000 young people joined. But the idea, as enlarged by General Sir Robert Baden-Powell, has in less time achieved greater popularity in England; the results have been such that we are justified in adopting his innovations. . . .

* * *

This is a time when the whole nation is turning toward the Outdoor Life, seeking in it the physical regeneration so needful for continued national existence—is waking to the fact long known to thoughtful men, that those live longest who live nearest to the ground, that is, who live the simple life of primitive times, divested, however, of the evils that ignorance in those times begot.

Consumption, the white man's plague since he has become a house race, is vanquished by the sun and air, and many ills of the mind also are forgotten, when the sufferer boldly takes to the life in tents.

Half our diseases are in our minds and half in our houses. We can safely leave the rest to the physicians for treatment.

Sport is the great incentive to Outdoor Life; nature study is the intellectual side of sport.

I should like to lead this whole nation into the way of living outdoors for at least a month each year, reviving and expanding a custom that as far back as Moses was deemed essential to the national well-being.

Not long ago a benevolent rich man, impressed with this idea, chartered a steamer and took some hundreds of slum boys up to the Catskills for a day in the woods. They were duly landed and told to "go in now and have a glorious time." It was like gathering up a netful of catfish and throwing them into the woods, saying, "Go and have a glorious time."

The boys sulked around and sullenly disappeared. An hour later, on being looked up, they were found in groups under the bushes, smoking cigarettes, shooting "craps," and playing cards,—the only things they knew.

Thus the well-meaning rich man learned that it is not enough to take men out-of-doors. We must also teach them to enjoy it. . . .

Nine leading principles are kept in view:

(1) This movement is essentially for *recreation.*

(2) *Camp-life.* Camping is the simple life reduced to actual practice, as well as the culmination of the outdoor life.

Camping has no great popularity to-day, because men have the idea that it is possible only after an expensive journey to the wilderness; and women that it is inconvenient, dirty, and dangerous.

These are errors. They have arisen because camping as an art is not understood. When intelligently followed camp-life must take its place as a cheap and delightful way of living, as well as a mental and physical saviour of those strained and broken by the grind of the over-busy world.

The wilderness affords the ideal camping, but many of the benefits can be got by living in a tent on a town lot, piazza, or even house-top.

(3) *Self-government.* Control from without is a poor thing when you can get control from within. As far as possible, then, we make these camps self-governing. Each full member has a vote in affairs.

(4) *The Magic of the Camp-fire.* What is a camp without a camp-fire? —no camp at all, but a chilly place in a landscape, where some people happen to have some things.

When first the brutal anthropoid stood up and walked erect—was man, the great event was symbolized and marked by the lighting of the first camp-fire.

For millions of years our race has seen in this blessed fire the means and emblem of light, warmth, protection, friendly gathering, council. All the hallow of the ancient thoughts, hearth, fireside, home, is centred in its glow, and the home-tie itself is weakened with the waning of the home-fire. Not in the steam radiator can we find the spell; not in the water coil; not even in the gas-log: they do not reach the heart. Only the ancient sacred fire of wood has power to touch and thrill the chords of primitive remembrance. When men sit together at the camp-fire, they seem to shed all modern form and poise, and hark back to the primitive—to meet as man and man—to show the naked soul. Your camp-fire partner wins your love, or hate, mostly your love; and having camped in peace together, is a lasting bond of union,—however wide your worlds may be apart.

The camp-fire, then, is the focal centre of all primitive brotherhood. We shall not fail to use its magic powers.

(5) *Woodcraft Pursuits.* Realizing that *manhood, not scholarship,* is the first aim of education, we have sought out those pursuits which develop the finest character, the finest physique, and which may be followed out of doors, which, in a word, *make for manhood.*

By nearly every process of logic we are led primarily to Woodcraft, that is, Woodcraft in its largest sense,—meaning every accomplishment of an all-round Woodman:—Riding, Hunting, Camper-craft, Scouting, Mountaineering, Indian-craft, Star-craft, Signalling, and Boating. To this we add all good Outdoor Athletics and Sports, including Sailing and Motoring, and Nature-Study, of which Wild Animal Photography is an important branch, but above all, Heroism.

About one hundred and fifty deeds or exploits are recognized in these various departments, and the members are given decorations that show what they achieved.

(6) *Honors by Standards.* The competitive principle is responsible for much that is evil. We see it rampant in our colleges to-day, where every effort is made to discover and develop a champion, while the great body of students is neglected. That is, the ones who are in need of physical development do not get it, and those who do not need it are over-developed. The result is much unsoundness of many kinds. A great deal of this would be avoided if we strove to bring all the individuals up to a certain standard. In our non-competitive tests the enemies are not *"the other fellows,"* but *time and space,* the forces of Nature. We try *not to down the others,* but *to raise ourselves.* A thorough application of this principle would end many of the evils now demoralizing college athletics. Therefore, all our honors are bestowed according to world-wide standards. (Prizes are not honors.)

(7) *Personal Decoration for Personal Achievements.* The love of glory is the strongest motive in a savage. Civilized man is supposed to find in high principle his master impulse. But those who believe that the men of our race, not to mention boys, are civilized in this highest sense, would be greatly surprised if confronted with figures. Nevertheless, a human weakness may be good material to work with. I face the facts as they are. All have a chance for glory through the standards, and we blazon it forth in personal decorations that all can see, have, and desire.

(8) *A Heroic Ideal.* The boy from ten to fifteen, like the savage, is purely physical in his ideals. I do not know that I ever met a boy that would not rather be John L. Sullivan than Darwin or Tolstoi. Therefore, I accept the fact, and seek to keep in view an ideal that is physical, but also clean, manly, heroic, already familiar, and leading with certainty to higher things.

(9) *Picturesqueness in Everything.* Very great importance should be attached to this. The effect of the picturesque is magical, and all the more subtle and irresistible because it is not on the face of it reasonable. The charm of titles and gay costumes, of the beautiful in ceremony, phrase, dance, and song, are utilized in all ways. . . .

It becomes part of the duty of any one who joins the Boy Scout movement as an official to get others also to interest themselves in it in a practical manner, because our object is to sow healthy seed not merely in a few thousand boys, but in a few million if possible.

For this purpose it is well that he should himself realize and be able to explain the aims and outside effects of our scheme.

In the first place we have to recognize that our nation is in need of help, from within, if it is to maintain its position as a leading factor for peace and prosperity among the other nations of the earth.

History shows us, that with scarcely an exception, every great nation, after climbing laboriously to the zenith of its power, has then apparently become exhausted by the effort, and has settled down in a state of repose, relapsing into idleness and into indifference to the fact that other nations were pushing up to destroy it, whether by force of arms or by the more peaceful but equally fatal method of commercial strangulation. In every case the want of some of that energetic patriotism which made the country has caused its ruin; in every case the verdict of history has been, "Death through bad citizenship." . . .

One sign of the disease (which was also one of the signs of decay in Rome before her fall) is the horde of unemployed leading miserable, wasted lives in all parts of the country—the great army of drones in our hive.

It is no longer a mere temporary excrescence, but is a growing tumor pregnant with evil for the nation.

These people, *having never been taught to look after themselves, or to think of the future or their country's good,* allow themselves to become slaves by the persuasive power of a few professional agitators whose living depends on agitating (whether it is needed or not); and blinded by the talk of these men they spurn the hand which provides the money, till they force employers to spend fortunes either in devising machinery that will take their place and will not then go on strike, or in getting in foreign labor, or in removing their business to other countries, leaving the agitators fat, but the mass of their deluded followers unemployed and starving and unable to provide for the crowds of children which they still continue improvidently to bring into the world. . . .

One of the causes of the downfall of Rome was that the people, being fed by the State to the extent of three-quarters of the population, ceased to have any thought or any responsibility for themselves or their children, and consequently became a nation of unemployed wasters. They frequented the circuses, where paid performers appeared before them in the arena, much as we see the crowds now flocking to look on at paid players playing football.

Football in itself is a grand game for developing a lad physically and also morally, for he learns to play with good temper and unselfishness, to play in his place and "play the game," and these are the best of training for any game of life. But it is a vicious game when it draws crowds of lads away from playing the game themselves to be merely onlookers at a few paid performers. I yield to no one in enjoyment of the sight of those splendid specimens of our race, trained to perfection, and playing faultlessly; but my heart sickens at the reverse of the medal—thousands of boys and young men, pale, narrow-chested, hunched-up, miserable specimens, smoking endless cigarettes, numbers of them betting, all of them learning to be hysterical as they groan or cheer in panic unison with their neighbors—the worst sound of all being the hysterical scream of laughter that greets any little trip or fall of a player. One wonders whether this can be the same nation which had gained for itself the reputation of being a stolid manhood, unmoved by panic or excitement, and reliable in the tightest of places.

Get the lads away from this—teach them to be manly, to play the game, whatever it may be, and not be merely onlookers and loafers.

In the eyes of some, these and many similar signs appear to indicate that we have arrived at the point of our existence where we may fold our hands and resign our life. But is not national life very like that of the individual?

How many a man in the case of sickness has given up all hope of recovery and has accordingly died, whereas another, by carrying out the spirit of our scouts' maxim, "Never say die till you're dead," has risen to recovery and renewed health and strength.

It is equally possible for us as a nation, by energetically plucking up spirit, recognizing our faults, and taking the proper remedies in time, not only to avoid becoming worse, but to rise to far greater power and to a potentiality for good in the world such as history has never seen.

2. The Dilemma of Urban Growth

In 1830 only one out of every fifteen Americans lived in a city of over 8,000 inhabitants. In 1900 it was one in every three. Ten years later approximately half the population was urban. From another perspective, there were 141 cities of 8,000 or more in the United States in 1860. By 1910 the figure was 778. Americans responded ambivalently to this basic environmental change. On the one hand, cities were the seats of intellect and refinement. They also seemed to many a new frontier—replete with opportunities. But on the debit side, cities were thought to spawn social disorder, immorality, and an indifference to the virtues of nature. The problem of the cities was not minor. Deeply-rooted values and traditions were involved, and the debate frequently became heated. In 1913 the *Atlantic Monthly* published two independently-written essays on the subject in the same issue. G. S. Dickerman addressed the liabilities of urbanization, and Mark Jefferson its advantages.

The Drift to the Cities
G. S. DICKERMAN

It is safe to take into consideration our losses as well as our gains. The thirteenth census tells of a decade of growth in the United States. In 1900 the population was less than seventy-six millions; in 1910 it is nearly ninety-two millions, an increase of about sixteen millions. In the list of 225 cities having over 25,000 inhabitants, all but three show an increase of population, and among the 1172 smaller cities having over 2500 inhabitants, the story is much the same. . . .

G. S. Dickerman, "The Drift to the Cities," *Atlantic Monthly,* 112 (Sept., 1913), 349–353.

The most surprising lapses are in the great states of the Mississippi Valley whose prosperity has been almost proverbial. In Missouri, with such growing centres as St. Louis and Kansas City, which together show an increase of 196,000, we find 71 counties out of 100 in which the population has declined. . . .

Not to pursue the record of particular states, it is enough to say that among the 2941 counties in all the states, we find 798 in which the population was less in 1910 than it had been ten years before. If we compare with this the record of the previous decade, we find that between 1890 and 1900 there were 378 counties in which there was a decline; and going back to the tenth census we find that between 1870 and 1880 the number was little over a hundred. This is interesting in connection with the fact that the increase of population in urban territory throughout the country in this decade was over eleven million and in the rural less than five million. It all points to a widespread movement from the farm to the town and the metropolis.

It was to be expected that a decline would appear in the products of the farm. The following are examples of this. The corn crop of 1910 was less than that of ten years before by 114,000,000 bushels. The wheat crop was greater on account of the better yield, but the number of acres on which it was grown was less by over 8,000,000. The apple crop was smaller by 27,876,000 bushels, and fewer small fruits were grown by 36,653,000 quarts. . . .

With such a decrease in crops, particularly those required for feeding animals, it was inevitable that there should be a falling off in the amount of livestock on farms. . . . The explanation is the decline of rural population in so many counties and the decrease in those products of the farm which are necessary to the feeding of these animals.

So the rising prices of beef, pork, and mutton are directly traceable to the decline of our rural population. It is the same, of course, with the rising prices of cereals, fruits, and all the other products of the farm. This touches other people besides those within the boundaries of the United States. Heretofore large quantities of bread-stuffs, meats, and fruit have been exported to other countries and have borne an important part in their sustenance. Of necessity there is a decrease in these exports. Higher prices must then follow in all the countries with which we have commercial relations, and wherever there is want of food we may expect the want to be aggravated. This is involved in our world-wide relationships at the present time.

There is a more serious consequence, however, than scarcity of food; it is lowering of character. Governor Eberhart of Minnesota tells of a visit he made to Minneapolis in a harvest emergency, for laborers to gather wheat. The farmers were at their wits' ends to save their crops. It was said that the city was full of the unemployed who were looking everywhere for jobs. He found them, as he says, 'seated on the park benches in all sections of the city and overflowing to the curb stones. Work, it seemed, could not be found. Some of the men were on the verge of starvation, and the charitable organizations of the city were taxed to their utmost capacity to provide for them.' It looked as if his task would be an easy one and he could take back as many men as he wished. He picked out his men and told them he wanted their help. They were eager for the chance and said they could do anything. He spoke of the service he had in mind in the country and on the farms, when instantly their faces fell and they were as glum as they had been before. Their answer was: 'We don't want to go to the country, boss. We don't want to live on a farm. There's nothin' for us there,—no life, no entertainment, no lights,—nothin' but monotony and work. We'd rather stay in the city and starve than go to the country an' have nothin' to do but work. No, sir, we stay right here.' And stay they did. He couldn't get one of them to go with him, and the farmers had to harvest their wheat as best they could while the city held in its grasp, unemployed, enough men to garner all the crops of the state.

We cannot suppose that Minneapolis was any worse than other cities in this particular. It is likely that a proposal of this sort would have been received by the unemployed in any one of a thousand American cities in much the same way. And that is the worst of it, for it means an essentially wrong attitude of mind in multitudes of people. Willingness to lie idle rather than to undertake anything they do not quite like, to hang on charity rather than to go where they are wanted and can be of use, with callous incapacity for hearing any call of duty or feeling any thrill of interest at a summons for help in an hour of somebody's crying necessity. That is the kind of men that our cities make, or too many such.

People flock to the cities for the advantages there offered, and find disadvantages. Parents sell their wholesome country homes because of their children, and go where there are grand churches, superior schools, and attractive libraries, to find themselves in close proximity to drinking saloons, dancehalls, gambling dens, and indescribable allurements to vice. Is that better for their boys and girls, or is the new atmosphere heavy with influences that are a peril? There are fifty churches in a city and a thousand saloons. The churches are open one day and two or three evenings in each week. The saloons are open every week-day all day long and far into the night. Boys and young men are not attracted to the churches. The saloons hold out all sorts of attractions to beguile them within their doors. What wonder that so many city boys grow up with disordered appetites and depraved tastes! A gentleman was recently heard to say, 'As I go along the street the sight of cigars in the store windows makes me want to smoke and I step in and buy when otherwise I should not think of it.' This gentleman is an eminent scholar, a principal of a boys' school, an advocate of reforms, and influential in church and society. If the temptation of the store windows was too much for him, can we expect his pupils to be proof against it?

Do we understand the extent to which these artificial appetites are being cultivated and what this means? With a lessening of the food-supply there comes a more constant resort to stimulants and narcotics. The hungry go for solace to drink and tobacco, sometimes to more powerful drugs. We can easily imagine that those loungers whom Governor Eberhart saw in the parks of Minneapolis were, most of them, habituated to these indulgences. But these practices grow in prevalence among all classes of people. They are not so common in the country, but are most rife in all our centres of population. And abundant provision is made for them. The prices of flour and meat may advance, but somehow the cost of whiskey and tobacco is kept within the reach of even the very poor. Cigarettes to-day do not cost more than half what they did ten years ago, and three or four times as many of them are used.

Some products of the farm have not decreased during this decade. Barley, which goes largely to breweries and distilleries, was grown on 3,228,000 more acres in 1910 than in 1900, the product was greater by 53,709,000 bushels, and the valuation by $50,826,000. Tobacco was grown on 193,451 acres more, its product was greater by 187,652,000 pounds, and its valuation by $47,315,000. We find too that while exports of bread-stuffs and meats have declined, it has not been so with tobacco; on the contrary, the export of leaf tobacco increased within the ten years including 1912 some 79,000,000 pounds.

Our Internal Revenue receipts offer a measure of the amount of these products. The taxes derived from distilled and malt liquors and from tobacco, as reported by the United States Commissioner, in 1912 amounted to $290,250,000. This was considerably more than the entire congressional appropriations for the army and navy; and in sixteen months these taxes pour into the treasury more than the estimated cost of the Panama Canal. These taxes have nearly doubled within twenty years, indicating how rapidly these habits of cultivating and indulging artificial appetites have been spreading throughout our country.

In a highly organized community there is a possibility that children will grow up to be like the parts of a machine fitting snugly into their little places and moving there with hardly a thought of what their life means; making of custom a slavery; bowing in craven fealty to a boss, to a business, a sect, an order, a party, any sort of fashionable convention, with never a sentiment of devotion to any burning truth or any grand cause, and with scarcely any recognition of those responsibilities which give to life its dignity and splendor. Many great human qualities come to their best in a life of comparative isolation. A big tree, an oak or elm, standing out in an open field, has a toughness of fibre, a spread of boughs and roundness of shape that are never seen in a tree that stands in the woods. So people get individuality by being much alone. They become self-reliant by relying on themselves. They gain clear opinions by thinking things over, and thinking them out to their necessary conclusions. They acquire inflexibility of purpose by facing obstacles and conquering them. The pioneers of our country and the fathers of the republic were such men. The projectors of great undertakings carried through triumphantly have acquired their power in this way. The country is the natural nursery of such qualities. People are wanted on the farms to raise corn and grow stock for the markets; but they are wanted there far more for the training of manhood and womanhood in moral worth, in religious sensibility, in all the traits of a strong, upright personality. In the future as never heretofore, our cities with their multiplying wealth and lavish luxury are likely to need the country for that steady renewal of their better life which shall keep them from relaxing into sensuality and sinking into decay.

Advantages
MARK JEFFERSON

One has heard so much of late years about the exodus from the country, in the United States, that it is time someone pointed out that no such exodus has taken place. Individuals leave some country places for the city or other country places, but generally speaking the country is gaining inhabitants

Mark Jefferson, "A Hopeful View of the Urban Problem," *Atlantic Monthly*, 112 (Sept., 1913), 353–358.

at a fairly rapid rate. These are not figures of speech, but rather figures from the Census. . . . As to rate of increase, our country dwellers have increased in the last decade by eleven per cent. The whole German Empire, cities and all, has only increased by thirteen. The American exodus from the country is one of the three great myths of the nineteenth century! . . .

Men and families have been lost to the country, but for one that has gone nine have come. Our population is a shifting one; many of those whom we see leaving one country district have merely gone to swell the country dwellers elsewhere. . . . Not an exodus from the country but the development of cities has been the phenomenon of the generation.

Now, this thing that has been happening is natural and normal in a nation taking possession of a land. We should not fail to note that the number of cities has grown as well as their population. Not merely are they three times as populous at the end of the decade as at the beginning, but over twice as numerous. The public mind has thought of the cities as if they had always been there, over against the country and independent of it; as if in matters concerning the growth of population everything were possible,—that the cities might have grown slower than the country, or that it was in some way to be expected that town and country should normally grow alike. As a matter of fact, our cities are the outcome of the growth of country population; are an outgrowth of the needs of the country people, first for exchange and distribution of products, second for some working over and manufacturing of those products; and they must grow faster than the country population that creates them, from the conditions of modern life and industry.

Thirty years ago, more than half our cities did not exist. The new ones number no less than 1303. These have not been 'gone to' by people from the country, but have just grown on their sites out of rural communities. Of course, part of the number is fictitious. With the discrimination between rural and urban communities at 2500, a 'country' community of 2490 becomes a 'city' on adding ten new inhabitants without any change of character. . . .

With us, cities are as sure to spring up with the increase of country population as the forests are to disappear. City and country are organically related. Crops cannot be grown without fields, nor exchanged and manufactured under the modern system of division of labor, without cities. Only in the rudest pioneer settlements do men dispense with this division of labor by doing everything painfully and badly on the farm. Such settlements are retarded and hampered until they have towns for the city part of the work. When we estimate that the average inhabitant of New York may have but a few score square feet for his own use, we are apt to forget that he can only exist on them because somewhere in the country there are acres of ground producing for him. . . .

Where the author lives, in southern Michigan, the farms of from forty to eighty acres have their houses strung along the highways at considerable distances. At road corners every few miles we may find a little cluster of them by a church or a school-house, and especially by a country corner-store. This is important in the life of the whole district for its social opportunities, but it lives on its usefulness as a point of local supply and collection. Here eggs and butter are brought from all the farms around. Every one obtains here his flour, sugar, tea, coffee, kerosene, lamps, common plates, rough cloth and clothing, hammers and nails; the things that some one within a few miles is certain to want every day. At longer intervals one comes on villages with better goods in larger assortments; things not so constantly needed; so that a wider clientèle must be appealed to for their sale. In the same way every county has its little city, with banks and higher schools and theatres and factories, and stores with costlier grades of furniture and clothing and objects of luxury. Here or in the village will be sold the farmer's crop. To them he will look for the culture he wants in the form of religion, of education for his family, or of social intercourse and entertainment. Here he and his wife hope to spend their last days, with the farm rented or worked by some one on halves. Each of these grades of communities has been created by the settling of the region. Each has grown as more forest was cut away; villages have grown into little cities, little cities have grown into large ones in which manufacturing becomes more and more important with size, for only in the large ones are assured ease of movement of raw and manufactured material and a constant supply of labor of varied training and capacity. The few really strategic points in the whole country, for interchange of commodities, will foster the growth of a few cities to overwhelming size. But all of these cities alike have their roots in the country fields. If the country folk ever really take it into their heads to flock to the cities, no city can either last or grow. . . .

Now, American farms are going to be smaller, but it will happen by the introduction of intensive methods of agriculture or by the taking up of the farms by Europeans who understand those methods. There are signs enough that the thing is happening already, but it is a slow process compared with the increase of the population. It is the nature of the case that the man in the field can raise the raw produce for seven or eight. That is about what he was doing in this country in 1900, and he will produce for more and more with every year. Between 1855 and 1894 the introduction of seven different machines used in raising and harvesting corn reduced the man-labor in a bushel of corn from four hours and thirty-four minutes to forty-one minutes. For a bushel of wheat the similar reduction has been from three hours and three minutes to ten minutes. To get the same produce from the ground, one man in the field suffices where then sixteen were needed. Of course such an application of machinery is ideal, and not attained in wide practice. The essential farm population must always be thin, and if it becomes too dense, economic forces tend to thin it at once. But the operations connected with the manufacture and interchange of commodities need not be kept near the fields. On the contrary, they can best be carried on under the conditions of village and city life, at points well placed for power and transportation.

City population normally adds a portion of the natural increase of the population of the country to its own increase: it must grow faster than the country population does. . . .

To the density of city population there is hardly any limit. Some wards in New York are settled at the rate of five hundred thousand people to the mile; all Manhattan island averages about a hundred thousand, but this is, of course, mere 'home space.'

There are many difficulties in drawing distinctions between city and country, as we must for statistical purposes. I have tried to lay emphasis above rather on their interrelation and essential unity, yet the line must be drawn somewhere. It was General Francis A. Walker, Director of the Census in 1870, who suggested 8000 as a critical size; all communities with fewer inhabitants than that being defined as 'rural.' The Twelfth Census reduced this number to 4000, the Thirteenth to 2500. What has been the effect of this change of standard on computations of country growth? Apparently to make country population *seem* to grow more slowly. . . .

If the 'city' minimum were set a little lower, the case might be made to look worse yet for the country.

The reductions in the limit to 4000 and 2500 appear to have been made with the eyes rather on the *rus* than on the *urbs*. Is a place of 2500 really a city? The dweller in one of 100,000 will hardly think so. Form of government is of course not a satisfactory means of distinguishing; but surely there is some common element in the usual notion of *city, citified,* and *urban* that can be used in defining. I think the words carry for all of us the idea of paved streets, compactly and continuously closed in by permanent buildings several stories high and pretty crowded with people. Public parks do not interrupt the city concept at all, nor do waterways which are used for traffic. The community at the mouth of the Charles is really one city, although governed by several mayors and councils.

Rural population lives in isolated houses. Such is the country population that I find widespread about here with a density of 31 to the square mile; but between this rural life and city life is another type, that of the village or small city. Village life is marked by a drawing together of homes; that is its distinction from the true country. Perhaps the greatest hardship of country life is the lonesomeness, above all for the women. The village is built up by this country longing for society, and the village appears therefore as soon as two houses stand side by side. When they are so clustered and grouped that they have no farms annexed, it is plain that the village has arrived. The space occupied is an essential part of the idea. Not how many are the people, but how near together do they live? The Michigan General Laws are suggestive when they authorize the incorporation as a village of any community that has at least 300 people on at least one square mile of ground.

The city appears in the growth of the village when the increasing material nearness of men brings about social repulsions. It is the delight of moving to the village that I may have neighbors; of going to the city that I need not know who my neighbors are. Material crowding of men has brought evils in its train against which the city must defend itself. To prevent vehicles from sticking in the mud of heavily traveled streets, the streets must be paved, and as further defenses we must now have city lighting, policing, sewerage, and water supply, all because there are now so many of us so near together.

The blessings of the village become curses with further growth, unless 'city' remedies are applied. The very crowding brings a thinning out at the centre. In the heart of the great modern cities nobody lives but janitors and caretakers of store and office buildings. While each of the twenty-odd square miles of Manhattan Island has more than a hundred thousand residents, the business centre, in Wards Two and Three near the southern tip of the island, has less than seven thousand to the mile. The great example of course is London, with its old 'City' steadily dwindling; but more than that, the central fifth of the whole County of London has fewer inhabitants with each decade, as shops and offices take the place of homes.

Country people live in isolated homes, village homes are neighborly, and the city defends its inmates from neighbors who may not be desired.

The line cannot be sharply drawn between them; the best thing to use is the average from the facts of many large cities. We learn from that how people do live in large cities.

From studies of many large cities in Europe as well as in America, it appears that a reasonable lower limit of density of population for a city is ten thousand people to a square mile. This is not far from the official average for American great cities. All areas continuously settled at the rate of over ten thousand to the mile are *cities;* all areas less densely settled, *villages,* until the houses come to be isolated, when we have reached the *country.* This throws Charlottenburg in with Berlin, Hoboken and Jersey City with New York, and makes Cambridge, Somerville, Chelsea, and Brookline essential parts of Boston, with a total population this year, 1913, of nine hundred thousand people.

Most of our cities contain City part, Village part, and Country part. So does Vienna, but most European cities have expanded beyond their limits and citified their suburbs. London has invaded several counties.

The land has been settled, population has been developed slowly in the country, as befits the sparse agricultural occupation of the land; in the cities, rapidly, at the demand and under the stimulus of country development. No exodus from the country has occurred except as the country, exuberant and life-giving, brings forth a population in excess of agricultural needs. This it is always doing, and with this surplus it creates the cities that supplement and crown the life of the land.

3. Rejuvenation Through Conservation

The first great surge of the American Conservation movement occurred during the Progressive period when the nation sensed a diminishing of the material abundance that had buoyed the prosperity of its youth. On May 13, 1908, at the invitation of President Theodore Roosevelt, over a thousand national leaders gathered at the White House for a conference. Gifford Pinchot, Roosevelt's Chief Forester, organized the dramatic meeting to publicize a new concept of resource management known as "sustained yield." With the aid of science and technology, the harvesting of natural resources would proceed more efficiently and, hopefully, longer. The decline of national greatness could thus be forestalled. What follows is Roosevelt's opening address to the conference.

Conservation of Natural Resources
THEODORE ROOSEVELT

Governors of the several States; and Gentlemen:

I welcome you to this Conference at the White House. You have come hither at my request, so that we may join together to consider the question of the conservation and use of the great fundamental sources of wealth of this Nation.

Theodore Roosevelt, "Opening Address by the President," *Proceedings of a Conference of Governors in the White House,* ed. Newton C. Blanchard (Washington, D.C., Government Printing Office, 1909), 3–10, 12.

So vital is this question, that for the first time in our history the chief executive officers of the States separately, and of the States together forming the Nation, have met to consider it. It is the chief material question that confronts us, second only—and second always—to the great fundamental questions of morality.

With the governors come men from each State chosen for their special acquaintance with the terms of the problem that is before us. Among them are experts in natural resources and representatives of national organizations concerned in the development and use of these resources; the Senators and Representatives in Congress; the Supreme Court, the Cabinet, and the Inland Waterways Commission have likewise been invited to the Conference, which is therefore national in a peculiar sense.

This Conference on the conservation of natural resources is in effect a meeting of the representatives of all the people of the United States called to consider the weightiest problem now before the Nation; and the occasion for the meeting lies in the fact that the natural resources of our country are in danger of exhaustion if we permit the old wasteful methods of exploiting them longer to continue.

With the rise of peoples from savagery to civilization, and with the consequent growth in the extent and variety of the needs of the average man, there comes a steadily increasing growth of the amount demanded by this average man from the actual resources of the country. And yet, rather curiously, at the same time that there comes that increase in what the average man demands from the resources, he is apt to grow to lose the sense of his dependence upon nature. He lives in big cities. He deals in industries that do not bring him in close touch with nature. He does not realize the demands he is making upon nature. For instance, he finds, as he had found before in many parts of this country, that it is cheaper to build his house of concrete than of wood, learning in this way only that he has allowed the woods to become exhausted. That is happening, as you know, in parts of this country at this very time.

Savages, and very primitive peoples generally, concern themselves only with superficial natural resources; with those which they obtain from the actual surface of the ground. As peoples become a little less primitive, their industries, although in a rude manner, are extended to resources below the surface; then, with what we call civilization and the extension of knowledge, more resources come into use, industries are multiplied, and foresight begins to become a necessary and prominent factor in life. Crops are cultivated; animals are domesticated; and metals are mastered.

We can not do any of these things without foresight, and we can not, when the nation becomes fully civilized and very rich, continue to be civilized and rich unless the nation shows more foresight than we are showing at this moment as a nation.

Every step of the progress of mankind is marked by the discovery and use of natural resources previously unused. Without such progressive knowledge and utilization of natural resources population could not grow, nor industries multiply, nor the hidden wealth of the earth be developed for the benefit of mankind.

From the first beginnings of civilization, on the banks of the Nile and the Euphrates, the industrial progress of the world has gone on slowly, with occasional set-backs, but on the whole steadily, through tens of centuries to the present day.

It never does advance by jumps, gentlemen. It always goes slowly. There are occasional set-backs, but on the whole it goes steadily.

But of late the rapidity of the process has increased at such a rate that more space has been actually covered during the century and a quarter occupied by our national life than during the preceding six thousand years that take us back to the earliest monuments of Egypt, to the earliest cities of the Babylonian plain.

Now, I ask you to think what that means; and I am speaking with historic literalness. In the development, the use, and therefore the exhaustion of certain of the natural resources, the progress has been more rapid in the past century and a quarter than during all preceding time of which we have record.

When the founders of this nation met at Independence Hall in Philadelphia the conditions of commerce had not fundamentally changed from what they were when the Phoenician keels first furrowed the lonely waters of the Mediterranean.

You turn to Homer—some of you did in your school days, even if you do not now—and you will see that he spoke, not of the Mediterranean but of one corner of the Egean only, as a limitless waste of water which no one had traversed. There is now no nook of the earth that we are not searching.

When our forefathers met in Independence Hall, the differences were those of degrees, not of kind, and they were not in all cases even those of degree. Mining was carried on fundamentally as it had been carried on by the Pharaohs in the countries adjacent to the Red Sea. Explorers now-a-days by the shores of the Red Sea strike countries that they call new, but they find in them mines, with sculptures of the Pharaohs, showing that those mines were worked out and exhausted thousands of years before the Christian era.

In 1776 the wares of the merchants of Boston, of Charleston, like the wares of the merchants of Nineveh and Sidon, if they went by water, were carried by boats propelled by sails or oars; if they went by land were carried in wagons drawn by beasts of draft or in packs on the backs of beasts of burden. The ships that crossed the high seas were better than the ships that three thousand years before crossed the Aegean, but they were of the same type, after all—they were wooden ships propelled by sails. There the difference was one of degree in our favor. On shore the difference was one of degree against us, for on land the roads, at the end of the eighteenth century, when this country became a nation, were not as good as the roads of the Roman Empire, while the service of the posts, at any rate prior to the days of Benjamin Franklin, was probably inferior. In the previous eighteen hundred years there had been a retrogression in roads and in postal service.

In [George] Washington's time anthracite coal was known only as a useless black stone; and the great fields of bituminous coal were undiscovered. As steam was unknown, the use of coal for power production was undreamed of. Water was practically the only source of power, save the labor of men and animals; and this power was used only in the most primitive fashion. But a few small iron deposits had been found in this country, and the use of iron by our countrymen was very small. Wood was practically the only fuel, and what lumber was sawed was consumed locally, while the forests were regarded chiefly as obstructions to settlement and cultivation. The man who cut down a tree was held to have conferred a service upon his fellows.

Such was the degree of progress to which civilized mankind had attained when this nation began its career. It is almost impossible for us in this day to realize how little our Revolutionary ancestors knew of the great store of natural resources whose discovery and use have been such vital factors in the growth and greatness of this Nation, and how little they required to take from this store in order to satisfy their needs.

Since then our knowledge and use of the resources of the present territory of the United States have increased a hundred-fold. Indeed, the growth of this Nation by leaps and bounds makes one of the most striking and important chapters in the history of the world. Its growth has been due to the rapid development, and alas that it should be said! to the rapid destruction of our natural resources. Nature has supplied to us in the United States, and still supplies to us, more kinds of resources in a more lavish degree than has ever been the case at any other time or with any other people. Our position in the world has been attained by the extent and thoroughness of the control we have achieved over nature; but we are more, and not less, dependent upon what she furnishes than at any previous time of history since the days of primitive man.

Yet our fathers, though they knew so little of the resources of the country, exercised a wise forethought in reference thereto. Washington clearly saw that the perpetuity of the States could only be secured by union, and that the only feasible basis of union was an economic one; in other words, that it must be based on the development and use of their natural resources. Accordingly, he helped to outline a scheme of commercial development, and by his influence an interstate waterways commission was appointed by Virginia and Maryland.

It met near where we are now meeting, in Alexandria, adjourned to Mount Vernon, and took up the consideration of interstate commerce by the only means then available, that of water; and the trouble we have since had with the railways has been mainly due to the fact that naturally our forefathers could not divine that the iron road would become the interstate and international highway, instead of the old route by water. Further conferences were arranged, first at Annapolis, and then at Philadelphia. It was in Philadelphia that the representatives of all the States met for what was in its original conception merely a waterways conference; but when they had closed their deliberations the outcome was the Constitution which made the States into a Nation. [Applause]

The Constitution of the United States thus grew in large part out of the necessity for united action in the wise use of one of our natural resources. The wise use of all our natural resources, which are our national resources as well, is the great material question of today. I have asked you to come together now because the enormous consumption of these resources, and the threat of imminent exhaustion of some of them, due to reckless and wasteful use, once more calls for common effort, common action.

We want to take action that will prevent the advent of a woodless age, and defer as long as possible the advent of an ironless age. [Applause]

Since the days when the Constitution was adopted, steam and electricity have revolutionized the industrial world. Nowhere has the revolution been so great as in our country. The discovery and utilization of mineral fuels and alloys have given us the lead over all other nations in the production of steel. The discovery and utilization of coal and iron have given us our railways, and have led to such industrial development as has never before been seen. The vast wealth of lumber in our forests, the riches of our soils and mines, the discovery of gold and mineral oils, combined with the efficiency of our transportation, have made the conditions of our life unparalleled in comfort and convenience.

A great many of these things are truisms. Much of what I say is so familiar to us that it seems commonplace to repeat it; but familiar though it is, I do not think as a nation we understand what its real bearing is. It is so familiar that we disregard it.

The steadily increasing drain on these natural resources has promoted to an extraordinary degree the complexity of our industrial and social life. Moreover, this unexampled development has had a determining effect upon the character and opinions of our people. The demand for efficiency in the great task has given us vigor, effectiveness, decision, and power, and a capacity for achievement which in its own lines has never yet been matched. So great and so rapid has been our material growth that there has been a tendency to lag behind in spiritual and moral growth [laughter and applause]; but that is not the subject upon which I speak to you today.

Disregarding for the moment the question of moral purpose, it is safe to say that the prosperity of our people depends directly on the energy and intelligence with which our natural resources are used. It is equally clear that these resources are the final basis of national power and perpetuity. Finally, it is ominously evident that these resources are in the course of rapid exhaustion.

This Nation began with the belief that its landed possessions were illimitable and capable of supporting all the people who might care to make our country their home; but already the limit of unsettled land is in sight, and indeed but little land fitted for agriculture now remains unoccupied save what can be reclaimed by irrigation and drainage—a subject with which this Conference is partly to deal. We began with an unapproached heritage of forests; more than half of the timber is gone. We began with coal fields more extensive than those of any other nation and with iron ores regarded as inexhaustible, and many experts now declare that the end of both iron and coal is in sight.

The mere increase in our consumption of coal during 1907 over 1906 exceeded the total consumption in 1876, the Centennial year. This is a striking fact: Thirty years went by, and the mere surplus of use of one year over the preceding year exceeded all that was used in 1876—and we thought we were pretty busy people even then. The enormous stores of mineral oil and gas are largely gone; and those Governors who have in their States cities built up by natural gas, where the natural gas has since been exhausted, can tell us something of what that means. Our natural waterways are not gone, but they have been so injured by neglect, and by the division of responsibility and utter lack of system in dealing with them, that there is less navigation on them now than there was fifty years ago. Finally, we began with soils of unexampled fertility, and we have so impoverished them by injudicious use and by failing to check erosion that their crop-producing power is diminishing instead of increasing. In a word, we have thoughtlessly, and to a large degree unnecessarily, diminished the resources upon which not only our prosperity but the prosperity of our children and our children's children must always depend.

We have become great in a material sense because of the lavish use of our resources, and we have just reason to be proud of our growth. But the time has come to inquire seriously what will happen when our forests are gone, when the coal, the iron, the oil, and the gas are exhausted, when the soils shall have been still further impoverished and washed into the streams, polluting the rivers, denuding the fields, and obstructing navigation. These questions do not relate only to the next century or to the next generation. One distinguishing characteristic of really civilized men is foresight; we have to, as a nation, exercise foresight for this nation in the future; and if we do not exercise that foresight, dark will be the future! We should exercise foresight now, as the ordinarily prudent man exercises foresight in conserving and wisely using the property which contains the assurance of well-being for himself and his children. We want to see a man own his farm rather than rent it, because we want to see it an object to him to transfer it in better order to his children. We want to see him exercise forethought for the next generation. We need to exercise it in some fashion ourselves as a nation for the next generation.

The natural resources I have enumerated can be divided into two sharply distinguished classes accordingly as they are or are not capable of renewal. Mines if used must necessarily be exhausted. The minerals do not and can not renew themselves. Therefore in dealing with the coal, the oil, the gas, the iron, the metals generally, all that we can do is to try to see that they are wisely used. The exhaustion is certain to come in time. We can trust that it will be deferred long enough to enable the extraordinarily inventive genius of our people to devise means and methods for more or less adequately replacing what is lost; but the exhaustion is sure to come.

The second class of resources consists of those which can not only be used in such manner to leave them undiminished for our children, but can actually be improved by wise use. The soil, the forests, the waterways come in this category. Every one knows that a really good farmer leaves his farm more valuable at the end of his life than it was when he first took hold of it. So with the waterways. So with the forests. In dealing with mineral resources, man is able to improve on nature only by putting the resources to a beneficial use which in the end exhausts them; but in dealing with the soil and its products man can improve on nature by compelling the resources to renew and even reconstruct themselves in such manner as to serve increasingly beneficial uses—while the living waters can be so controlled as to multiply their benefits.

Neither the primitive man nor the pioneer was aware of any duty to posterity in dealing with the renewable resources. When the American settler felled the forests, he felt that there was plenty of forest left for the sons who came after him. When he exhausted the soil of his farm, he felt that his son could go West and take up another. The Kentuckian or the Ohioan felled the forest and expected his son to move west and fell other forests on the banks of the Mississippi; the Georgian exhausted his farm and moved into Alabama or to the mouth of the Yazoo to take another. So it was with his immediate successors. When the soil-wash from the farmer's field choked the neighboring river, the only thought was to use the railway rather than the boats to move produce and supplies. That was so up to the generation that preceded ours.

Now all this is changed. On the average the son of the farmer of today must make his living on his father's farm. There is no difficulty in doing this if the father will exercise wisdom. No wise use of a farm exhausts its fertility. So with the forests. We are over the verge of a timber famine in this country, and it is unpardonable for the Nation or the States to permit any further cutting of our timber save in accordance with a system which will provide that the next generation shall see the timber increased instead of diminished.

Just let me interject one word as to a particular type of folly of which it ought not to be necessary to speak. We stop wasteful cutting of timber; that of course makes a slight shortage at the moment. To avoid that slight shortage at the moment, there are certain people so foolish that they will incur absolute shortage in the future, and they are willing to stop all attempts to conserve the forests, because of course by wastefully using them at the moment we can for a year or two provide against any lack of wood. That is like providing for the farmer's family to live sumptuously on the flesh of the milch cow. Any farmer can live pretty well for a year if he is content not to live at all the year after.

We can, moreover, add enormous tracts of the most valuable possible agricultural land to the national domain by irrigation in the arid and semi-arid regions, and by drainage of great tracts of swamp land in the humid regions. We can enormously increase our transportation facilities by the canalization of our rivers so as to complete a great system of waterways on the Pacific, Atlantic, and Gulf coasts and in the Mississippi Valley, from the Great Plains to the Alleghenies, and from the northern lakes to the mouth of the mighty Father of Waters. But all these various uses of our natural resources are so closely connected that they should be coordinated, and should be treated as part of one coherent plan and not in haphazard and piecemeal fashion.

It is largely because of this that I appointed the Waterways Commission last year, and that I sought to perpetuate its work. There are members of the coordinate branch present. The reason this meeting takes place is because we had that waterways commission last year. I had to prosecute the work by myself. I have asked Congress to pass a bill giving some small sum of money for the perpetuation of that Commission. If Congress does not act, I will perpetuate the Commission anyway, [Great applause] but of course it is a great deal better that Congress should act; it enables the work to be more effectively done. I hope there will be action. But the Commission will go ahead.

I wish to take this opportunity to express in heartiest fashion my acknowledgment to all the members of the Commission. At great personal sacrifice of time and effort they have rendered a service to the public for which we cannot be too grateful. Especial credit is due to the initiative, the energy, the devotion to duty, and the farsightedness of Gifford Pinchot, [Great applause] to whom we owe so much of the progress we have already made in handling this matter of the coordination and conservation of natural resources. If it had not been for him this convention neither would nor could have been called.

We are coming to recognize as never before the right of the Nation to guard its own future in the essential matter of natural resources. In the past we have admitted the right of the individual to injure the future of the Republic for his own present profit. In fact there has been a good deal of a demand for unrestricted individualism, for the right of the individual to injure the future of all of us for his own temporary and immediate profit. The time has come for a change. As a people we have the right and the duty, second to none other but the right and duty of obeying the moral law, of requiring and doing justice, to protect ourselves and our children against the wasteful development of our natural resources, whether that waste is caused by the actual destruction of such resources or by making them impossible of development hereafter.

Any right thinking father earnestly desires and strives to leave his son both an untarnished name and a reasonable equipment for the struggle of life. So this Nation as a whole should earnestly desire and strive to leave to the next generation the national honor unstained and the national resources unexhausted. . . .

Finally, let us remember that the conservation of our natural resources, though the gravest problem of today, is yet but part of another and greater problem to which this Nation is not yet awake, but to which it will awake in time, and with which it must hereafter grapple if it is to live—the problem of national efficiency, the patriotic duty of insuring the safety and continuance of the Nation. [Applause.] When the People of the United States consciously undertake to raise themselves as citizens, and the Nation and the States in their several spheres, to the highest pitch of excellence in private, State, and national life, and to do this because it is the first of all the duties of true patriotism, then and not till then the future of this Nation, in quality and in time, will be assured.

4. The Virtues of Nature

The 1908 Conservation Conference expressed an overwhelmingly utilitarian attitude toward nature. In a sense, Gifford Pinchot and his colleagues were only extending the conquering-developing emphasis of the pioneers with emphasis on greater efficiency. Yet for other Americans, especially intellectuals and city dwellers, this kind of conservation stopped far short of realizing the highest benefits from the natural environment. Among those who spoke for the aesthetic, spiritual, psychological, and other "soft" values of nature, few equaled the eminence of Charles W. Eliot, president emeritus of Harvard University at the time he wrote this essay.

The Need of Conserving the Beauty and Freedom of Nature
CHARLES W. ELIOT

The past hundred years have supplied civilized mankind with a complete demonstration that the evils which attend the growth of modern cities and the factory system are too great for the human body to endure; yet these evils are the consequences, or results, of nineteenth-century civilization, and particularly of that form of liberty which the first half of the century developed—individualism. Within the last 40 years a different form of liberty, the liberty of association and collective action, has begun

Charles W. Eliot, "The Need of Conserving the Beauty and Freedom of Nature in Modern Life," *National Geographic*, 26 (July, 1914), 67, 69, 71, 73.

to check some of the evils fostered by individualism, and so to improve the human environment.

The sources of the evils which afflict the population massed in cities are partly physical and partly mental or moral. The collective energies of society are now actively directed to the amelioration of bad physical conditions, and considerable improvements in this respect have already been made; and more are in sight. The study, even, of remedies for wrong mental and moral conditions has hardly begun: yet these are fundamental evils which must be eradicated, if improved physical conditions are to produce their desired effects.

It is therefore a very practical and urgent inquiry: What influences in the environment of civilized mankind make for mental health, for wholesome interests, for rational pleasures, and for exalting delight in the beauty, grace, and splendor of nature?

By far the most important social study today is the study of the means of improving men's emotion and thought environment from earliest youth to age. These means are both negative and positive—on the one hand they must shut out poisonous excitements and injurious pleasures, on the other they must develop all wholesome mental interests and enjoyable activities of observation, memory, and imagination.

In order to cure the destructive evils of present urban life and the factory system, it will not be enough to restrict the vices, to diminish the pressure of poverty, to prevent destructive diseases, and prolong the average human life. The human environment must be not only negatively but positively improved; so that the whole people may have the opportunity to cultivate healthy tastes and interests, to acquire just ideals of pleasantness and beauty, and to learn the value toward tranquil happiness of that living with nature which city congestion has within a single generation made almost impossible for multitudes.

While the exclusion of bad influences needs to be unremitting, the good influences—fortunately for crowded urban populations—need not all be incessantly in action. An occasional holiday in a city park or garden, a week-end in the country now and then, or a fortnight's vacation in summer may make deep and lasting mental impressions, and supply both children and adults with wholesome material to fill the mind and direct its energies for months and years.

Hence the importance of better city and suburban planning, of public reservations of all sorts in city and state, and of national parks and monuments. All these modes of public action tell not only on the physical well-being of both urban and rural populations, but on the mental training of children and on the cultivation in the whole population of thoroughly healthy spiritual interests and uplifting enjoyments, both individual and social.

The profession of landscape architecture is going to be—indeed, it already is—the most direct professional contributor to the improvement of the human environment in the twentieth century, because it is devoted not only to the improvement of housing and of town and city designing, but also to the creation, preservation, and enlargement of opportunities for human enjoyment of mountains and valleys, hills and plains, forests and flowers, ponds and water-courses, spring blossoms and autumn tints, and the wild life of birds and other animals in their natural haunts. These are the things that city dwellers need to have opportunities to see and enjoy; these are the things that serve as antidotes to the unwholesome excitements and tensions of modern city life; these are the delights which, by occupying the mind and satisfying the spirit, keep out degrading thoughts and foul desires.

That good environment can modify favorably the effects of heredity is as true of nations as of individuals. The vital question of modern life is how to feed the mental health and spiritual growth of multitudes. In the modern world life is tightly packed against life, and one life is interwoven with many others. Neither freedom of mind nor health of body can be secured in isolation; for both blessings the individual must hereafter be dependent on social or collective action.

The present evils of city life and the factory system—bad conditions which civilization has itself created—have developed their destructive forces in this country in spite of the schools and churches and of free political institutions, and in spite of many happy influences from art, poetry, music, and the drama. Clearly, society needs to develop a new and better environment for the general life—an environment favorable to both bodily and mental health and to the attainment of genuine happiness—not of mere momentary excitements, pleasures, and gratifications, but of solid contentment, and the lasting satisfactions of life enjoyed in quietness and peace. What are the means of compassing this end?

The readiest means is good planning of city, town, and landscape—first applied to areas still open, and then gradually to areas already occupied in undesirable ways. The new planning must take into account the interests of the whole community, as well as the interests of individual owners, the social or collective interest always prevailing.

The immediate objects to be sought are more light and air for dwellings, offices, shops, and factories, and thus a spreading out of cities; the transfer of factories to suburbs and to country sites along the lines of railway; the multiplication of playgrounds and open decorated areas, and above all the attachment of a piece of arable or garden ground to every family dwelling. Many of these results can certainly be attained; and indeed much work of this sort is already started in regulating the height of buildings, transferring factories and setting up new plants in smaller towns, enlarging school-yards, and creating public parks and gardens.

The housing problem for mechanics and operatives has already been solved in a business way by the English Garden City. In cities already too compactly built and with too lofty structures the improvement of the human environment must await better understanding of life's needs or change of taste in populations now unwholesomely congested. With the diffusion of knowledge concerning healthy and happy conditions for family life and the industrial life of the laborious masses this reformation of our cities and manufacturing towns will surely come about, but in coming about it must take account of something more than water supplies, sewers, and street lights; it must take account of beauty and of all that brings cheerfulness and social happiness.

The collective force of the community must further supply the means of making rural and landscape pleasures occasionally accessible to city populations by means of parks and gardens which illustrate all forms of open-country beauty and permit the occasional enjoyment by city families or larger urban groups of the outdoor pleasures which woods, shrubberies, gardens, and broad fields can give. All city dwellers greatly need these occasional delights, and Americans more than any other people; for they have become accustomed to an indoor life, and have come to rely on electricity as a substitute for sunlight, and mechanical ventilation as an equivalent for fresh air. Even the richer sort of Americans are often content to live in houses in which at least one-third of the cubical contents cannot be used without artificial light the year round, and to occupy offices in which electricity has to reinforce sunlight during the greater part of the year.

The proper use of the natural materials for creating on public ground fine landscapes, gardens, and scenes of rural beauty involves an extensive study of these materials. The landscape architect must know how to use a near or distant prospect of hills and woods. He must know the trees, shrubs, and herbaceous plants valuable in landscape or in gardens, or along walks and drives where thousands of people daily pass. He must know all the native materials for creating scenes of beauty, and all the imported materials which have proved available in the climate of the reservation he plans. And in order that the landscape architect may have the opportunity to study these materials, society must furnish places where they may be assembled, appropriately used, and thoroughly tested.

In other words, the collective force of society should be used to provide and maintain living collections of these materials of landscape and garden beauty, where climate, soil, and scenery make it possible to assemble, cultivate, and exhibit them advantageously. The botanic gardens and arboretums which universities and governments maintain do not fully answer this purpose, although they contribute to it; because the lay-out of the botanical gardens and arboretums is made for a scientific purpose quite different from that which directs the thoughts of the landscape architect.

There is another source of keen enjoyment for city people which should be provided for when parks, gardens, and playgrounds are constructed for their pleasure, namely, the natural interest in animal life as well as vegetable life. Most men and nearly all women take a keen interest in bird life—in the migration, nesting, family life, and feeding habits of birds, both land birds and sea fowl. It is one of the advantages of suburban over city life that many varieties of birds can be seen and studied in the suburbs. The collective force of society, therefore, should be exerted to preserve all the species of birds which are profitable, not only for food and crop protection, but also for the stirring of human sympathy and delight in their colors, songs, and alert, sprightly ways. The provision of sanctuaries for birds, of closed spaces as well as closed seasons, is a highly expedient use of the collective protective force of society against individual destroyers of bird life.

The government of the United States has begun to use effectively its constitutional powers for improving the environment of the people by conserving broad scenes of extraordinary natural beauty and single beautiful or striking objects which, without the protection afforded them by government, might be lost to future generations. The national parks are reserved by act of Congress; the President, by executive order, may and does order the preservation of smaller areas or single objects under the title of national monuments. State legislatures have begun to provide State reservations, and have authorized municipalities, or special districts, to acquire both large and small parks. Chartered bodies of trustees have been authorized by State legislatures to acquire and hold considerable areas for perpetual public use.

On the beautiful island of Mount Desert, not far from the northeastern extremity of the Atlantic coast of the United States, there is at this moment opportunity for establishing a national monument of unique interest and large serviceableness. The island is the loftiest piece of land on the Atlantic coast of the United States, and has a sharply differentiated surface of hills and valleys, a climate midway between that of the neighboring lands and that of the surrounding sea, abundant water, and in favorable spots a highly productive soil, well suited for growing a wide variety of trees, flowering shrubs, and herbaceous plants belonging to the temperate and subarctic regions of the world.

Private initiative and enterprise have long since demonstrated the peculiar fitness of the Mount Desert climate and soils for horticultural and arboricultural uses, and leading botanists and garden experts have testified to the remarkable thriftiness of plants grown upon the island, as well as to the unusual beauty and rich coloring of their blooms.

A body of trustees, called the "Hancock County Trustees of Public Reservations," has already acquired the wooded slopes and rocky summits of many of the principal hills, and holds them for perpetual public enjoyment. Possession, too, has been secured by public-spirited private persons of considerable areas exceptionally fitted for the growth and exhibition of all varieties of trees, shrubs, and herbaceous plants which the landscape architect might use in developing all across the continent, in northern climates, parks and gardens for the enjoyment of city populations. Here, too, all the bird-food plants could be appropriately cultivated and bird sanctuaries provided. The cultivated tracts would have a noble background of rocky cliffs and lofty hills, and down the valleys and gorges visitors would look out from time to time over the near bays or the distant ocean. Here, in short, could be brought together under highly favorable conditions and in great variety the botanical and zoölogical materials of the landscape and garden designer.

If the government of the United States should set aside as a national monument a large area on this picturesque and unique island, it would help to consecrate for all time to the improvement of the human environment one of the most beautiful and interesting regions in the whole country; and in so doing it would take appropriate part in resisting and overcoming the destructive influences on modern civilization of urban life and the factory system.

The powers of the national government have thus far been exerted to these conservation ends chiefly in the Far West, where population is sparse and the evils of city life and the factory system are little developed. Is it not just and highly expedient that these beneficent powers should now be exerted in the East, where manufacturing industries occupy the major part of the population and the destructive effects of city life have long been manifest?

5. Environmental Tastes

The American idea of "progress" traditionally meant eliminating the natural environment and replacing it with something man-made. Skyscrapers rose while hills were sliced away. The smokestacks of mills and factories came to dominate the view and their emissions to pollute the air. People learned to adapt to the new conditions, living and working as best they could in urban situations. But the need for nature persisted. City planners and park commissioners designed "green belts" around metropolitan areas in order to break the hold of the artificial environment. Communities and industries willing to bear the expense, landscaped highways and railroad stations, tempering machines with gardens. Zoning laws reinforced social preferences, restricting the individual.

The historic environment was also a matter of concern. Pioneer log cabins were restored, relocated, and landscaped in a manner believed suitable to their original condition. The preservation of Revolutionary landmarks such as battlefields and forts served to foster patriotism. Such visible remains *were* history in the mind of the average citizen. Even a single, natural object, such as an ancient tree, might be coveted in some circles and defended against destruction. But the main thrust toward development and transformation of the environment received only token checks before 1916. The overwhelmingly utilitarian emphasis of American culture did not yet allow much reverence for the land itself.

54

1. TRANSFORMING THE LANDSCAPE:
    Sluicing down Seattle's hills in 1907.

2. THE SYNTHETIC SKYLINE: *Pittsburgh, 1909.*

3. PEOPLE IN CITIES: *Slum backyard about 1910.*

4. GREEN BELTS: *Park system proposed for Washington, D.C., 1901.*

5. BEAUTIFICATION: *Landscaped railroad station,
St. David's, Pennsylvania.*

58

6. THE VISIBLE PAST: *Pioneer cabin, Letchworth Park, New York.*

7. HISTORICAL LANDMARKS AND PATRIOTISM:
Restored barracks, Fort Ticonderoga, New York.

8. NATURE AS HISTORY: *225-year-old Inwood tulip tree, Spuyten Duyvil Creek near the Hudson River, New York.*

6. Rural Uplift and Nature Education

From his position as Dean of the Agricultural School at Cornell University, Liberty Hyde Bailey carried on an extended campaign to check the decreasing influence of nature in American civilization. From 1901 to 1903 he edited *Country Life in America,* using its pages to argue that the optimum environment was one which combined the best of both city and country. He was among the first to extol the suburb. He also sought to make farm life more attractive and, to this end, served as a member of the President's Commission on Country Life in 1908 and 1909. Another Bailey cause was the promotion of nature education for city children. Borrowing some of the ideas of John Dewey's progressive education, he developed a program for overcoming the growing unreality of the natural world. Near the end of his career Bailey arrived at a philosophy of love and respect for what he called "the holy earth."

Country Life
LIBERTY HYDE BAILEY

There is a growing interest in country life: this journal [*Country Life in America*] would be its representative.

The interest in country life is various. Many persons are drawn to it because it is release from the city. Sooner or later every busy man longs for a quiet nook in the country where he may be at peace. He wants a

Liberty Hyde Bailey, "What This Magazine Stands For," *Country Life in America,* 1 (Nov., 1901), 24–25; Bailey, *The Nature-Study Idea* (New York, Doubleday, Page and Co., 1903), 5, 14–19.

country residence. Every year the outflux to the country is greater and farther reaching. The city may not satisfy the soul.

To others, country life is nature for nature's sake. It is contact with living and growing things. The spirit of nature-love, under one name or another, is taking firm hold on our people. It is the spirit of pleasant inquiry, of intellectual enthusiasm, of moral uplift. Its associations are with things that are clean and true.

Others, by choice or chance, are permanent country residents. They are farmers or horticulturists, or they are professional or business men who live in villages and rural cities. Spread out a map of North America. Note the mere dots that represent the cities; contrast the immense expanses of the country.

Only when we love the country is country life worth the living. Contentment and satisfaction of soul are beyond all questions of pecuniary reward. Ultimately, they dominate all things. We would clasp hands with every person who loves the country, and we would engender that love in persons who love it not; and thus would we come into sympathy with all mankind.

We would preach the sermon of the out-of-doors, where men are free. We would lead the way to the place where there is room, and where there are sweet, fresh winds. We would relieve the cramped and pent-up life with visions of things that every one may have for only the trouble of opening his eyes. We would tell him where the wild geranium blows and what it means. To the person who resides permanently in the country, we would give a broader view and a closer intimacy with what he has. We would show him the dandelion. We would put him into harmony with his environment.

We intend that our work shall be more than sentiment. We believe that we have also an economic and social mission. The cities are congested; the country has room. We would check the influx into the cities by opening the eyes of the country man to see the country. We would show him his advantages. The abjectly poor live in the cities. One does not starve in the country.

We shall not make a technical agricultural or horticultural journal; yet we stand for the elevation and betterment of farming in its best and broadest sense, because the fundamental thing in a self-sustaining country life is agriculture. We want to encourage home-building outside the city, and we shall give instruction in those kindly agricultural arts that have to do with the making of a country home, whether the home is a summer residence, a farmhouse, a rich man's mansion or a workman's cottage. We shall make sketches of farms and gardens. We shall endeavor to portray the artistic in rural life.

We desire to develop the beautiful spots in our country. We would lend our influence in the preservation of natural scenery and historic places. Whilst we are concerned primarily with country life, we shall consider it within our sphere to discuss all matters of urban improvement that have to do with parking and planting. We desire to coöperate with improvement organizations, historical associations, horticultural and agricultural societies.

To attain all these ideals, we must make a magazine that is artistic and that enlists the best literary talent of the day. We shall endeavor to make the publication worth reading and preserving. It will also be a journal of record. It will discuss the rural progress of the time. It will make note of the current writings on nature and farming, both American and foreign. It will take particular account of horticultural matters, since these things usually are intimately associated with the home. Connected with the editorial management are greenhouses and a farm, from which reports can be made on the novelties in plants. It will also be a journal of comment. It will express an editorial opinion on the movements, political or otherwise, that intimately affect country living.

There is intrinsic worth in the country. Many of us see the country through stained-glass windows and admire the color for a moment, then forget. "Country Life in America" is edited in the country. It is a country magazine for the country man, and for the city man who wants to know the country; it is not a city magazine that sees the country afar off and takes it for granted. It is not a vacation journal. We hope that the smell of the soil will be on its pages.

What, then, is our field? To extend and emphasize the interest in country life; to point the way to nature; to portray the beauty of the land that lies beneath the open sky; to lure to health and relaxation; to stay the congestion of the city; to raise the tone of American farming; to offer specific help and advice to the homemaker, the vacation-seeker, the gardener, the farmer, the nature-teacher, the naturalist; to take account of current rural events, to record progress, and to make note of the literature; to make the country the complement of the city; to sound some sweet and joyous note that shall relieve the tension of our eager lives.

More than half the people of North America live in the country. Bulletin 65 of the Twelfth United States Census (1900) shows a population in "incorporated places" of 47.1 per cent of the total. The remaining 53 per cent lives in the open country or in small hamlets and villages.

The "incorporated places," in which the 47 per cent lives, include rural villages as well as cities, and many of these persons are essentially country people. Only 37.3 per cent of the population of the United States (Bulletin 70) lives in places of 4,000 people and upwards.

How many of our people are farmers it is difficult to determine. Many business men are also farmers, although they may not appear as farmers in the census. In 1890, there were 8,305,286 persons occupied as farmers, dairymen, apiarists and farm laborers out of the twenty-two and three-fourths millions people engaged in all occupations. Aside from these there were more than seventy-two thousand gardeners, florists and nurserymen. What proportion of the people actually live on farms is also difficult of determination. Not all farmers live on their farms. There is a strong tendency, which seems to be growing, for farmers to live in villages. But wherever these people live, they are concerned with the problems of the country as distinguished from those of the city. It is true that the proportion of persons who live in cities is constantly increasing; it is also true that interest in the country and in all rural affairs is extending at the same time. There is room in the country for endless development. There are opportunities for full and useful lives. It is surprising how thinly populated and how undeveloped the open country is. Farms are remarkable for the small numbers of people whom they employ. The eight and one-third million farmers of the Eleventh Census worked about four and a half million farms; that is, there were about two workers to a farm. Not only the half of the people who live in the country, but fully half of the other half, is interested in country life. For all these people, we believe that this magazine has a mission.

It was not many years ago that people lived in the suburbs as a matter of economy. Now they live in these parts because higher ideals may often be attained here. From reports personally obtained from twenty-eight of the largest cities in America, North, South, East and West, it was estimated that during two recent years over $420,000,000 had been invested in private purchases and the development of lands adjacent to large cities, for suburban operations. Over $60,000,000 were reported to have been voted by trolley and railroad companies to extend their service beyond the limits of these cities. Nearly half a billion of dollars, therefore, were invested in two years in the proposed development of suburban properties, in addition to the millions of dollars already so invested.

It is becoming more and more apparent that the ideal life is that which combines something of the social and intellectual advantages and physical comforts of the city with the inspiration and the peaceful joys of the country. If, for business reasons, the tendency of population is concentrative, for living it is distributive. The greater part of the summer exodus countryward is the expression of a growing and genuine interest in the country and in nature, and is deeper and more far-reaching than mere fad or fashion. The enormous investment that is made in country homes is itself a conservative influence and tends to the permanence of the outdoor movement. This movement is having a most beneficial effect on agriculture, in raising the ideals of country living.

Aside from all this, there is an independent revival of interest in agriculture itself. The teachings of science are being felt. Business methods are being applied. The country is improving.

The growth of literature pertaining to plants and animals and the out-of-doors is one of the most emphatic and significant movements of the time. As an indication of the interest on the part of the public in reading matter appertaining to country life, it may be recorded that there were published in the United States within fifteen months one hundred and forty-two books devoted to outdoor topics. Not one of these books has been what the publishers call a failure; a number have sold 20,000 copies; some 40,000; others 50,000; and at least one 60,000 copies. Publishing houses prepare special catalogues of outdoor literature. Added to this, is the rapidly growing literature of agriculture and its allied arts. The old days of distrust in "book-farming" have come to an end. Farm literature of the present day is vital, resourceful, scientific, entertaining. The demand for it is increasing. Much of it will outlive its generation.

Only by means of a large correspondence can we hope to keep in touch with the many interests that are concerned in country living. We desire to have a close personal relation with our constituents. These constituents will be largely the makers of the magazine. Correspondence addressed to the publishers or editor will receive careful attention. We are especially anxious to interest every expert photographer who cares for country living or the beautiful in nature.

Nature-Study
LIBERTY HYDE BAILEY

Nature-study is not science. It is not knowledge. It is not facts. It is spirit. It is concerned with the child's outlook on the world.

Nature-study will endure, because it is natural and of universal application. Methods will change and will fall into disrepute; its name will be dropped from curriculums; here and there it will be encased in the schoolmaster's "method" and its life will be smothered; now and then it will be overexploited; with many persons it will be a fad: but the spirit will live. . . .

It is one of the marks of the evolution of the race that we are coming more and more into sympathy with the objects of the external world. These things are a part of our lives. They are central to our thoughts. The happiest life has the greatest number of points of contact with the world, and it has the deepest feeling and sympathy for everything that is. The best thing in life is sentiment; and the best sentiment is that which is born of the most accurate knowledge. I like to make this application of Emerson's injunction to "hitch your wagon to a star"; but it must not be forgotten that one must have the wagon before one has the star. Mere facts are dead, but the meaning of the facts is life. The getting of information is but the beginning of education. "With all thy getting, get understanding."

Of late years there has been a rapidly growing feeling that we must live closer to nature; and we must perforce begin with the child. We attempt to teach this nature-love in the schools, and we call the effort nature-study. It would be better if it were called nature-sympathy.

As yet there are no codified methods of teaching nature-study. The subject is not a formal part of the curriculum; and thereby it is not perfunctory. And herein lies much of its value—in the fact that it cannot be reduced to a system, is not cut and dried, cannot become a part of rigid school methods. Its very essence is spirit. It is as free as its subject-matter, as far removed from the museum and the cabinet as the skeleton is from the living animal.

It thus transpires that there is much confusion as to what nature-study is, because of the different attitudes of its exponents; but these different attitudes are largely the reflections of different personalities and the working out of different methods. There may be twenty best ways of teaching nature-study. It is essentially the expression of one's outlook on the world. We must define nature-study in terms of its purpose, not in terms of its methods. It is not doing this or that. It is putting the child into. intimate and sympathetic contact with the things of the external world. Whatever the method, the final result of nature-study teaching is the development of a keen personal interest in every natural object and phenomenon.

There are two or three fundamental misconceptions of what nature-study is or should be; and to these we may now give attention.

Fundamentally, nature-study is seeing what one looks at and drawing proper conclusions from what one sees; and thereby the learner comes into personal relation and sympathy with the object. It is not the teaching of science—not the systematic pursuit of a logical body of principles. Its object is to broaden the child's horizon, not, primarily, to teach him how to widen the boundaries of human knowledge. It is not the teaching of botany or entomology or geology, but of plants, insects and fields. But many persons who are teaching under the name of nature-study are merely teaching and interpreting elementary science.

Again, nature-study is studying things and the reason of things, not about things. It is not reading from nature-books. A child was asked if she had ever seen the great dipper. "Oh, yes," she replied, "I saw it in my geography." This is better than not to have seen it at all; but the proper place to have seen it is in the heavens. Nature-readers may be of the greatest use if they are made incidental and secondary features of the instruction; but, however good they may be, their influence is pernicious if they are made to be primary agents. The child should first see the thing. It should then reason about the thing. Having a concrete impression, it may then go to the book to widen its knowledge and sympathies. Having seen mimicry in the eggs of the aphis on the willow or apple twig, or in the walking-stick, the pupil may then take an excursion with Wallace or Bates to the tropics and there see the striking mimicries of the leaf-like insects. Having seen the wearing away of the boulder or the ledge, he may go to Switzerland with Lubbock and see the mighty erosion of the Alps. Now and then the order may be reversed with profit, but this should be the exception: from the wagon to the star should be the rule.

Yet again, nature-study is not the teaching of facts for the sake of the facts. It is not the giving of information merely—notwithstanding the fact that some nature-study leaflets are information leaflets. We must begin with the fact, to be sure, but the lesson is not the fact but the practical application to the daily life, for the object is the effort to train the mind and the sympathies. It is a common notion that when the subject-matter is insects, the pupil should be taught the life-histories of injurious insects and how to destroy the pests. Now, nature-study may be equally valuable whether the subject is the codlin-moth or the ant; but to confine the pupil's attention to insects that are injurious to man is to give him a distorted and untrue view of nature. A bouquet of daisies does not represent a meadow. Children should be interested more in seeing things live than in killing them. Yet I would not emphasize the injunction, "Thou shalt not kill." Nature-study is not recommended for the explicit teaching of morals. I should prefer to have the child become so much interested in living things that it would have no desire to kill them. The gun and sling-shot and fish-pole will be laid aside because the child does not like them any more. We have been taught that one must make collections if he is to be a naturalist. But collections make museums, not naturalists. The scientist needs these collections; but it does not follow that children always need them. To be taught how to kill is to alienate the pupil's affection and sympathy from the object he is studying. It may be said that it is necessary to kill insects; the farmer had this thought in mind when he said to one of our teachers: "Give us more potato-bug and less pussy willow." It is true that we must fight insects, but that is a matter of later practice, not of education. It should be an application of knowledge, not a means of acquiring it. It may be necessary to have war, but we do not teach our children to shoot their playmates.

Nature-study is not merely the adding of one more thing to a curriculum. It is not coördinate with geography or reading or arithmetic. Neither is it a mere accessory, or a sentiment, or an entertainment, or a tickler of the senses. It is not "a study." It is not the addition of more "work." It has to do with the whole point of view of elementary education, and therefore is fundamental. It is the full expression of personality. It is the practical working out of the extension idea that has been so much a part of our time. More than any other recent movement, it will reach the masses and revive them. In time it will transform our ideals and then transform our methods.

Nature-study stands for directness and naturalness. It is astonishing, when one comes to think of it, how indirect and how unrelated to the lives of pupils much of our education has been. Geographies begin with the earth, and finally, perhaps, come down to some concrete and familiar object or scene that the pupil can understand. Arithmetic has to do with brokerage and partnerships and partial payments and other things that mean nothing to the child. Botany has to do with cells and protoplasm and cryptograms. History deals with political affairs, and only rarely comes down to physical facts and to those events that have to do with the real lives of the people; and yet political and social affairs are only the results or expressions of the way in which people live. Readers begin with mere literature or with stories of things that the child will never see or do. Of course these statements are meant to be only general, as illustrating what is even yet a great fault in educational methods. There are many exceptions, and these are becoming commoner. Surely, the best education is that which begins with the materials at hand. A child asks what a stone is before it asks what the earth is.

7. Responses to the Vanishing Frontier

It was with a considerable sense of shock that Americans of the early twentieth century realized many of the forces which had shaped their national character were disappearing. Primary among these was the frontier. The Census of 1890 had officially pronounced pioneering dead, and three years later Frederick Jackson Turner wrote an obituary, but not until the turn of the century did American thought absorb the full meaning of this environmental change. In the following essay novelist Frank Norris comments on several attempts by Americans to find surrogate frontiers and ends with a suggestion of yet another. For California trail rider George Evans, however, the old frontier had not vanished; but only receded further into the mountains. A determined vacationer could still find wilderness conditions, but Evans' attitude toward them stood in sharp contrast to that of the typical pioneer.

The Frontier Gone at Last
FRANK NORRIS

Suddenly we have found that there is no longer any Frontier. Until the day when the first United States marine landed in China we had always imagined that out yonder somewhere in the West was the border land where civilization disintegrated and merged into the untamed. Our skirmish line was there, our posts that scouted and scrimmaged with

Frank Norris, "The Frontier Gone at Last," *World's Work,* 3 (1902), 1728–1731.

the wilderness, a thousand miles in advance of the steady march of civilization.

And the Frontier has become so much an integral part of our conception of things that it will be long before we shall all understand that it is gone. We liked the Frontier; it was romance, the place of the poetry of the Great March, the firing line where there was action and fighting, and where men held each other's lives in the crook of the forefinger. Those who had gone out came back with tremendous tales, and those that stayed behind made up other and even more tremendous tales.

When we—we Anglo-Saxons—busied ourselves for the first stage of the march, we began from that little historic reach of ground in the midst of the Friesland swamps, and we set our faces Westward, feeling no doubt the push of the Slav behind us. Then the Frontier was Britain and the sober peacefulness of land where are the ordered, cultivated English farmyards of today was the Wild West for the Frisians of that century; and for the little children of the Frisian peat cottages, Hengist was the Apache Kid and Horsa Deadwood Dick—freebooters, law-defiers, slayers-of-men, epic heroes, blood brothers if you please to Boone and Bowie.

Then for centuries we halted and the van closed up with the firing line and we filled all England and all Europe with our clamor because for a while we seemed to have gone as far Westward as it was possible; and the checked energy of the race reacted upon itself, rebounded as it were, and back we went to the Eastward again—crusading, girding at the Mohammedan, conquering his cities, breaking into his fortresses with mangonel, siege engine and catapult—just as the boy shut indoors finds his scope circumscribed and fills the whole place with the racket of his activity.

But always, if you will recall it, we had a curious feeling that we had not reached the ultimate West even yet, that there was still a Frontier. Always that strange sixth sense turned our heads toward the sunset; and all through the Middle Ages we were peeking and prying at the Western horizon, trying to reach it, to run it down, and the queer tales about Vineland and that storm-driven Viking's ship would not down.

And then at last a naked savage on the shores of a little island in what is now our West Indies, looking Eastward one morning, saw the caravels, and on that day the Frontier was rediscovered, and promptly a hundred thousand of the most hardy rushed to the skirmish-line and went at the wilderness as only the Anglo-Saxon can.

And then the skirmish-line decided that it would declare itself independent of the main army behind and form an advance column of its own, a separate army corps, and no sooner was this done then again the scouts went forward, went Westward, pushing the Frontier ahead of them, scrimmaging with the wilderness, blazing the way. At last they forced the Frontier over the Sierra Nevada down to the edge of the Pacific. And here it would have been supposed that the Great March would have halted again as it did before the Atlantic, that here at last the Frontier ended.

But on the first of May, eighteen hundred and ninety-eight, a gun was fired in the Bay of Manila, still further Westward, and in response the skirmish-line crossed the Pacific, still pushing the Frontier before it. Then came a cry for help from Legation Street in Peking and as the first boat bearing its contingent of American marines took ground on the Asian shore, the Frontier—at last after so many centuries, after so many marches, after so much fighting, so much spilled blood, so much spent treasure, dwindled down and vanished; for the Anglo-Saxon in his course of empire had circled the globe and had brought the new civilization to the old civilization, had reached the starting point of history, the place from which the migrations began. So soon as the marines landed there was no longer any West, and the equation of the horizon, the problem of the centuries for the Anglo-Saxon was solved.

So, lament it though we may, the Frontier is gone, an idiosyncrasy that has been with us for thousands of years, the one peculiar picturesqueness of our life is no more. We may keep alive for many years yet the idea of a Wild West, but the hired cowboys and paid rough riders of Mr. William Cody are more like "the real thing" than can be found today in Arizona, New Mexico or Idaho. Only the imitation cowboys, the college-bred fellows who "go out on a ranch" carry the revolver or wear the concho. The Frontier has become conscious of itself, acts the part for the Eastern visitor; and this self-consciousness is a sign, surer than all others, of the decadence of a type, the passing of an epoch. The Apache Kid and Deadwood Dick have gone to join Hengist and Horsa and the heroes of the Magnusson Saga.

But observe. What happened in the Middle Ages when for awhile we could find no Western Frontier? The race impulse was irresistible. March we must, conquer we must, and checked in the Westward course of empire we turned Eastward and expended the restless energy that by blood was ours in conquering the Old World behind us.

Today we are the same race, with the same impulse, the same power and, because there is no longer a Frontier to absorb our overplus of energy, because there is no longer a wilderness to conquer and because we still must march, still must conquer, we remember the old days when our ancestors before us found the outlet for their activity checked and, rebounding, turned their faces Eastward, and went down to invade the Old World. So we. No sooner have we found that our path to the Westward has ended than, reacting Eastward, we are at the Old World again, marching against it, invading it, devoting our overplus of energy to its subjugation.

But though we are the same race, with the same impulses, the same blood-instincts as the old Frisian marsh people, we are now come into a changed time and the great word of our century is no longer War but Trade.

Or if you choose it is only a different word for the same race-characteristic. The desire for conquest—say what you will—was as big in the breast of the most fervid of the Crusaders as it is this very day in the most peacefully-disposed of American manufacturers. Had the Lion-Hearted Richard lived today he would have become a "leading representative of the Amalgamated Steel Companies" and doubt not for one moment that he would have underbid his Manchester rivals in the matter of bridge girders. Had Mr. Andrew Carnegie been alive at the time of the preachings of Peter the Hermit he would have raised a company of *gens-d'armes* sooner than all of his brothers-in-arms, would have equipped his men better and more effectively, would have been first on the ground before Jerusalem, would have built the most ingenious siege engine and have hurled the first cask of Greek-fire over the walls.

Competition and conquest are words easily interchangeable, and the whole spirit of our present commercial crusade to the Eastward betrays itself in the fact that we cannot speak of it but in terms borrowed from the glossary of the warrior. It is a commercial "invasion," a trade "war," a "threatened attack" on the part of America; business is "captured," opportunities are "seized," certain industries are "killed," certain former monopolies are "wrested away." Seven hundred years ago a certain Count Baldwin, a great leader in the attack of the Anglo-Saxon Crusaders upon the Old World, built himself a siege engine which would help him enter the beleaguered city of Jerusalem. Jerusalem is beleaguered again today, and the hosts of the Anglo-Saxon commercial crusaders are knocking at the gates. And now a company named for another Baldwin—and for all we know a descendant of the count—leaders of the invaders of the Old World, advance upon the city, and, to help in the assault, build an engine —only now the engine is no longer called a *mangonel*, but a locomotive.

The difference is hardly of kind and scarcely of degree. It is a mere matter of names, and the ghost of Saladin watching the present engagement might easily fancy the old days back again.

So perhaps we have not lost the Frontier after all. A new phrase, reversing that of Berkeley's, is appropriate to the effect that "Eastward the course of commerce takes its way," and we must look for the lost battleline not toward the sunset, but toward the East. And so rapid has been the retrograde movement that we must go far to find it, that scattered firing-line, where the little skirmishes are heralding the approach of the Great March. We must already go further afield than England. The main body, even to the reserves, are intrenched there long since, and even continental Europe is to the rear of the skirmishers.

Along about Suez we begin to catch up with them where they are deepening the great canal, and we can assure ourselves that we are fairly abreast of the most distant line of scouts only when we come to Khiva, to Samarcand, to Bokhara and the Trans-Baikal country.

Just now one hears much of the "American commercial invasion of England." But adjust the field glasses and look beyond Britain and search for the blaze that the scouts have left on the telegraph poles and mile posts of Hungary, Turkey, Turkey in Asia, Persia, Beloochistan, India and Siam. You'll find the blaze distinct and the road, though rough hewn, is easy to follow. Prophecy and presumption be far from us, but it would be against all precedent that the Grand March should rest forever upon its arms and its laurels along the Thames, the Mersey and the Clyde, while its pioneers and Frontiersmen are making roads for it to the Eastward.

Is it too huge a conception, too inordinate an idea to say that the American conquest of England is but an incident of the Greater Invasion, an affair of outposts preparatory to the real manœuvre that shall embrace Europe, Asia, the whole of the Old World? Why not? And the blaze is ahead of us, and every now and then from far off there in the countries that are under the rising sun we catch the faint sounds of the skirmishing of our outposts. One of two things invariably happens under such circumstances as these: either the outposts fall back upon the main body or the main body moves up to the support of its outposts. One does not think that the outposts will fall back.

And so goes the great movement, Westward, then Eastward, forward and then back. The motion of the natural forces, the elemental energies, somehow appear to be thus alternative—action first, then reaction. The tides ebb and flow again, the seasons have their slow vibrations, touching extremes at periodic intervals. Not impossibly, in the larger view, is the analogy applicable to the movements of the races. First Westward with the great migrations, now Eastward with the course of commerce, moving in a colossal arc measured only by the hemispheres, as though upon the equator a giant dial hand oscillated, in gradual divisions through the centuries, now marking off the Westward progress, now traveling proportionately to the reaction toward the East.

Races must follow their destiny blindly, but is it not possible that we can find in this great destiny of ours something a little better than mere battle and conquest, something a little more generous than mere trading and underbidding? Inevitably with constant change of environment comes the larger view, the more tolerant spirit, and every race movement, from the first step beyond the Friesland swamp to the adjustment of the first American theodolite on the Himalayan watershed, is an unconscious lesson in patriotism. Just now we cannot get beyond the self-laudatory mood, but is it not possible to hope that, as the progress develops, a new patriotism, one that shall include all peoples, may prevail? The past would indicate that this is a goal toward which we trend.

In the end let us take the larger view, ignoring the Frieslanders, the Anglo-Saxons, the Americans. Let us look at the peoples as a people and observe how inevitably as they answer the great Westward impulse the true patriotism develops. If we can see that it is so with all of them we can assume that it must be so with us, and may know that mere victory in battle as we march Westward, or mere supremacy in trade as we react to the East is not after all the great achievement of the races but patriotism. Not our selfish present-day conception of the word, but a new patriotism, whose meaning is now the secret of the coming centuries.

Consider then the beginnings of patriotism. At the very first, the seed of the future nation was the regard of family; the ties of common birth held men together and the first feeling of patriotism was the love of family. But the family grows, develops by lateral branches, expands and becomes the clan. Patriotism is the devotion to the clan, and the clansmen will fight and die for its supremacy.

Then comes the time when the clans, tired of the roving life of herders, halt a moment and settle down in a chosen spot, the tent becoming permanent evolves the dwelling house, and the encampment of the clan becomes at last a city. Patriotism now is civic pride, the clan absorbed into a multitude of clans is forgotten; men speak of themselves as Athenians not as Greeks, as Romans not as Italians. It is the age of cities.

The city extends its adjoining grazing fields, they include outlying towns, other cities, and finally the State comes into being. Patriotism no longer confines itself to the walls of the city, but is enlarged to encompass the entire province. Men are Hanoverians or Wurtemburgers not Germans; Scots or Welsh not English; are even Carolinians or Alabamans rather than Americans.

But the States are federated, pronounced boundaries fade, State makes common cause with State and at last the nation is born. Patriotism at once is a national affair, a far larger, broader, truer sentiment than that first huddling about the hearthstone of the family. The word "brother" may be applied to men unseen and unknown, and a countryman is one of many millions.

We have reached this stage at the present, but if all signs are true, if all precedent may be followed, if all augury may be relied on and the tree grow as we see the twig is bent, the progress will not stop here.

By war to the Westward the family fought its way upward to the dignity of the nation, by reaction Eastward the nation may in patriotic effect merge with other nations, and others and still others, peacefully, the bitterness of trade competition may be lost, the business of the nations seen as a friendly *quid pro quo,* give and take arrangement, guided by a generous reciprocity. Every century the boundaries are widening, patriotism widens with the expansion, and our countrymen are those of different race, even different nations.

Will it not go on, this epic of civilization, this destiny of the races, until at last and at the ultimate end of all, we who now arrogantly boast ourselves as Americans, supreme in conquest, whether of battle-ship or of bridge-building, may realize that the true patriotism is the brotherhood of man and know that the whole world is our nation and simple humanity our countrymen?

The Wilderness
GEORGE S. EVANS

The wilderness hath charms. To go to it is to return to the primitive, the elemental. It is reached by the trail, the oldest thoroughfare of man. The trail breathes out the spirit of romance.

It may date back to the days when the aborigines gave chase to the deer and the elk beneath the branches of the leafy forest. In pioneer

George S. Evans, "The Wilderness," *Overland Monthly,* 43 (1904), 31–33.

days, the trail may have had its sanctity invaded by a white-skinned cavalcade, intent on finding gold. It has probably felt the hoofs of a steed carrying a fugitive from justice into a wild fastness. Over it have passed the strongest, bound to the hunting grounds to kill them venison. Over it passes in procession horses and men, carrying supplies to the cattle station, or the sheep-herder.

The trail winds around and up mountains, whose heads touch heaven. It makes its way down leafy forest aisles; it leads past trickling springs, surrounded by moss-covered bowlders; it penetrates Nature's Titanic quarries; it crosses the range where cloud and wind, frost and snow, contend with boulder and dwarf timber.

The question of transportation of supplies over the trail is solved by the bronco, the pack-saddle and the diamond hitch, of men by the horse and saddle.

The wilderness still exists. Man has ravaged and plundered the earth in large measure, but there are still great tracts of wilderness where bear and deer and cougar wander as in the days of old. From the southern line of Mendocino County in California, bounded on the west by the sea, and on the east by the eastern wall of the Coast Range, running north for league after league lies a great tract of comparatively untamed wilderness. Here and there on the edge of this land is a settler's clearing marred by burnt, gnarled stumps. A few winding roads connect scattered villages. But go far enough, even these disappear. Press on, and you come to the true wilderness. Mountains clad in cloaks of forest verdure, rise like giants. Rough peaks flout high their banners of snow. Scarred and furrowed canyon sides are covered with an almost impenetrable thicket of brush. Little streams trickle down over rocks, through grassy glades to join the mad foam creek at the bottom of the gorge. Mountain lakes and pools glimmer. Forest oceans mingle with the sky.

Away off, far from the haunts of man, you pitch your camp by some cool spring. Your horse has brought you over the trail safely. The supplies have arrived without accident. The air is bracing. Mountain piled on mountain, vast wastes of forest verdure, boulders heaped on boulders, tracts of brush and leafy glades mark this primeval waste—a workshop of the gods.

Dull business routine, the fierce passions of the market place, the perils of envious cities become but a memory. At first you are appalled by the immensity of the wilderness. You do not seem to be a part of the waste. You do not seem to fit into the landscape. The rocks have equanimity, the mountains ruggedness, the trees sturdiness, the wind savagery. You have none of these attributes. You are awe stricken, meek, filled with wonder. Your guide has lived in the wilderness for years. He is not awed by it, but seems to blend into it, to be a part and parcel of it. He has taken on the attributes of the wild and rugged land.

Almost imperceptibly a sensation of serenity begins to take possession of you. You explore deep canyons, climb vast mountains, penetrate shaggy forests, follow the meanderings of wild, turbid streams. You begin to take on some of the characteristics of the denizens of the woods. Your step becomes lighter, your eyesight keener, your hearing more acute. You think of the civilization you have left behind. Seen through the eyes of the wilderness, how stupid and insane it all seems. The mad eagerness of money-seeking men, the sham pleasures of conventional society, the insistence upon the importance of being in earnest over trifles, pall on you when you think of them.

Your blood clarifies; your brain becomes active. You get a new view of life. You acquire the ability to single out the things worth while. Your judgment becomes keener.

Another stage in your wilderness development arrives. You learn how simple life is when reduced to its elements. The complexity of the life you have left behind becomes apparent. Slowly, surely, you become like the land you are in. When you first reached the wilderness you wondered why the sheepherders and packers were wild and rugged like the country they inhabited. It seemed as though men living in such a land should be meek and humble. You never had stopped to think that a stupid, conventional society made men stupid and conventional. You now perceive that man is the product of his environment. From worship of Nature you pass to toleration of it. You know that while Nature sits enthroned in the midst of this mountain kingdom, man needs but the words "gold here" to spur him into a campaign ending in the dethronement of the monarch. At the touch of the magic words "gold here" the trees would go down like wheat before the sickle, the rock heaps of the ages would be rent asunder by the blast, streams would be harnessed, mountains tunneled—man enthroned. And now you have become like your environment. You have the equanimity of the rocks, the ruggedness of the mountains, the sturdiness of the oaks, the relentless savagery of the wind.

The wilderness is moody. At times the silence is terrifying. Again storms spring up, the reverberation of the thunder calls to mind the shaggy gods of the Norse. You hear the rush and roar of the gale through the tree-tops, the crash of falling trees struck by lightning, the spiteful spat of the rain. Springs rise and rivulets become torrents. At other times fires break out, and ruin and devastation reap a harvest. A forest fire is one of the most terrifying spectacles ever witnessed. The flames rush and roar; they flare up dry trees, and hold a holocaust over fallen logs. Over the noise of the conflagration can be heard the crash of falling trees and limbs. Then the wilderness, after the fire, takes on a sombre mood, sicklied o'er by the sullen cast of repose.

The noises of the wilderness at night are many. Far below you can hear the music of the water flowing over stones. The wind rushing through the trees sounds like beating surf. The shrill bark of the fox, the melancholy yelp of the coyote reverberate.

Overhead the stars shine with brilliance. Constellations traced by shepherd astronomers of Chaldea are visible through the gauze-like foliage of trees standing in the days when Hyksos kings sat enthroned at Thebes. The astronomers and the kings have gone, but the stars and the trees remain.

The pastimes of men in the wilderness are of the manly order. Those who delight in the chase here can pass hours filled with exciting incidents. To pit your human ingenuity against the ingenuity of the animal, to capture him at his own game, is invigorating and refreshing. You realize that if the life of each of the dwellers in the woods was written, you would have an epic. The wilderness teems with life. The deer leaps in the woodland. The sullen bear haunts dark canyons. The crested jay hawk makes the air vocal with his chattering. The raucous bark of the tree squirrel arouses you from your slumber. Down at the bottom of the canyon where the trout stream flows is another manifestation of life. Trout haunt the shady pools. The water ouzel flits from rock to rock. The mink and the otter lie in wait for their prey along the leafy banks. Flocks of quail come down out of the brush to the creek side to quench their thirst.

The wilderness is filled with tragedy. Never a creature there dies a natural death. From birth till death every dweller in the wilderness is surrounded by a cloud of danger. One by one the weak succumb to the strong. A perpetual warfare is carried on. You perceive that Nature is neutral: she neither fears nor hates.

Whenever the light of civilization falls upon you with a blighting power, and work and pleasure become stale and flat, go to the wilderness. The wilderness will take hold on you. It will give you good red blood; it will turn you from a weakling into a man. It will give you a broad view of human nature and enlist your sympathies in its behalf. When your pack train leaves the dusty road and "hits the trail," you will acquire new courage to live your life. You will get new strength. You will soon behold all with a peaceful soul.

8. Fundamental Frontier Virtues

Rancher, big game hunter, and historian of the American West, Theodore Roosevelt knew better than most of his contemporaries that the nation was advancing into a frontierless middle age. The implications were chilling. Remedies or alternatives had to be found. "As our civilization grows older and more complex," Roosevelt said, "we need a greater and not a lesser development of the fundamental frontier virtues." But how could this be obtained without the chance to pioneer in the wilderness? Roosevelt's answer is to be found in the speech he delivered at a Chicago men's club seven months before the end of the nineteenth century. The address comes as close as any of his pronouncements to outlining the philosophy with which he guided his own life.

The Strenuous Life
THEODORE ROOSEVELT

In speaking to you, men of the greatest city of the West, men of the State which gave to the country Lincoln and Grant, men who preëminently and distinctly embody all that is most American in the American character, I wish to preach, not the doctrine of ignoble ease, but the doctrine of the strenuous life, the life of toil and effort, of labor and strife; to preach that highest form of success which comes, not to the man who desires mere easy peace, but to the man who does not shrink from danger, from hardship, or from bitter toil, and who out of these wins the splendid ultimate triumph.

A life of slothful ease, a life of that peace which springs merely from lack either of desire or of power to strive after great things, is as little worthy of a nation as of an individual. I ask only that what every self-respecting American demands from himself and from his sons shall be demanded of the American nation as a whole. Who among you would teach your boys that ease, that peace, is to be the first consideration in their eyes—to be the ultimate goal after which they strive? You men of Chicago have made this city great, you men of Illinois have done your share, and more than your share, in making America great, because you neither preach nor practice such a doctrine. You work yourselves, and you bring up your sons to work. If you are rich and are worth your salt, you will teach your sons that though they may have leisure, it is not to be spent in idleness; for wisely used leisure merely means that those who possess it, being free from the necessity of working for their livelihood, are all the more bound to carry on some kind of non-remunerative work in science, in letters, in art, in exploration, in historical research—work of the type we most need in this country, the successful carrying out of which reflects most honor upon the nation. We do not admire the man of timid peace. We admire the man who embodies victorious effort; the man who never wrongs his neighbor, who is prompt to help a friend, but who has those virile qualities necessary to win in the stern strife of actual life. It is hard to fail, but it is worse never to have tried to succeed. In this life we get nothing save by effort. Freedom from effort in the present merely means that there has been stored up effort in the past. A man can be freed from the necessity of work only by the fact that he or his fathers before him have worked to good purpose. If the freedom thus purchased is used aright, and the man still does actual work, though of a different kind, whether as a writer or a general, whether in the field of politics or in the field of exploration and adventure, he shows he deserves his good fortune. But if he treats this period of freedom from the need of actual labor as a period, not of preparation, but of mere enjoyment, even though perhaps not of vicious enjoyment, he shows that he is simply a cumberer of the earth's surface, and he surely unfits himself to hold his own with his fellows if the need to do so should again arise. A mere life of ease is not in the end a very satisfactory life, and, above all, it is a life which ultimately unfits those who follow it for serious work in the world.

In the last analysis a healthy state can exist only when the men and women who make it up lead clean, vigorous, healthy lives; when the children are so trained that they shall endeavor, not to shirk difficulties, but to overcome them; not to seek ease, but to know how to wrest triumph from toil and risk. The man must be glad to do a man's work, to dare and endure and to labor; to keep himself, and to keep those dependent upon him. The woman must be the housewife, the helpmeet of the homemaker, the wise and fearless mother of many healthy children. In one of Daudet's powerful and melancholy books he speaks of "the fear of maternity, the haunting terror of the young wife of the present day." When such words can be truthfully written of a nation, that nation is rotten to the heart's core. When men fear work or fear righteous war, when women fear motherhood, they tremble on the brink of doom; and well it is that they should vanish from the earth, where they are fit subjects for the scorn of all men and women who are themselves strong and brave and high-minded.

As it is with the individual, so it is with the nation. It is a base untruth to say that happy is the nation that has no history. Thrice happy is the nation that has a glorious history. Far better it is to dare mighty things, to win glorious triumphs, even though checkered by failure, than to take rank with those poor spirits who neither enjoy much nor suffer much, because they live in the gray twilight that knows not victory nor defeat. If in 1861 the men who loved the Union had believed that peace was the end of all things, and war and strife the worst of all things, and had acted up to their belief, we would have saved hundreds of thousands of lives, we would have saved hundreds of millions of dollars. Moreover, besides saving all the blood and treasure we then lavished, we would have prevented the heartbreak of many women, the dissolution of many homes, and we would have spared the country those months of gloom and shame when it seemed as if our armies marched only to defeat. We could have avoided all this suffering simply by shrinking from strife. And if we had thus avoided it, we would have shown that we were weaklings, and that we were unfit to stand among the great nations of the earth. Thank God for the iron in the blood of our fathers, the men who upheld the wisdom of Lincoln, and bore sword or rifle in the armies of Grant! Let us, the children of the men who proved themselves equal to the mighty days, let us, the children of the men who carried the great Civil War to a triumphant conclusion, praise the God of our fathers that the ignoble counsels of peace were rejected; that the suffering and loss, the blackness of sorrow and despair, were unflinchingly faced, and the years of strife endured; for in the end the slave was freed, the Union restored, and the mighty American republic placed once more as a helmeted queen among nations.

We of this generation do not have to face a task such as that our fathers faced, but we have our tasks, and woe to us if we fail to perform them! We cannot, if we would, play the part of China, and be content to rot by inches in ignoble ease within our borders, taking no interest in what goes on beyond them, sunk in a scrambling commercialism; heedless of the higher life, the life of aspiration, of toil and risk, busying ourselves only with the wants of our bodies for the day, until suddenly we should find, beyond a shadow of question, what China has already found, that in this world the nation that has trained itself to a career of unwarlike and isolated ease is bound, in the end, to go down before other nations which have not lost the manly and adventurous qualities. If we are to be a really great people, we must strive in good faith to play a great part in the world. We cannot avoid meeting great issues. All that we can determine for ourselves is whether we shall meet them well or ill. In 1898 we could not help being brought face to face with the problem of war with Spain. All we could decide was whether we should shrink like cowards from the contest, or enter into it as beseemed a brave and high-spirited people; and, once in, whether failure or success should crown our banners. So it is now. We cannot avoid the responsibilities that confront us in Hawaii, Cuba, Porto Rico, and the Philippines. All we can decide is whether we shall meet them in a way that will redound to the national credit, or whether we shall make of our dealings with these new problems a dark and shameful page in our history. To refuse to deal with them at all merely amounts to dealing with them badly. We have a given problem to solve. If we undertake the solution, there is, of course, always danger that we may not solve it aright; but to refuse to undertake the solution simply renders it certain that we cannot possibly solve it aright. The timid man, the lazy man, the man who distrusts his country, the over-civilized man, who has lost the great fighting, masterful virtues, the ignorant man, and the man of dull mind, whose soul is incapable of feeling the mighty lift that thrills "stern men with empires in their brains"—all these, of course, shrink from seeing the nation undertake its new duties; shrink from seeing us build a navy and an army adequate to our needs; shrink from seeing us do our share of the world's work, by bringing order out of chaos in the great, fair tropic islands from which the valor of our soldiers and sailors has driven the Spanish flag. These are the men who fear the strenuous life, who fear the only national life which is really worth leading. They believe in that cloistered life which saps the hardy virtues in a nation, as it saps them in the individual; or else they are wedded to that base spirit of gain and greed which recognizes in commercialism the be-all and end-all of national life, instead of realizing that, though an indispensable element, it is, after all, but one of the many elements that go to make up true national greatness. No country can long endure if its foundations are not laid deep in the material prosperity which comes from thrift, from business energy and enterprise, from hard, unsparing effort in the fields of industrial activity; but neither was any nation ever yet truly great if it relied upon material prosperity alone. All honor must be paid to the architects of our material prosperity, to the great captains of industry who have built our factories and our railroads, to the strong men who toil for wealth with brain or hand; for great is the debt of the nation to these and their kind. But our debt is yet greater to the men whose highest type is to be found in a statesman like Lincoln, a soldier like Grant. They showed by their lives that they recognized the law of work, the law of strife; they toiled to win a competence for themselves and those dependent upon them; but they recognized that there were yet other and even loftier duties—duties to the nation and duties to the race.

We cannot sit huddled within our own borders and avow ourselves merely an assemblage of well-to-do hucksters who care nothing for what happens beyond. Such a policy would defeat even its own end; for as the nations grow to have ever wider and wider interests, and are brought into closer and closer contact, if we are to hold our own in the struggle for naval and commercial supremacy, we must build up our power without our own borders. We must build the isthmian canal, and we must grasp the points of vantage which will enable us to have our say in deciding the destiny of the oceans of the East and the West.

So much for the commercial side. From the standpoint of international honor the argument is even stronger. The guns that thundered off Manila and Santiago left us echoes of glory, but they also left us a legacy of duty. If we drove out a mediæval tyranny only to make room for savage anarchy, we had better not have begun the task at all. It is worse than idle to say that we have no duty to perform, and can leave to their fates the islands we have conquered. Such a course would be the course of infamy. It would be followed at once by utter chaos in the wretched islands themselves. Some stronger, manlier power would have to step in and do the work, and we would have shown ourselves weaklings, unable to carry to successful completion the labors that great and high-spirited nations are eager to undertake.

The work must be done; we cannot escape our responsibility; and if we are worth our salt, we shall be glad of the chance to do the work— glad of the chance to show ourselves equal to one of the great tasks set modern civilization. . . .

I preach to you, then, my countrymen, that our country calls not for the life of ease but for the life of strenuous endeavor. The twentieth century looms before us big with the fate of many nations. If we stand idly by, if we seek merely swollen, slothful ease and ignoble peace, if we shrink from the hard contests where men must win at hazard of their lives and at the risk of all they hold dear, then the bolder and stronger peoples will pass us by, and will win for themselves the domination of the world. Let us therefore boldly face the life of strife, resolute to do our duty well and manfully; resolute to uphold righteousness by deed and by word; resolute to be both honest and brave, to serve high ideals, yet to use practical methods. Above all, let us shrink from no strife, moral or physical, within or without the nation, provided we are certain that the strife is justified, for it is only through strife, through hard and dangerous endeavor, that we shall ultimately win the goal of true national greatness.

9. Use *Versus* Beauty

It is sometimes possible to settle conflicts between utilitarian and aesthetic values by considering them as separate entities. Thus one building is intended as an art museum; another, a factory. Each has its own clientele. Or one tract of land is preserved as a national park for its scenic values; another is used to grow potatoes or support a highway. The separation formula works when there is sufficient space to satisfy all parties. But in an either-or situation the latent tension in American culture between use and beauty bursts forth.

One such explosion occurred in 1913 in connection with the Hetch Hetchy Valley in Yosemite National Park. It quickly became apparent that the same valley could not serve at the same time as wilderness and reservoir. In the exchanges before a committee of the United States House of Representatives, the varying criteria for making difficult environmental decisions were fully aired. Gifford Pinchot was the former Chief Forester and "Mr. Conservation" to his generation. James D. Phelan had been mayor of San Francisco until 1902 and had originally applied for the use of Hetch Hetchy on behalf of the city. Edmund A. Whitman was a Boston lawyer representing the Society for the Protection of National Parks and, he claimed, "the public of the United States." Robert Underwood Johnson, whose letter Whitman read to the committee, was a poet and an editor of the genteel *Century* magazine.

The Hetch Hetchy Dam Site
AN EXCHANGE OF VIEWS

The CHAIRMAN.* In deference to Mr. [Gifford] Pinchot's wishes, as he desires to leave the city, he will be permitted to address the committee at this time if there is no objection.

Mr. PINCHOT. Mr. Chairman and gentlemen of the committee, my testimony will be very short. I presume that you very seldom have the opportunity of passing upon any measure before the Committee on the Public Lands which has been so thoroughly thrashed out as this one. This question has been up now, I should say, more than 10 years, and the reasons for and against the proposition have not only been discussed over and over again, but a great deal of the objections which could be composed have been composed, until finally there remains simply the one question of the objection of the Spring Valley Water Co. I understand that the much more important objection of the Tuolumne irrigation districts have been overcome. There is, I understand, objection on the part of other irrigators, but that does not go to the question of using the water, but merely to the distribution of the water. So we come now face to face with the perfectly clean question of what is the best use to which this water that flows out of the Sierras can be put. As we all know, there is no use of water that is higher than the domestic use. Then, if there is, as the engineers tell us, no other source of supply that is anything like so reasonably available as this one; if this is the best, and, within reasonable limits of cost, the only means of supplying San Francisco with water, we come straight to the question of whether the advantage of leaving this valley in a state of nature is greater than the advantage of using it for the benefit of the city of San Francisco.

Now, the fundamental principle of the whole conservation policy is that of use, to take every part of the land and its resources and put it to that use in which it will best serve the most people, and I think there can be no question at all but that in this case we have an instance in which all weighty considerations demand the passage of the bill. There are, of

* Scott Ferris, Representative from Oklahoma. [Ed.]

U.S. Congress, House of Representatives, Committee on the Public Lands, Hearings, *Hetch Hetchy Dam Site*, 63rd Cong., 1st Sess. (June 25–28, July 7, 1913), 25, 26, 28, 29, 165, 166, 213, 214, 235–38.

course, a very large number of incidental changes that will arise after the passage of the bill. The construction of roads, trails, and telephone systems which will follow the passage of this bill will be a very important help in the park and forest reserves. The national forest telephone system and the roads and trails to which this bill will lead will form an important additional help in fighting fire in the forest reserves. As has already been set forth by the two Secretaries, the presence of these additional means of communication will mean that the national forest and the national park will be visited by very large numbers of people who cannot visit them now. I think that the men who assert that it is better to leave a piece of natural scenery in its natural condition have rather the better of the argument, and I believe if we had nothing else to consider than the delight of the few men and women who would yearly go into the Hetch Hetchy Valley, then it should be left in its natural condition. But the considerations on the other side of the question to my mind are simply overwhelming, and so much so that I have never been able to see that there was any reasonable argument against the use of this water supply by the city of San Francisco. . . .

Mr. RAKER.* Taking the scenic beauty of the park as it now stands, and the fact that the valley is sometimes swamped along in June and July, is it not a fact that if a beautiful dam is put there, as is contemplated, and as the picture is given by the engineers, with the roads contemplated around the reservoir and with other trails, it will be more beautiful than it is now, and give more opportunity for the use of the park?

Mr. PINCHOT. Whether it will be more beautiful, I doubt, but the use of the park will be enormously increased. I think there is no doubt about that.

Mr. RAKER. In other words, to put it a different way, there will be more beauty accessible than there is now?

Mr. PINCHOT. Much more beauty will be accessible than now.

Mr. RAKER. And by putting in roads and trails the Government, as well as the citizens of the Government, will get more pleasure out of it than at the present time?

Mr. PINCHOT. You might say from the standpoint of enjoyment of beauty and the greatest good to the greatest number, they will be conserved by the passage of this bill, and there will be a great deal more use of the beauty of the park than there is now.

* John E. Raker, Representative from California. [Ed.]

Mr. RAKER. Have you seen Mr. John Muir's criticism of the bill? You know him?

Mr. PINCHOT. Yes, sir; I know him very well. He is an old and a very good friend of mine. I have never been able to agree with him in his attitude toward the Sierras for the reason that my point of view has never appealed to him at all. When I became Forester and denied the right to exclude sheep and cows from the Sierras, Mr. Muir thought I had made a great mistake, because I allowed the use by an acquired right of a large number of people to interfere with what would have been the utmost beauty of the forest. In this case I think he has unduly given away to beauty as against use.

Mr. RAKER. Would that be practically the same as to the position of the Sierras [sic] Club?

Mr. PINCHOT. I am told that there is a very considerable difference of opinion in the club on this subject.

Mr. RAKER. Among themselves?

Mr. PINCHOT. Yes, sir.

Mr. RAKER. You think then, as a matter of fact, that the provisions of this bill carried out would relieve the situation; in other words, that there is no valid objection which they could make?

Mr. PINCHOT. That is my judgment. . . .

The CHAIRMAN. Mr. Phelan, please state what official connection you have had with the city of San Francisco.

Mr. PHELAN. I was mayor of San Francisco for five years, my term ending in 1902.

The CHAIRMAN. Are you connected with the administration in any way now?

Mr. PHELAN. No, sir; except as a member of this commission which has been sent to Washington, appointed by the mayor of San Francisco, to represent in part the city of San Francisco in this water investigation. I am also a library trustee, but the water investigation has nothing to do with books. The mayor asked me to appear because I am familiar with the needs of the city of San Francisco, where I was born and of which I have been ever since a resident, and because during my incumbency of the office of mayor the first filings were made on this Hetch Hetchy Valley and on the Tuolumne River. I have also participated in the several hearings which have been had on this subject. I realize that the committee has gone into all the questions at this hearing, and I do not wish to delay the committee a moment longer than is necessary, so I will only emphasize the fact that the needs of San Francisco are pressing and urgent. San

Francisco is expanding with tremendous rapidity due to the development of the interior of California and to the prospect of the early opening of the canal and the building of the exposition, and already, notwithstanding the threat of a water famine, the outlying district, which never before was developed, is being cut up into suburban tracts.

A large number of our population has been lost to Oakland, Alameda, and Berkeley, by reason of the fact that we have never had adequate facilities either of transportation or of water supply to meet what would otherwise be a demand for residences on the peninsula. There are disadvantages in crossing the bay. So San Francisco, the chief Federal city on the Pacific coast, asks the Federal Government for assistance in this matter by grant and not by money. It has obligated itself to pay $70,000,-000 for a water supply. We have endeavored to satisfy the needs of the irrigationists in good faith, as well as the local water monopoly, and we come this year to Washington, I think, with the good will of those heretofore opposed, possibly with the exception of the gentlemen who are devoted to the preservation of the beauties of nature.

As Californians, we rather resent gentlemen from different parts of the country outside of California telling us that we are invading the beautiful natural resources of the State or in any way marring or detracting from them. We have a greater pride than they in the beauties of California, in the valleys, in the big trees, in the rivers, and in the high mountains. We have the highest mountain in the United States in California, Mount Whitney, 15,000 feet above the sea, as we have the lowest land, in Death Valley, 300 feet below the sea. We have the highest tree known in the world, and the oldest tree. Its history goes back 2,000 years, I believe, judged by the internal evidences; as we have the youngest in the world, Luther Burbank's plumcot.

All of this is of tremendous pride, and even for a water supply we would not injure the great resources which have made our State the playground of the world. By constructing a dam at this very narrow gorge in the Hetch Hetchy Valley, about 700 feet across, we create, not a reservoir, but a lake, because Mr. Freeman, who has studied the situation in Manchester or Birmingham, where there is a similar case, has shown that by planting trees or vines over the dam, the idea of a dam, the appearance of a dam, is entirely lost; so, coming upon it, it will look like an emerald gem in the mountains; and one of the few things in which California is deficient, especially in the Sierras, is lakes, and in this way we will contribute, in a large measure, to the scenic grandeur and beauty of California. I suppose nature lovers, suspecting a dam there not made by the Creator, will think it of no value, in their estimation, but I submit, man can imitate the Creator—a worthy exemplar.

Mr. GRAHAM.* In that they are mistaken by a dam site?

Mr. PHELAN. They are mistaken by a dam site, and after it is con-- structed, as somebody said, not wishing to be outdone in profanity, "It will be the damdest finest sight you ever saw."

I remember the story of John Hay's Little Breeches, which describes the old fellow, who, believing in nothing that was religious or good, and having been told, after his child recovered, that he had wandered away in the woods and must have been restored by the angels, said:

> To restore the life of a little child and to bring him back to his own,
> Is a darn sight better business than loafing 'round the throne.

To provide for the little children, men, and women of the 800,000 popu- lation who swarm the shores of San Francisco Bay is a matter of much greater importance than encouraging the few who, in solitary loneliness, will sit on the peak of the Sierras loafing around the throne of the God of nature and singing His praise. A benign father loves his children above all things. There is no comparison between the highest use of the water— the domestic supply—and the mere scenic value of the mountains. When you decide that affirmatively, as you must, and then, on top of that, that we are not detracting from the scenic value of the mountains, but enhanc- ing it, I think there is nothing left to be said. That is all.

The CHAIRMAN. Are there any gentlemen here who wish to speak in opposition to the bill?

Mr. WHITMAN. I am one of them. . . .

There is no doubt that the building of the roads which they [the San Francisco engineers] propose will facilitate the ability to get in there, but my proposition is that they will find that there will not be any reason to go in there, except for people who want to go in and look at the lake and come out again.

Mr. KENT.* Well, if it should be made a popular camping ground, what provision could be made for taking care of the people? The minute you popularize a camping ground and make it available for a vast number of people, you immediately destroy the very element which originally made it attractive as a camping ground, because you must provide camp regulations, install a water supply, provide sanitary arrangements, and then the character of the camping site is entirely changed.

Mr. WHITMAN. I suppose that applies to the Yosemite Valley itself,

---

* James M. Graham, Representative from Illinois. [Ed.]
* William Kent, Representative from California.

and yet large numbers do go in there, feed their stock, and camp at the present time.

Mr. LA FOLLETTE.* A tract 2 miles long and half a mile wide would be only about 2,400 acres, and if a tract of that size was camped upon by a large number of people they would generate all kinds of filth and typhoid for the people below.

Mr. WHITMAN. That might be the fate of it, but it is the only camping ground in that part of the region, and it is the only spot open for the people.

Mr. LA FOLLETTE. I am willing to grant that, but I am looking at the matter from the broad viewpoint of the people. Not one hundredth of 1 per cent of the people of the United States will ever go in there. On the other hand, if one-fiftieth or a hundredth part of the people of the United States, or even of California, were to go in there, it would be a vast camp ground instead of a thing of beauty. That change would take place within a year. For that reason, looking at it from a practical viewpoint, I do not believe the people of the United States care very much whether it is kept for a playground or not, when in all probability only one one-hundredth of 1 per cent of the people of the country would ever go in there. . . .

If I had my way about it, they would build the dam immediately as high as they could, to store every gallon of water flowing there. . . .

I can not believe that the flooding of 1,500 acres will destroy all that vast area of scenery. I think if they go in there to see it and if anything is said derogatory to the dam, their attention should be called to the fact that the water is required for the irrigation of thousands of acres of land, and is also required to meet the domestic and economic needs of a great city, and when they come to realize that I should think their æsthetic taste could stand a little shock. . . .

Mr. WHITMAN. You are asked to consider this park as it is at present, with almost nobody using it. Very little attention has been given to what may happen to this park by the year 2000. On the other hand, the city desires to focus your attention to the year 2000 for its water supply. They are getting along and can get along perfectly comfortably for a good many years for their local supply, but it is the year 2000 they want you to look to. If you look to the year 2000 in one way, I pray you to look to it in the other. What will that park be and what will the use of it be to the American public, winter and summer, in the year 2000?

Now, I have said nothing about nature. I have tried to put this thing

* William L. La Follette, Representative from Washington.

on a practical ground, which will appeal to the American citizen, and I do not want to add anything as to nature. But I have a letter here addressed to the chairman of this committee from Robert Underwood Johnson, who was, with Mr. John Muir, the original cause of the establishment of this park, and he has put this matter so admirably in his letter that, as a few concluding words, I should like to read it. There is not very much of it. He says:

New York, June 25, 1913

Hon. Scott Ferris, M. C.,
Chairman House Committee on the Public Lands,
Washington, D. C.

Dear Sir:

I thank you for the courtesy of your telegram of the 23d informing me of the plans of the committee for the hearings on the bill of Mr. Raker (H. R. 112) to grant the Hetch Hetchy and Lake Eleanor Valleys to San Francisco for reservoir purposes.

I deeply regret that pressing private business here makes it apparently impossible for me to appear in person before the committee. I therefore respectfully submit for the consideration of its members some points which I think germane to the bill. My remarks will deal not with mechanical data, but with what I and I believe the vast majority of the intelligent public regard as higher and not less pertinent considerations.

There never was a time when there was a more urgent necessity for our country to uphold its best ideals and its truest welfare against shortsighted opportunism and purely commercial and local interests. The history of the country presents a thousand examples of the sacrifice of the good of all to the advantage of a part, and the waste of national resources at the dictation of selfish parties under specious pretexts. The enormous amounts of money lost to the Government for the enrichment of individuals in the careless disposition of the public lands and forests would have liquidated the public debt a hundred times over and have made life easier for every citizen of the United States in the past century and down to the present day. It is the subordination of the ideal to the material, the greater future to the lesser present, that has set us apart as the most wasteful and imprudent of nations. In 1889–90 came an awakening, largely through the efforts of John Muir, discoverer of the Muir Glacier, a man combining in himself the ideal and the practical as have few men of our day. It was he who awakened the administration of President Harrison to the necessity of conserving the public forests instead of giving them over to the tender mercies of the chance comer.

The first step of importance in this awakening was the establishment of the Yosemite National Park, which led to the immense reservations made by the Harrison administration under the law of March 3, 1891, and to further reservations by each succeeding President, until at last the headwaters of all the great western streams are measurably secure against the perils of forest denudation. I think it is not too much to say that no Representative should consider himself competent to decide a question involving the dismemberment of a great national park until he has read the book of the late George P. Marsh, formerly American minister to Italy, entitled "Nature as Modified by Human Action," a work of singular imaginative force, in which the author, as early as 1850, pleaded with his countrymen to put an end to the passive policy of forest destruction, from which every Mediterranean country has suffered disastrously. Unless one can view the subject in the light of history and with the eye of imagination, he will remain indifferent to the large considerations involved in giving away to a corporation the use and control of fully half of the most beautiful of all our national parks.

What is at stake is not merely the destruction of a single valley, one of the most wonderful works of the Creator, but the fundamental principle of conservation. Let it be established that these great parks and forests are to be held at the whim or advantage of local interests and sooner or later they must all be given up. One has only to look about to see the rampant materialism of the day. It can only be overcome by a constant regard for ideas and for the good of the whole country now and hereafter. The very sneers with which this type of argument is received are a proof of the need of altruism and imagination in dealing with the subject. The time has not yet come to substitute for our national motto those baleful words, "Let us eat, drink, and be merry, for to-morrow we die."

The opponents of the Hetch Hetchy scheme maintain that their position is not inimical to the true interests of San Francisco. They say if there were no other source of good and abundant water for the city they would willingly sacrifice the valley to the lives and the health of its citizens. The records of the hearing before the Senate Committee on Public Lands two or three years ago show that two official representatives of the city (one, ex-Mayor Phelan) confessed that the city could get water anywhere along the Sierra if she would pay for it. This is the crux of the whole matter. The assault upon the integrity of the park has this purpose—to get something for nothing. Mr. Freeman, the engineer employed by the city, has also stated that it is physically possible to get water anywhere along the Sierra. The elaborate published examination of the Hetch Hetchy resources bears the proportion, let us say, of 30 or 50 to 1 to all the information concerning other sources. It has not been demonstrated that Hetch Hetchy is the only available source, but only that it might be the cheapest. On this point we hold that while we are willing to die for the lives or the health of the citizens of San Francisco, we are not willing to die for their pockets.

We believe, moreover, that a larger measure of attention should be given to the question of filtration. I have already called your attention to the system in operation at Toledo, under which typhoid fever has almost disappeared, and to the abandonment by the city of London of its project of a supply from the Welsh Mountains in favor of the same system of filtration. I earnestly suggest that the advantages of this method be made the subject of an official examination during the present summer by United States Government experts, for if such a system be feasible, it would be folly to destroy the valley and dismember the park to have it discovered later that they must, after all, be abandoned for a method both better and cheaper.

The opponents of the bill invite your careful attention to the fact that whereas at first the scheme was put forward as one appealing to humane instincts—to provide a great city with potable water—it is now clearly seen to be aiming at quite another purpose—the production of power for use and for sale. This is commercialism pure and simple, and the far-reaching results of this disposition of the national parks when the destruction of their supreme features is involved, is something appalling to contemplate.

I have not yet spoken of the great recreative, curative, and hygienic uses of the park. It contains three considerable camping spots—the Yosemite Valley, now greatly crowded every summer; the Tuolumne Meadows, and the Hetch Hetchy. The second is much more difficult of access than the third, and both would be withdrawn from public use by the operation of the proposed bill, for it would be idle to take the valley for a reservoir without giving to the city full control of the watershed, since a single case of typhoid infection would endanger the health of the city. The population of the San Joaquin Valley, in the hot and dusty summer, increasingly frequent the park as campers. These would be deprived of the use of these wonderful scenes. As for the general public of travelers, that take so much money to California in quest of beauty—for it, there would be only a phantom valley, sunken, like the fabled city of Brittany, while the 20 miles of the most wonderful rapids in the world, the cascades of the Tuolumne, would be virtually eclipsed. I am aware that in certain quarters one who contends for the practical value of natural beauty is considered a "crank," and yet the love of beauty is the most dominant trait in mankind. The moment anyone of intelligence gets enough to satisfy the primal needs of the physical man, he begins to plan for something beautiful—house, grounds, or a view of nature. Could this be capitalized in dollars, could some alchemy reveal its value, we should not hear materialists deriding lovers of nature, with any effect upon legislators. Without this touch of idealism, this sense of beauty, life would only be a race for the trough.

I have only time for one other point. In 1890 when I appealed to Senator George Hearst to support the bill creating the Yosemite National Park, a project which, as is well known, was first proposed by me to Mr. Muir in 1889, and was jointly urged by us upon Congress, that practical Senator assented with alacrity, and in effect said: "The chief use of that region is for water for irrigation purposes and for its scenery. It has been prospected over many times and there are no precious metals worth speaking of. The forests are more valuable to hold water for irrigation than as timber. Indeed I should favor reserving the whole of the Sierra down to Mount Whitney." I reported this last remark to Gen. Noble, President Harrison's Secretary of the Interior, and toward the close of the administration the whole of that region was reserved. I believe California would not consent to give up the great reservations. Moreover, I believe that the people of the State are opposed to the destruction of the Hetch Hetchy, and that this can be demonstrated if the bill can be delayed until the December session.

I have the honor to remain, respectfully yours,

Robert Underwood Johnson

Mr. WHITMAN (continuing). . . .

In conclusion, I wish there was some way in which this committee could see the Hetch Hetchy Valley itself. If you should see it for your-selves I know you would have an entirely different view of it than my poor efforts have been able to give you. I thank you very much for your kind attention.

The CHAIRMAN. Mr. Whitman, may I ask you a few questions?

Mr. WHITMAN. Certainly.

The CHAIRMAN. I have not interrupted you very much. You are aware of the fact that, right at the beginning of the hearing, we called here the Secretary of the Interior and the Secretary of Agriculture?

Mr. WHITMAN. Yes.

The CHAIRMAN. And the Director of the Geological Survey?

Mr. WHITMAN. Yes.

The CHAIRMAN. And the Director of the Reclamation Service, and the Chief of the Forest Service, and Hon. Gifford Pinchot, said to be the best authority on conservation in the whole United States? And you were present during that part of the hearings?

Mr. WHITMAN. I was, sir.

The CHAIRMAN. I believe you will agree with me that, in each and every instance, their views were at variance with yours?

Mr. WHITMAN. Their opinions, so far as they were based on the infor-mation before them, were.

The CHAIRMAN. Yes; I believe you will agree that we had before us here the Army board, men of standing and high character, who were sent out there to make a personal examination of this matter?

Mr. WHITMAN. Yes, sir.

The CHAIRMAN. And did go there. And that, to sum it up tersely, their conclusion was that this was the most available supply, and that it should be done now. Were those not practically the words spoken here by Col. Biddle?

Mr. WHITMAN. His opinion seemed to be that, inasmuch as this water was necessary for irrigation, it should be given to the city for domestic supply.

The CHAIRMAN. At the outset of your statement you conceded a shortage of water to San Francisco, did you not?

Mr. WHITMAN. There is a temporary shortage due to an unfortunate controversy which has gone on for some years between the company and the city whereby the necessary facilities which have been extended have not been adequate.

The CHAIRMAN. You are aware of the fact that California has eleven Members of Congress here in their delegation?

Mr. WHITMAN. I think so.

The CHAIRMAN. And that no one of them has been here and said anything other than in commendation of this action, are you not?

Mr. WHITMAN. I have not heard any very strong opposition, sir.

The CHAIRMAN. Do you not really think that it is assuming a good deal of responsibility for a resident of Cambridge, Mass.—even for a learned and distinguished lawyer that you are—to set up your judgment against that array of talent and array of officials and of Representatives in Congress who have gone into the question the same as yourself?

Mr. WHITMAN. So far as it is a question of opinion I agree with you; so far as it is a question of fact, I have endeavored to present such considerations of fact as to show that their opinion has not been based upon consideration of the existing facts.

PART TWO

ARTS

10. Styles of Decoration and Design

The ways people design their implements and decorate their homes is an excellent source of information about the taste and values of their time and place. Early twentieth century America inherited an "official" aesthetics which equated beauty with ornateness, and frequently with European styles. Louis C. Tiffany's silver and enamel hand mirror in the shape of a peacock is in the old tradition of elegance. A New York jeweler, Tiffany catered to the genteel tastes of the rich and established. Unconsciously beautiful in a radically different sense was the highly functional valve designed by the Eastwood Manufacturing Company of Belleville, New Jersey. But such vernacular expressions were not accorded the status of art even by their creators.

The mode of interior decoration selected for the homes of the very rich reflected the desire to consume as conspicuously as possible in a manner sanctioned by European tradition. The principal object of such decoration was not the collection of art for its own sake but rather as a showpiece testifying to the status of the collector. Thus the 250 room mansion, "Biltmore," that Richard Morris Hunt designed for the Vanderbilts was lavishly furnished with the most expensive array of canvases, tapestries, books, statuary, and historic treasures money could buy. George Washington Vanderbilt, heir to the railroad fortune of his grandfather Cornelius, personally scoured Europe for his prizes and opened his "country home" shortly before the turn of the century. At the other end of the social scale, other Americans merely tried to survive in garbage-littered slums.

At the same time there were those who strove for a more functional style of decoration that would be truer to native American tastes. One result was the living room of the residence Frank Lloyd Wright designed for Avery Coonley in 1908. Wright's own home, built on a bluff above the Wisconsin River in 1911, was decorated in a deliberately primitive style.

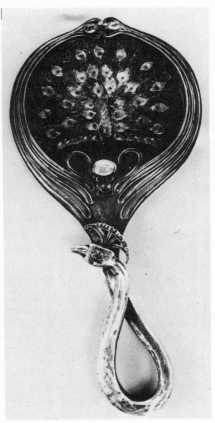

2. THE FUNCTIONAL:
    *Eastwood Manufacturing
    Company, valve
    handle, about 1900.*

1. THE ORNATE:
    *Lewis C. Tiffany,
    hand mirror,
    about 1900.*

3. THE OSTENTATIOUS I:
    Second landing of the Grand Staircase,
    "Biltmore," Ashville, North Carolina.

4. THE OSTENTATIOUS II: *Library, "Biltmore."*

5. THE OSTENTATIOUS III: *Banquet Hall, "Biltmore."*

6. SURVIVAL: *Slum kitchen about 1910.*

7. THE CLEAN LINE: *Living room, Avery Coonley residence by Frank Lloyd Wright, Riverside, Illinois.*

8. THE DELIBERATELY PRIMITIVE: *Living room, Frank Lloyd Wright's Taliesin I, Spring Green, Wisconsin.*

11. Wealth Against Taste

In 1904 the editors of the magazine *House Beautiful* launched a series of articles on the artistic taste of the very rich as manifested in the interior decoration of their homes. Accepted aesthetics received a thorough lampooning. In the face of such withering criticism, it became increasingly difficult to equate refinement with costly artifacts and ornaments. Gradually the way was cleared for simpler, more functional, more American styles.

The Poor Taste of the Rich

It is customary in many schools to teach English by means of incorrect sentences; to give examples of false construction, and to show on another blackboard similar sentences correctly written. Distinguished educators have questioned this method, claiming that the mind should be trained by reading and writing correct English only.

The policy of the *House Beautiful* has been based on a similar theory; that the good only should be illustrated, and that examples of faulty house furnishings should be carefully avoided.

Some mistakes in English are so flagrant that they are valuable as object lessons; some houses are so atrocious that they are valuable as warnings. A few examples of blunders in the grammar of architecture and decoration are herewith reproduced for the benefit of our readers. . . .

Cheap ugliness is bad enough, but costly ugliness is a crime, for the responsibility of the rich man is greater than that of his poorer brother.

Anonymous, "The Poor Taste of the Rich," *House Beautiful*, 17 (Dec., 1904), 20, 21, 23 (Feb., 1905), 19–21.

His opportunities to improve public taste are so vast that he cannot neglect them without violating a sacred trust. Is there one millionaire in ten who recognizes this responsibility, or who fulfils this trust? Is there one costly palace in fifty that is not an outrage against good taste? Is there one expensive residence in a hundred that is an object lesson in the beautiful?

Finally, is there one cottage in this broad land that can compare in ugliness and vulgarity with the millionaire's house which we have chosen as a text for our first sermon on *The Poor Taste of the Rich*—a sub-heading of which might run: *The Compensations of Poverty*.

We do not question the rich man's right to his mansion. It is his duty to build a costly house. The man of wealth who lives in miserly surroundings is evading his responsibility quite as much as the man who builds a monument of ugliness in brown stone and plush. Both are offenders. One does not use his opportunities; the other misuses them.

It is the rich man's duty to build the great house, and it is his duty to build it worthily. Every advantage that money can give is within his reach; every opportunity to create a beautiful house is his by right of wealth. When he erects a monstrosity in marble or stone he is corrupting public morals as well as taste. One of the greatest evils of our modern civilization is the aping of the rich by the poor. Sham and pretence thrive in this mad struggle for appearances. The genuine cannot be acquired and so the false is accepted. The vulgarity of the mansion is copied a hundred fold, copied in cheap material that has but one advantage—it cannot last.

The millionaire walks in the glare of the lime-light. The privacy enjoyed by men in humbler walks of life is denied him. He may hide his movements in Wall street, but he cannot hide his house. Stone walls and high hedges are powerless against the X-ray of public curiosity. He may make a fetish of privacy, seeking it with a persistency second only to his desire for greater gain, but he cannot attain it. His house is in a measure public property. It is a curse of riches, possibly the penalty of riches that their possessor is always in the public eye. The cut of his clothes, the number of his servants, the pattern of his furniture are matters of absorbing interest. We read these items daily in our newspapers; we hear them discussed continually.

If the millionaire is to occupy so much of our horizon, it behooves him to use his influence for good. He may endow colleges and found libraries, and yet, by reason of his house, fail as a public benefactor. The house lives after him; unlike its imitations, it is not built for a day.

All millionaires' houses are not of the same class. Some are worse than others. Perhaps the rich man has acquired his wealth quickly and wishes to impress the public with the fact. His house will express but one thing, *money*. Perhaps he wishes to avoid the public; he lives abroad and his house is merely a storage place for the treasures of dismantled palaces. It is a jumble of costly furniture and rare tapestries; things beautiful in themselves but producing only confusion and discord when crowded together within the walls of one American house. It is a museum, not a home, and without the wise classifications and dignity of a real museum.

There are many such houses in our land. They are, like the Bradley-Martin type, object lessons in the mis-direction of riches. Built solely to house a collection of costly antiques, they can have no value as *beautiful homes*, but they might be made to have a value of another kind. They could at least be consistent. We do not quarrel with the rich man for turning his house into a would-be museum; we quarrel with him for the jumble of styles, periods, and countries that he gathers together under one roof. Houses of this class suggest the mansion of Silas Higbee, the ham magnate, who made his fortune in Chicago and then moved to New York to spend it. His creator, Harry Leon Wilson, describes the house in his novel, "The Spenders."

"The door of the Higbee domain is of polished mahogany, set between lights of antique verte Italian glass and bearing an ancient brass knocker. From the reception-room, with its wall of green Empire silk, one passes through a foyer hall of Cordova leather hangings to the drawing-room. Opposite the entrance is a mantel of carved Caen stone faced with golden Pavanazzo marble, with old Roman andirons of gold, ending in the fleur-de-lis. The walls are hung with blue Florentine silk embossed in silver. Beyond a bronze grille is the music-room, a library done in Hungarian oak, a billiard-room, a smoking-room. The latter has walls of red damask and a mantel with 'Post Tenebras Lux' cut into one of its marble panels, a legend which the worthy lessee of all this splendor is wont to gaze at with respectful admiration."

Another novelist has described the exterior of a similar house. In "The Celebrity," by Winston Churchill, a newly-made millionaire points with pride to his mansion. "I had all these ideas I gathered knocking about the world and I gave them to Willis of Philadelphia to put together for me. But he's honest enough not to claim the house. Take for instance the minaret business on the west, I picked that up from a mosque in Algiers. The oriel just this side is whole-cloth from Haddon Hall, and the galleried porch next it is from a French château. Some of the features on the south are from a Buddhist temple in Japan. Only a little blending and grouping were necessary. Now get the effect. Did you ever see another house like it?"

The . . . house of Mr. Bradley-Martin [is] sufficient to illustrate the point in hand. Ostentation is expressed in every detail; pretence is written across every line. The rooms are faulty architecturally. The doors and ceilings are bad. The furnishings suggest the upholstery department of the country store. The rugs are commonplace. The draperies are execrable. Enter the Hall of the Bradley-Martin abode and gaze upon the mis-spent millions. Behold the ceiling, the walls, the furniture, the rugs, the draperies, and note the discord. The ceiling is good in itself—full of dignity and well constructed—a copy of a Medici ceiling in Florence; but it fits neither the walls nor the furniture. The walls are not much of anything; a weak imitation of a French period, poorly drawn and badly colored. The fine Empire chairs are as much out of place in this setting as a fine jewel in a brass mounting. They are a hundred years later than the walls and nearly two centuries behind the ceiling. Silas Higbee in his New York palace could not approach this hop-skip-and-jump of periods.

Note the ugly, trifling, commonplace lamps and ornaments, with their suggestion of the basement bargain counter! Gaze upon the grille and the drapery of the staircase and ponder deeply. This festoon with its ball fringe is the crowning point in the jumble. It is the final touch of the ridiculous. In a poor man's house it would be pathetic. In its present setting it must make the angels weep. As you walk from room to room in the Bradley-Martin mansion you will find the looped drapery with the ball fringe at every turn. You cannot escape it. It has left its mark on every window and every door. Its disfiguring hand is on the chairs, the couches—even the beds.

Passing from the Hall you enter the Drawing-room. More money; less taste. The upholstered ceiling, the tortured walls, the bedecked and begilded furniture, the costly and trumpery ornaments wage a continual battle. All the nations of Europe are represented in this apartment and they keep up an international warfare. The Russian sledge swears at the Japanese porcelains; the Japanese porcelains are not on speaking terms with the Chinese bronzes; the French furniture hurls invectives at the German draperies. How restful! How livable! Count the cost—the thousands expended here and rejoice that you *cannot* go and do likewise.

As a special feeling for the fitness of things note the sledge, typical of frozen ice fields, filled with palms from the tropics, and resting on the skin of a man-eating tiger. Retrace your footsteps, walking gingerly so that you may not demolish several thousand dollars' worth of bric-à-brac by a chance misstep. Ponder what it must be to thus pirouette three hundred and sixty-five days in the year—and be thankful for providential poverty.

As bedrooms express the real personality of their owners, not being in any sense show places—so the Bradley-Martin chambers reveal the true taste of their occupants. Here we see the commonplace shorn of some of its glitter. The commercially cheap is placed side by side with the costly.

Beginning with the Louis XV room study carefully the details, the hanging-lamp, the table with its useless trifles, the gilded cupid upholding the frenzied canopy. Louis XV did some one say? The decorators of Louis' court would be moved to tears could they but see the crimes committed in their name. There is nothing typical of this style except a few pieces of furniture and they are travesties. The ornate beds placed upon a *carpeted* dais have the outlines of the great style they seek to copy but that is all. The real spirit of the period is lacking. What little Louis XV feeling there is in the room is totally destroyed by the awful ceiling, the cheap and insecure table and the weird and very modern draperies. The walls have a suggestion of the style under consideration but their treatment robs them of any dignity.

For mis-applied energy the Empire bedroom is an impressive object lesson. Here is some fine old furniture ruined by a hopeless mixture of the commonplace:—The beautiful bedstead is disfigured by an astonishing canopy which suggests a huge lampshade. The couch of noble proportions, ornamented with the torch and wreath, is hidden beneath a chenille covering. The Empire divan of fine lines is marred by a sofa pillow. The undoubted beauty of the walls is spoiled by a weak and meaningless ceiling.

The chintz bedroom can hardly be taken seriously. A simple brass bed of indifferent pattern is bedraped and befringed until its lines are almost effaced. Heaven never designed beds of this kind for canopies. But balled and fringed canopies are the Bradley-Martin hall-mark, and no bed, be it ever so humble, can escape.

Make note of these five interiors. Study them as children study examples of incorrect English. They are colossal examples of errors in house furnishings. They break every law of decoration; violate every principle of home-making. They were planned and executed by money— undistracted by thought of comfort, taste, or harmony. The result is a monument to ugliness and the poor taste of the rich.

We would not ask the occupants of the modern house decorated in this bygone fashion to dress in harmony with the background. We would not ask Mr. Millionaire, after a day of frenzied finance, to exchange his business suit for an elaborate costume of lace and velvet, or to don high-heeled shoes and a curled wig; nor would we ask Madame Millionaire to greet her lord in sweeping satins and towering headgear. But we would ask for a truer understanding of the mission of a house. If a home is merely an exhibition place, wherein may be gathered the remnants of European palaces; a place to house works of art and the spoils of foreign travel; a place in which the professional decorator is to exercise his unlicensed fancy; a place in which to astonish the rich and to make envious the poor—if the home is to be this *thing,* then the Burrage house, and all others of its class, are eminently successful. If the home, on the other hand, is something else; if it stands for other things than money; if it is representative of something in our national life; if, coming nearer the heart of the matter, it is typical of the lives of those that spend their years within its walls—then the Burrage house, and all others like it, are rank failures. They fail lamentably, and they fail the more and the harder because they represent so many, many dollars.

The millionaire's duty? Does he know it, or, knowing it, heed it? Does he build with one thought beyond the cost, one thought beyond display, one thought beyond the desire to astonish the world with the magnitude of his undertaking? The millionaire who builds otherwise should have a monument erected to his memory, although a monument would be unnecessary, for the house would be a monument. He need endow no colleges, found no libraries, build no churches. In erecting the house he would have fulfilled his part as a public benefactor, and could rest secure in the world's verdict.

There may be such millionaires and such houses, but they are as rare as green carnations. Meanwhile, houses of the Bradley-Martin, the Clarence Mackay, and A. C. Burrage types are so numerous that at the mere phrase "a millionaire's house" the imagination paints a colossal edifice, sumptuous within and without, bedecked and begilded, and while beautiful in many ways, producing in its entirety an ugly dreariness that makes a simple cottage, by comparison, seem a thing of beauty.

Who would choose as a life companion a house like one of these, when simplicity, charm, peace, and true beauty were to be had for a fragment of the money bestowed on the rich man's abode? Who would live in rooms where every mantel was a copy of one in some crumbling palace, and every piece of furniture associated with some dead and gone monarch? The beds of kings were made for kings. How uneasy must sometimes lie the heads of those that rest beneath these canopies of silk and lace!

Does the humorous side of the picture ever occur to the millionaire? The droll incongruity of transplanting royal furniture to a democratic land, and placing it in an American citizen's house, or of copying the furniture where originals are impossible, and thus sitting, eating, and sleeping on royal reproductions.

As the millionaire unfolds his morning paper, seated in a Marie Antoinette chair, his hand resting on a Louis XIV table, and his eyes fixed on a Henry IV cabinet, does a touch of the humorous enter the situation? As he passes through the hall, with its woodwork from the palace of Lorenzo the Magnificent, its shields and cross-swords from the armory of Philip of Spain, its furniture from a dismantled château, and steps into his carriage, does the mirth of the occasion occur to him? Probably not. It is all so impressive, so gorgeous, so expensive; it has all been secured at the outlay of so much time and money, it must of necessity leave nothing to be desired. And complacent Mr. Millionaire drives away. His duty to his country ended when he signed the checks that made all this magnificence possible.

When Madame Millionaire sits in her Louis XV bedroom, with its rose Du Barry hangings, and its furniture copied from models in the Grand Trianon, is she troubled by a sense of the unfitness of things? The harmony here is greater than in any other part of the house, for consistency in royal furnishings is not difficult to attain in a bedroom. The professional decorator has done his work well, and the room is fit for a queen. For a queen, yes—but for the wife of an American citizen. Is there not an affectation in the every-day use of this gilded grandeur? The canopied bed, the elaborate curtains, the furniture of ormolu and satinwood ornamented with painted ladies in the guise of peasants? Is not Madame Millionaire masquerading as truly as the ladies of Louis's court who are depicted on table, and bureau, and commode? They play at peasantry: she plays at royalty. They lived in an artificial age when the chief zest of life lay in pretending to be something they were not. The age was their excuse. Madame Millionaire lives in an age when sincerity and simplicity cry to heaven, and when show and pretense are no longer in repute. Therefore, the gilded furniture, the painted cupids and simpering ladies, the hangings which once belonged to a king's favorite, are a huge sham. They cannot in any way express the personality of their present owner. They are untrue to the present age, to the house in which they are placed, and to the individuality of all who come in contact with them. They were a perfect expression of the life of their day and they cannot be severed from it.

There is the sham of makeshift furnishings. False this and false that. Wood painted to look like metal; metal treated to look like wood. Cotton that pretends to be satin: satin that pretends to be something else. And there are shams of another kind: things, real in themselves, genuine so far as their construction is concerned, but false nevertheless. False because they are placed where they do not belong; false because they are made to serve purposes for which they were never intended; false because they represent a mode of life entirely remote from present-day conditions. The shams of the rich man's house are of the latter class. There is nothing about his furniture, his hangings, his tapestries, that is not real, and yet they are false. They are untrue to American life, to American thought, to American ideals. They were a part of a past age, and they cannot be separated from it. So long as the age cannot be reproduced, why reproduce its accessories? Why seek to incorporate into the life of the twentieth century the household gods of the seventeenth and eighteenth centuries? Have we no atmosphere of our own that we needs must resurrect an atmosphere as lifeless as the hands that created it?

Let us accord all justice to the beautiful furniture of the great French periods. The furniture-makers of the seventeenth and eighteenth centuries must rank with the painters of that age. Boulle, Cressent, Gouthière, Cafferi, Roentgen are equal with Lebrun, Mignard, Lancret, and Watteau. One body of men worked with paint and canvas, and the other with wood and metal. Both produced works of art.

Let us accord all admiration to these marvelous pieces of handicraft in satinwood and ormolu, in mahogany and marquetry, in amboyna and gilded lacquer. The consoles, cabinets, bureaus, commodes, secrétaires, and tables have a beauty that has never been surpassed. They are museum pieces in the real sense of the word, and in museums they belong. They represent the life of the reigns with which they were associated far better than the pictures of the period, and as such they have a value far beyond that of the painted canvas—although the canvas may show us the costumes of the day with the fidelity of a miniature.

Let us study these masterpieces as we would study the histories of France, and if we be millionaires let us place them in our private museums. But in our homes, whether we be rich or poor, let us seek to make our surroundings an expression of our own times.

We hear a great deal about the lack of a national style in architecture.

Could we not hear to our advantage something about the absence of a national style in decoration? The colonial style, both in architecture and decoration, is our finest national expression—but it is eighteenth, not twentieth, century, and it does not meet the needs of our present complex· life.

The simplicity of the colonial period, however, does not appeal to the millionaire. The absence of glitter renders it unfit for him. It does not represent the dollar mark sufficiently. It may do for others, but not for one whose house must be a monument to millions. And so it happens that the country is full of dwarfed palaces and cut-down castles; of interiors that speak of everything save the life of the present day; halls with carved ceilings and mosaic floors, marble stairways and splashing fountains, suits of chain-mail and gilded cupids; drawing-rooms with the golden glitter of Versailles, Fontainebleau, and Grand Trianon combined, furniture that is reminiscent of a half dozen monarchs—Francis I, Louis XIV, Louis XV, and Louis XVI, Napoleon and Charles X—walls that fit neither floors nor ceilings and that have nothing in common with the draperies, clocks that are French, statues that are Italian, porcelains that are Japanese and Chinese; dining-rooms with the magnificence of a dozen Old World apartments, walls hung in Spanish leather, ceilings of the Elizabethan period, mantels of the Italian Renaissance, furniture of old Flemish oak, and paintings of the modern French school; libraries that are museums of rare furniture and costly bric-à-brac, but never book-rooms, although the shelves are lined with priceless volumes in gold and fine leather; bedrooms that are as regal as those belonging to Marie Antoinette and Josephine, but lacking in every essential that makes for rest and peace.

These French, Italian, old English, Flemish, and Oriental homes, built in a democratic land, are not without a mission. They exemplify the poor taste of the rich more clearly than volumes on the subject; and finally, they preach contentment with a lot in life as remote from that of the millionaire as one pole is from the other.

12. Conflicting Philosophies of Architecture

The American discussion of the role of the artist and the meaning of art was sharply focused in the field of architecture. On one side were traditionalists like Ralph Adams Cram for whom even the Renaissance was too modern. Cram's taste ran to the medieval, the Gothic, and he conceived of its restoration in American building style as a matter of paramount importance to the survival of civilization itself. Like his contemporary Henry Adams, Cram looked back nostalgically to a time many centuries past when faith and absolute law anchored men's lives. At the other end of the spectrum in architecture stood Frank Lloyd Wright—a disciple of nature rather than history and of pragmatic functionalism rather than rigid adherence to fixed law. Born in Wisconsin in 1869, Wright rose to leadership of the "Chicago School" of architectural innovators. But his ideas were slow to receive recognition as pioneering a new, native aesthetics.

The Ministry of Art
RALPH ADAMS CRAM

By the words "The Ministry of Art" I mean that function which I think art has performed, and always can perform, as an agency working toward the redemption of human character; and in this aspect (which is, of course, only one of several) it takes on something of that quality which characterizes the ministers of the Christian Church. . . .

And this I conceive to be the highest function of the artist and the art

Ralph Adams Cram, *The Ministry of Art* (Boston, Houghton Mifflin Co., 1914), viii–xiii, 46–50, 53, 54, 61–63.

that is his agency of operation. Not that I would for a moment make this an exclusive property; art has sufficient reason for existence in its quality as a creator of simple, sensuous joy and refreshment; as a beneficent force expressing itself through—and absolutely restricted to—pure beauty. As, however, each material thing in the universe has its sacramental quality, expressing a secret spiritual grace through an outward and visible form, from the crystalline snowflake that symbolizes the fancy of playful angels working under inexorable law, to the mind of man which is but the crude, material type of the very Mind of God, so abstract art may do more than make life beautiful (at times), in that it can act symbolically, tropically, sacramentally, and so become the supreme means of expressing, and of inciting and exalting, those emotions which transcend experience and may not in any degree find voice through those channels of expression which are entirely adequate for the purposes of the intellect.

In this aspect the master of art (the word "artist" has acquired a sickly connotation which almost rules it out of use in this connection) wields a power of most astonishing magnitude, and he may, if he likes, become through his works one of the greatest agencies of righteousness and light, and, conversely, he may too easily become the servant of damnation. That he has so often become the latter is less his own fault, perhaps, than that of society itself, which, when it periodically strikes its downward course, becomes actually poisonous, and very swiftly metamorphoses the best of arts and the most willing of artists into Circean beasts. If the master of art himself, and the world he would serve, were more clearly and persistently convinced of the great educational, expressive, and dynamic force of art as art and as a sacramental agency, it is even possible that, though they might not be avoided, the depths to which civilization periodically falls might not be so abysmal as history records, the crests more enduring and prolonged, the nodal points less closely set together.

And now again, as the descending curve meets the ascending swell and we confront a crossing of tendencies with all this ever has implied of cross-currents and confusion, it is particularly important that the higher aspects of art in all its forms should be brought to mind, while we call upon it to exercise its just and unique functions of expression and education. There is a new strength in all the arts, as always happens when the power that created them is losing force, and while this cannot possibly arrest the fall of one dynasty or the rise of the other, it has a great part to perform, if it wholly realizes itself, in giving expression to all that is worth preserving in an era so fast becoming history, and in bridging the inevitable chasm now opening between one definite epoch and the next. In the interregnum we may expect a general breakdown of what we now consider a triumphant civilization, but the artist has the same part to play here that was so splendidly performed by the monasteries of the Dark Ages. In his work, whatever it may be, he must record and preserve all that was and is best in a shattered era, that this may be carried over into the next and play its new part, no longer of conservation but of re-creation.

So, in a sense, the artist stands as a minister in minor orders, and so his life and acts take hold of that sacramentalism that is the foundation of both the Church and the world: if he plays his part honestly and as one so charged with duties and privileges, he may see the art to which he is sworn become once more, not only a great recorder of true civilization, but the surety of its eventual restoration.

The Gothic restoration means, a returning to other days—not for the retrieving of pleasant but forgotten forms, but for the recovery of those impulses in life which made these forms inevitable. . . . The Gothic restoration is neither a fad nor a case of stylistic predilections. . . .

We think it better art than anything the Renaissance ever produced; but back of this is either a clear conviction or a dim instinct (one is as good as the other as an incentive) that the power that expressed itself through Gothic forms was a saner and more wholesome and altogether nobler thing than that which expressed itself through the art of the Renaissance and all that has succeeded it. . . .

We may assume that at least from 1950 on we, or our descendants, shall confront a revolution of the same nature, during which what we now call "modern civilization" (which may be dated roughly from the fall of Constantinople in 1453) will dissolve and disappear as completely as the Roman Empire vanished at the first node after the birth of Christ, the Carolingian empire at the second, and mediævalism at the third; while what takes its place will be as radically different as happened in each of these historic instances. . . .

Half the so-called reforms of to-day, and those most loudly acclaimed and avidly accepted, are really no more than the desperate efforts of a dying force to prolong for an hour its pitiful existence, to postpone for a day its inevitable plunge into the sea of oblivion. On the other hand, the other half,—who shall estimate its vast significance, its illimitable dynamic force? Under its varied forms lie the promise and potency of a new era, a new epoch of civilization; and I honestly think the great question that confronts every man to-day, and that must be promptly answered is

"On which wave are you riding?" If on that whose crest loomed in the immediate past, then you are riding down the swift glissade of dissolution and your day is nearly done; if [on the Gothic restoration] then before you lifts an ascent that cannot be checked and whose cresting is perhaps two or three centuries ahead. . . .

This, then, is the significance of the contemporary Gothic restoration, and we who believe in it, who give it our most earnest support, do so less as artists than as missionaries, confident that if we can bring it back, even at first on the old lines, we shall have been working in the service of humanity.

Shall we rest there? Shall we restore a style, and a way of life, and a mode of thought? Shall we re-create an amorphous mediævalism and live listlessly in that fool's paradise? On the contrary. When a man finds himself confronting a narrow stream, with no bridge in sight, does he leap convulsively on the very brink and then project himself into space? If he does he is very apt to fail of his immediate object, which is to get across. No; he retraces his steps, gains his running start, and clears the obstacle at a bound. This is what we architects are doing when we fall back on the great past for our inspiration; this is what, specifically, the Gothicists are particularly doing. We are getting our running start, we are retracing our steps to the great Christian Middle Ages, not that there we may remain, but that we may achieve an adequate point of departure; what follows must take care of itself.

And, by your leave, in following this course we are not alone, we have life with us; for at last life also is going backward, back to gather up the golden apples lost in the wild race for prizes of another sort, back for its running start, that it may clear the crevasse that startlingly has opened before it. Beyond this chasm lies a new field, and a fair field, and it is ours if we will. The night has darkened, but lightened toward dawn; there is silver on the edges of the hills and promise of a new day, not only for architects, but for every man.

In the Cause of Architecture
FRANK LLOYD WRIGHT

Radical though it be, [my work] is dedicated to a cause conservative in the best sense of the word. At no point does it involve denial of the elemental law and order inherent in all great architecture; rather, it is a declaration of love for the spirit of that law and order, and a reverential recognition of the elements that made its ancient letter in its time vital and beautiful.

Primarily, Nature furnished the materials for architectural motifs out of which the architectural forms as we know them to-day have been developed, and, although our practice for centuries has been for the most part to turn from her, seeking inspiration in books and adhering slavishly to dead formulae, her wealth of suggestion is inexhaustible; her riches greater than any man's desire. I know with what suspicion the man is regarded who refers matters of fine art back to Nature. I know that it is usually an ill-advised return that is attempted, for Nature in external, obvious aspect is the usually accepted sense of the term and the nature that is reached. But given inherent vision there is no source so fertile, so suggestive, so helpful æsthetically for the architect as a comprehension of natural law. As Nature is never right for a picture so is she never right for the architect—that is, not ready-made. Nevertheless, she has a practical school beneath her more obvious forms in which a sense of proportion may be cultivated, when Vignola and Vitruvius fail as they must always fail. It is there that he may develop that sense of reality that translated to his own field in terms of his own work will lift him far above the realistic in his art; there he will be inspired by sentiment that will never degenerate to sentimentality and he will learn to draw with a surer hand the ever-perplexing line between the curious and the beautiful.

A sense of the organic is indispensable to an architect; where can he develop it so surely as in this school? A knowledge of the relations of form and function lies at the root of his practice; where else can he find the pertinent object lessons Nature so readily furnishes? Where can he

Frank Lloyd Wright, "In the Cause of Architecture," *Architectural Record*, 23 (March, 1908), 155–157, 165.

study the differentiations of form that go to determine character as he can study them in the trees? Where can that sense of inevitableness characteristic of a work of art be quickened as it may be by intercourse with nature in this sense?

In 1894 . . . I formulated the following "proportions." I set them down here much as they were written then, although in the light of experience they might be stated more completely and succinctly.

I.—Simplicity and Repose are qualities that measure the true value of any work of art.

But simplicity is not in itself an end nor is it a matter of the side of a barn but rather an entity with a graceful beauty in its integrity from which discord, and all that is meaningless, has been eliminated. A wild flower is truly simple. Therefore:

1. A building should contain as few rooms as will meet the conditions which give it rise and under which we live, and which the architect should strive continually to simplify; then the ensemble of the rooms should be carefully considered that comfort and utility may go hand in hand with beauty. Beside the entry and necessary work rooms there need be but three rooms on the ground floor of any house, living room, dining room and kitchen, with the possible addition of a "social office"; really there need be but one room, the living room with requirements otherwise sequestered from it or screened within it by means of architectural contrivances.

2. Openings should occur as integral features of the structure and form, if possible, its natural ornamentation.

3. An excessive love of detail has ruined more fine things from the standpoint of fine art or fine living than any one human shortcoming —it is hopelessly vulgar. Too many houses, when they are not little stage settings or scene paintings, are mere notion stores, bazaars or junk-shops. Decoration is dangerous unless you understand it thoroughly and are satisfied that it means something good in the scheme as a whole, for the present you are usually better off without it. Merely that it "looks rich" is no justification for the use of ornament.

4. Appliances or fixtures as such are undesirable. Assimilate them together with all appurtenances into the design of the structure.

5. Pictures deface walls oftener than they decorate them. Pictures should be decorative and incorporated in the general scheme as decoration.

6. The most truly satisfactory apartments are those in which most or all of the furniture is built in as a part of the original scheme considering the whole as an integral unit.

II.—There should be as many kinds (styles) of houses as there are kinds (styles) of people and as many differentiations as there are different individuals. A man who has individuality (and what man lacks it?) has a right to its expression in his own environment.

III.—A building should appear to grow easily from its site and be shaped to harmonize with its surroundings if Nature is manifest there, and if not try to make it as quiet, substantial and organic as She would have been were the opportunity Hers.

We of the Middle West are living on the prairie. The prairie has a beauty of its own and we should recognize and accentuate this natural beauty, its quiet level. Hence, gently sloping roofs, low proportions, quiet sky lines, suppressed heavy-set chimneys and sheltering overhangs, low terraces and out-reaching walls sequestering private gardens.

IV.—Colors require the same conventionalizing process to make them fit to live with that natural forms do; so go to the woods and fields for color schemes. Use the soft, warm, optimistic tones of earths and autumn leaves in preference to the pessimistic blues, purples or cold greens and grays of the ribbon counter; they are more wholesome and better adapted in most cases to good decoration.

V.—Bring out the nature of the materials, let their nature intimately into your scheme. Strip the wood of varnish and let it alone—stain it. Develop the natural texture of the plastering and stain it. Reveal the nature of the wood, plaster, brick or stone in your designs; they are all by nature friendly and beautiful. No treatment can be really a matter of fine art when these natural characteristics are, or their nature is, outraged or neglected.

VI.—A house that has character stands a good chance of growing more valuable as it grows older while a house in the prevailing mode, whatever that mode may be, is soon out of fashion, stale and unprofitable.

Buildings like people must first be sincere, must be true and then withal as gracious and lovable as may be.

Above all, integrity. The machine is the normal tool of our civilization, give it work that it can do well—nothing is of greater importance. To do this will be to formulate new industrial ideals, sadly needed. . . .

As for the future—the work shall grow more truly simple; more expressive with fewer lines, fewer forms; more articulate with less labor; more plastic; more fluent, although more coherent; more organic. It shall grow not only to fit more perfectly the methods and processes that are called upon to produce it, but shall further find whatever is lovely or of good repute in method or process, and idealize it with the cleanest, most virile stroke I can imagine. As understanding and appreciation of life matures and deepens, this work shall prophesy and idealize the character of the individual it is fashioned to serve more intimately, no matter how inexpensive the result must finally be. It shall become in its atmosphere as pure and elevating in its humble way as the trees and flowers are in their perfectly appointed way, for only so can architecture be worthy its high rank as a fine art, or the architect discharge the obligation he assumes to the public—imposed upon him by the nature of his own profession.

13. Buildings and Values

Palatial mansions, largely imitative of European homes, were in vogue at the turn of the century. The archetype was the "Biltmore," near Asheville, North Carolina. Situated on 125,000 acres of prime forested land it commanded a sweeping view of the Blue Ridge. The value of the estate in 1900 was close to $100,000,000. The criterion of urban elegance at the time was represented by the Clark town house in New York City, which flaunted its baroque grandeur across the street from a set of billboards.

American public architecture had long been marred by imitation and incongruity. Ralph Adams Cram built medieval castles. Nothing could have been less suitable as a monument for Abraham Lincoln than the Greek temple Henry Bacon designed, but the log cabin in which Lincoln originated was not deemed "beautiful" by the cultural arbiters.

Louis Sullivan revolted against all this. Believing that the form of a building should be related to its function (and that beauty might stem from this relationship), Sullivan designed the Carson Pirie Scott department store in Chicago with a steel beam frame and unprecedented large windows. The hold of the old aesthetics on the building, however, was apparent in the elaborate ornamentation of the doorway. Taking up where Sullivan left off, Frank Lloyd Wright became the controversial giant of American architecture. Clean, bold lines, and an emphasis on naturalness marked his public and private buildings. Of his own home near Spring Green, Wisconsin, Wright wrote that "the buildings become a brow for the hill itself." Local rock and wood furnished the construction material and the grounds were purposefully left in an unlandscaped condition. Here, after three centuries of imitation, was *American* architecture.

1. PALACES FOR THE VERY RICH:
   "Biltmore," Ashville, North Carolina, 1895 (Richard Morris Hunt).

2. GOTHIC IMITATION: *Graduate College, Princeton, New Jersey, 1911–1913 (Ralph Adams Cram).*

3. GREEK IMITATION:
Lincoln Memorial, Washington, D.C., 1917 (Henry Bacon).

126

4. THE BAROQUE: *Clark Mansion, New York City, 1901–1903.*

5A. TOWARD FUNCTIONALISM: *Carson Pirie
Scott Store, Chicago, 1904 (Louis Sullivan).*

5B. *Detail of doorway ornament, Carson Pirie Scott
Store, Chicago, 1904 (Louis Sullivan).*

6. FUNCTIONALISM: *Larkin Building, Buffalo, New York, 1903 (Frank Lloyd Wright).*

7. *F. C. Robie Residence, Chicago,*
Illinois, 1909 (Frank Lloyd Wright).

8. BLENDING WITH THE LANDSCAPE: *Taliesin I,*
Spring Green, Wisconsin, 1911–1914 (Frank Lloyd Wright).

9. NATURALNESS: *Exterior detail, Taliesin I,*
Spring Green, Wisconsin, 1911–1914 (Frank Lloyd Wright).

14. Literary Rebellion

The *Smart Set,* founded in 1900, was one of the many "little" magazines that carried on an assault against established literary and moral norms. In 1908 an obscure newspaper writer named Henry L. Mencken joined its staff. As Mencken began to review books and comment generally on the times, it soon became evident that here was no ordinary mind. Mencken made bold to assail any and every convention; his iconoclasm became legendary. Nothing was too exotic or naughty for the *Smart Set*—"A Magazine for Minds That Are Not Primitive," as its slogan advertised. Along with his fellow editor, George Jean Nathan, Mencken and his sarcastic pen gave the establishment little rest.

Mush for the Multitude
HENRY L. MENCKEN

Midway between the tales of persecution and passion that address themselves frankly to servant girls, country school-teachers and the public stenographers in commercial hotels and those works of popular romance which yet hang hazardously, as it were, upon the far-flung yardarms of beautiful letters—midway, as I say, between these wholly atrocious and quasi-respectable evangels of amour and derring-do, there floats a literature vast, gaudy and rich in usufructs, which outrages all sense and probability without descending to actual vulgarity and buffoonery, and so manages to impinge agreeably upon that vast and

Henry L. Mencken, "Mush for the Multitude," *Smart Set,* (Dec., 1914).

money-in-pocket public which takes instinctively a safe, middle course in all things, preferring Sousa's band to either a street piano or the Boston Symphony Orchestra, and *The New York Times* to either the *Evening Journal* or the *Evening Post,* and Dr. Woodrow Wilson to either Debs or Mellon, and dinner at six o'clock to either dinner at noon or dinner at eight-thirty, and three children (two boys and a girl) to either the lone heir of Fifth Avenue or the all-the-traffic-can-bear hatching of the Ghetto, and honest malt liquor to either Croton water or champagne, and Rosa Bonheur's "The Horse Fair" to either Corot's *"Danse de Nymphes"* or a "Portrait of a Lady" from the *Police Gazette,* and fried chicken to either liver or terrapin, and a once-a-week religion to either religion every day or no religion at all, and the Odd Fellows to either the Trappists or the Black Hand, and a fairly pretty girl who can cook fairly well to either a prettier girl who can't cook a stroke or a good cook who sours the milk.

To make an end, the public I refer to is that huge body of honest and right-thinking folk which constitute the heart, lungs and bowels of this great republic—that sturdy multitude which believes in newspapers, equinoctial storms, trust-busting, the Declaration of Independence, teleology, the direct primary, the uplift, trial by jury, monogamy, the Weather Bureau, Congress and the moral order of the world—that innumerable caravan of middling, dollar-grubbing, lodge-joining, quack-ridden folk which the Socialists sneer at loftily as the *bourgeoisie,* and politicians slobber over as the bulwark of our liberties. And, by the same token, the meridional, intermediate literature that I speak of is that literature without end which lifts its dizzy pyramids from the book-counters in the department stores, and from which, ever and anon, there emerges that prize of great price, the best-seller. The essence of this literature is sentiment, and the essence of that sentiment is hope. Its aim is to fill the breast with soothing and optimistic emotions—to make the fat woman forget that she is fat—to purge the tired business man of his bile, to convince the flapper that Douglas Fairbanks may yet learn to love her, to prove that this dreary old world, as botched and bad as it is, might yet be a darn sight worse.

I offer *The Rosary, Soldiers of Fortune, Laddie, The Helmet of Navarre, Little Lord Fauntleroy, Freckles, Eben Holden* and *V. V's. Eyes* as specimens, and so pass on to the latest example, to wit, *Bambi,* by Marjorie Benton Cooke. By the time this reaches you, I have no doubt, *Bambi* will be all the rage in your vicinage. You will be hearing about it on all sides. You will see allusions to it in your evening paper. You will observe it on the desk of your stenographer. Your wife (if you belong to the gnarled and persecuted sex) will be urging you to read it and mark it well. You yourself (if you are fair and have the price) will be wearing a Bambi petticoat or a Bambi collar or a pair of Bambi stockings or a Bambi something-more-intimate-still. Such, alas, is the course that best-sellers run! They permeate and poison the atmosphere of the whole land. It is impossible to get away from them. They invade the most secure retreats, even the very jails and alms-houses. Serving thirty days myself, under the Sherman Act, during the late rage for *The Salamander,* I had it thrust upon me by the rector of the bastile, and had to read it to get rid of him.

Wherefore, in sympathy, as it were, I have ploughed through *Bambi* in time to tell you what it is about before you have to read it yourself, thus hoping to save you from the dangers of too much joy. It is a tale, as you may suspect, of young love, and the heroine is a brilliant young lady named Miss Francesca Parkhurst, the daughter of Professor James Parkhurst, Ph.D., the eminent but somehow balmy mathematician. Professor Parkhurst, as Bambi herself says, knows more about mathematics than the man who invented them, but outside the domain of figures his gigantic intellect refuses to function. Thus he always forgets to go to his lecture-room unless Bambi heads him in the right direction at the right hour, and if it were not for her careful inspection of his make-up, he would often set off with his detachable cuffs upon his ankles instead of upon his wrists, and the skirts of his shirt outside instead of inside his pantaloons. In a word, this Professor Parkhurst is the standard college professor of the best-sellers—the genial jackass we know and love of old. The college professor of the stern, cold world, perhaps, is a far different creature: I once knew one, in fact, who played the races and was a first-rate amateur bartender, and there is record of another who went into politics and clawed his way to a very high office. But in romance, of course, no such heretics are allowed. The college professor of prose fiction is always an absent-minded old boob, who is forever stumbling over his own feet, and he always has a pretty daughter to swab up his waistcoat after he has dined, and to chase away the *ganovim* who are trying to rob him, and to fill his house with an air of innocent and youthful gayety.

Naturally enough, this Professor Parkhurst of our present inquest is not at all surprised when sweet Bambi tells him that she has decided to marry young Jarvis Jocelyn, the rising uplifter, nor even when she tells him that Jarvis knows nothing about it, nor even when she kidnaps Jarvis while he is in a state of coma and sends for a preacher and marries him on the spot, nor even when she puts him to bed *a cappella* on the third floor of the house, and devotes her honeymoon to gathering up and sorting out the flying pages of the Great Drama that he is writing. College professors of the standard model do not shy at such doings. Like babies in arms, they see the world only as a series of indistinct shadows. It would not have made much impression upon Professor Parkhurst had Bambi invited the ashman to dinner or flavored the soup with witch-hazel or come to the meal herself in a bathing-suit. And so it makes very little impression upon him when she shanghais Jarvis and internes the poor fellow in the garret and kicks up a scandal that shakes the whole town. He is dimly conscious that something is going on, just as an infant is dimly conscious that it is light at times and dark at times, but further than that he recks and wots not.

Well, well, we must be getting on! What does Bambi do next? Next she grabs a pencil and a pad of paper and dashes off a short story of her own, with herself, Jarvis and the professor as its characters. Then she tires of it and puts it away. Then, one day, she picks up a New York magazine containing an offer of $500 cash for the best short story submitted in competition. Then she gets out her story, has it typewritten and sends it in. Then—what! have you guessed it? Clever you are, indeed! Yes, even so: then she wins the prize. And then, tucking Jarvis under her arm, she goes to New York and tries to sell the Great Drama. And then she spends a week of sitting in the anterooms of theatrical managers. And then, her story being published under a *nom de plume*, she finds herself an anonymous celebrity and is hospitably received by the genial Bob Davis, editor of *Munsey's*. And then another and much slimmer magazine editor—no doubt G. J. Nathan, thinly disguised—falls in love with her and gives her many valuable pointers. And then Charles Frohman proposes to have her story dramatized, and she lures him into offering Jarvis the job, and then pitches in and helps to perform it. And then the play makes a tremendous hit on Broadway, and she confesses the whole plot, and Jarvis falls desperately in love with her, and we part from them in each other's arms.

A sweet, sweet story. A string of gum-drops. A sugar-teat beyond compare. Of such great probabilities, of such searching reports of human motive and act, the best-seller is all compact. If you have a heart, if you can feel and understand, if your cheers for the true, the good and the beautiful are truly sincere, then this one will squeeze a tear from your leaden eye and send it cascading down your nose. And if, on the contrary, you are one of those cheap barroom cynics who think it is smart to make game of honest sentiment and pure art, then it will give you the loud, coarse guffaw that you crave. But do not laugh too much, dear friend, however hard your heart, however tough your hide. The mission of such things as *Bambi* is, after all, no mean one. Remember the fat woman—how it will make her forget that she is fat. Remember the tired business man—how it will lift him out of his wallow and fill him with a noble enthusiasm for virtue and its rewards. Remember the flapper— how it will thrill her to the very soles of her feet and people her dreams with visions of gallant knights and lighten that doom which makes her actual beau a baseball fan and corrupts him with a loathing for litera- ture and gives him large, hairy hands and a *flair* for burlesque shows and freckles on his neck. And so to other things.

15. Rebellion in Music

Music was one of the slowest arts to respond to the call of the wild. Blues, ragtime, and their hybrid offspring—jazz—existed for years on a level far below recognized "culture." The establishment would have none of this "coon" music, associating it with immorality and licentiousness. But by 1915 some champions of the new music could be found among American intellectuals. Putting unfavorable connotations aside, they simply *listened* to the intriguing sounds and began to tap their feet. Soon after Hiram K. Moderwell wrote this essay the whole nation would swing to jazz and America would proudly export a native music to an admiring world.

Ragtime
HIRAM K. MODERWELL

It has been nearly twenty years, and American ragtime is still officially beyond the pale. As the original and indigenous type of music of the American people, as the one type of American popular music that has persisted and undergone constant evolution, one would think it might receive the clammy hand of fellowship from composers and critics. There is very little evidence that these gentlemen have changed their feeling about it in the last ten years. Then they asserted that it was "fortunately on the wane"; now they sigh that it will be always with us. That is the only difference.

Hiram K. Moderwell, "Ragtime," *New Republic,* 4 (Oct. 16, 1915), 284–286.

I can't feel satisfied with this. I can't help feeling that a person who doesn't open his heart to ragtime somehow isn't human. Nine out of ten musicians, if caught unawares, will like this music until they remember, that they shouldn't. What does this mean? Does it mean that ragtime is "all very well in its place?" Rather that these musicians don't consider that place *theirs*. But that place, remember, is in the affections of some 10,000,000 or more Americans. Conservative estimates show that there are at least 50,000,000 copies of popular music sold in this country yearly, and a goodly portion of it is in ragtime.

And these musicians prefer to regard themselves as beings apart. This is a pretty serious accusation for the musician to level against himself. I don't mean that wherever 10,000,000 Americans agree on a thing they are necessarily right. Their sentimental ballads are the mere dregs of Schubert and Franz Abt. But ragtime is a type of music substantially new in musical history. It has persisted, grown, evolved in many directions, without official recognition or aid. You may take it as certain that if many millions of people persist in liking something that has not been recognized by the schools, there is vitality in that thing. The attitude toward folk-music at the beginning of the nineteenth century was very similar. A Russian folk-song was no less scorned in the court of Catherine the Great than a ragtime song in our music studios to-day. Yet Russian folk-song became the basis of some of the most vigorous art-music of the past century, and no musician speaks of it to-day except in terms of respect. The taste of the populace is often enough toward the shoddy and outworn. But when the populace creates its own art without official encouragement, then let the artists listen. I haven't a notion whether ragtime is going to form the basis of an "American school of composition." But I am sure that many a native composer could save his soul if he would open his ears to this folk-music of the American city.

But the schools have their reply. "Ragtime is not new," they say. "It is merely syncopation, which was used by Haydn and Mozart, Beethoven and Brahms, and is good, like any other musical material, when it is used well." But they are wrong. *Ragtime is not "merely syncopation."* It is a certain sort of syncopation—namely, a persistent syncopation in one part conflicting with exact rhythm in another. But of course this definition is not enough. Ragtime has its flavor that no definition can imprison. No one would take the syncopation of a Haydn symphony to be American ragtime. "Certainly not," replies the indignant musician. Nor the syncopation of any recognized composer. But if this is so, then ragtime *is* new. You can't tell an American composer's "art-song" from any mediocre art-song the world over. (Permit me to pass over the few notable exceptions.) You can distinguish American ragtime from the popular music of any nation and any age.

In the first instance the love of ragtime is a purely human matter. You simply can't resist it. I remember hearing a negro quartet singing "Waiting for the Robert E. Lee," in a café, and I felt my blood thumping in tune, my muscles twitching to the rhythm. I wanted to paraphrase Shakespeare—

> "The man who hath no ragtime in his soul,
> Who is not moved by syncopated sounds" . . .

and so on. If any musician does not feel in his heart the rhythmic complexities of "The Robert E. Lee" I should not trust him to feel in his heart the rhythmic complexities of Brahms. This ragtime appeals to the primitive love of the dance—a special sort of dance in which the rhythm of the arms and shoulders conflicts with the rhythm of the feet, in which dozens of little needles of energy are deftly controlled in the weaving of the whole. And if musicians refuse to recognize it, as they once refused to recognize Russian folk-music, they criticize not ragtime, but themselves.

But ragtime is also "good" in the more austere sense of the professional critic. I cannot understand how a trained musician can overlook its purely technical elements of interest. It has carried the complexities of the rhythmic subdivision of the measure to a point never before reached in the history of music. It has established subtle conflicting rhythms to a degree never before attempted in any popular or folk-music, and rarely enough in art-music. It has shown a definite and natural evolution—always a proof of vitality in a musical idea. It has gone far beyond most other popular music in the freedom of inner voices (yes, I mean polyphony) and of harmonic modulation. And it has proved its adaptability to the expression of many distinct moods. Only the trained musician can appreciate the significance of a style which can be turned to many distinct uses. There is the "sentimental manner," and the "emotional manner" and so on; but the style includes all the manners, and there have not been so many styles in musical history that they couldn't be counted on a few people's fingers.

It may be that I am deceived as to the extent of ragtime's adaptability. But I think of the rollicking fun of "The International Rag," the playful delicacy of "Everybody's Doing It," the bustling laziness of "Waiting for the Robert E. Lee," the sensual poignancy of "La Seduction" tango, and the tender pathos of "The Memphis Blues." Each of these pieces has its peculiar style—in the narrower sense—deftly carried out. And I know that we are dealing here with a set of musical materials which have no more than commenced their job of expressing a generation.

We must admit that current ragtime is deficient on the melodic side. Some of the tunes are strong, but many of the best ragtime pieces have little beyond their rhythmic energy and ingenuity to distinguish them. If we had a folk-song tradition in America our popular melodies, doubtless, would not be so permeated with vulgarity. The words, also, too often have the chief vice of vulgarity—sluggish conventionality—without its chief virtue, the generous warmth of everydayness. And this latter quality, when it exists, resides not so much in the words themselves, as in the flavor of the songs, the uninspired but tireless high spirits of the American people.

But ragtime words have at least one artist quality of the highest rank. They fit the music like a glove. These songs appeal to the people who expect to sing them, a people who have no oratorio or grand opera tradition behind them, and who come quite naturally to the ideal of wedded music and verse which Wagner had to struggle for against his whole generation. I shouldn't be surprised, in fact, if the origin of the "rag" is to be found in the jerky quality of the English—or shall we say American—language, which found in the negroes its first naïve singers. One of the negro "spirituals" runs thus:

> "An' he gave them commishun to fly,
>   Brudder Lass'rus!
> An' he gave them commishun to fly."

The tune, as always in negro songs, follows the exact accent of the spoken words. But just imagine what Messrs. Moody and Sankey would have done to them!

As you walk up and down the streets of an American city you feel in its jerk and rattle a personality different from that of any European capital. This is American. It is in our lives, and it helps to form our characters and condition our mode of action. It should have expression in art, simply because any people must express itself if it is to know itself. No European music can or possibly could express this American personality. Ragtime I believe does express it. It is to-day the one true American music.

16. Rebellion in Poetry

Poetry was one of the last cultural media to feel the force or rebellion. It was not until 1912 that a few dissatisfied young poets gathered in Chicago and New York's Greenwich Village to court the muse in their own way. In their eyes the past was dead; vitality lay in spontaneity, self-expression, and innovation. The most important organ of the Chicago rebellion was *Poetry;* its moving spirit and editor, Harriet Monroe. As a promoter of the "new" poetry, Miss Monroe proved ideal. Her high standing among the social elite of Chicago eased the tension between the establishment, with its potential for patronage, and the rebellious writers. Indeed Miss Monroe actually secured money from conservative businessmen to support avant-garde verse. Two of her prize discoveries were young Middle Western poets: Vachel Lindsay and Carl Sandburg. Their unprecedented content and disregard of traditional verse form elicited howls of protest from old-line critics but injected new vigor into American poetry.

Two Editorials
HARRIET MONROE

THE MOTIVE OF THE MAGAZINE

In the huge democracy of our age no interest is too slight to have an organ. Every sport, every little industry requires its own corner, its own voice, that it may find its friends, greet them, welcome them.

The arts especially have need of . . . an entrenched place, a voice of

Harriet Monroe, "The Motive of the Magazine," *Poetry*, 1 (Oct., 1912), 26–28; Harriet Monroe, "The New Beauty," *Poetry*, 2 (April, 1913), 22–25.

power, if they are to do their work and be heard. For as the world grows greater day by day, as every member of it, through something he buys or knows or loves, reaches out to the ends of the earth, things precious to the race, things rare and delicate, may be overpowered, lost in the criss-cross of modern currents, the confusion of modern immensities.

Painting, sculpture, music are housed in palaces in the great cities of the world; and every week or two a new periodical is born to speak for one or the other of them, and tenderly nursed at some guardian's expense. Architecture, responding to commercial and social demands, is whipped into shape by the rough and tumble of life and fostered, willy-nilly, by men's material needs. Poetry alone of all the fine arts, has been left to shift for herself in a world unaware of its immediate and desperate need of her, a world whose great deeds, whose triumphs over matter, over the wilderness, over racial enmities and distances, require her ever-living voice to give them glory and glamour.

Poetry has been left to herself and blamed for inefficiency, a process as unreasonable as blaming the desert for barrenness. This art, like every other, is not a miracle of direct creation, but a reciprocal relation between the artist and his public. The people must do their part if the poet is to tell their story to the future; they must cultivate and irrigate the soil if the desert is to blossom as the rose.

The present venture is a modest effort to give to poetry her own place, her own voice. The popular magazines can afford her but scant courtesy —a Cinderella corner in the ashes—because they seek a large public which is not hers, a public which buys them not for their verse but for their stories, pictures, journalism, rarely for their literature, even in prose. Most magazine editors say that there is no public for poetry in America; one of them wrote to a young poet that the verse his monthly accepted "must appeal to the barber's wife of the Middle West," and others prove their distrust by printing less verse from year to year, and that rarely beyond page-end length and importance.

We believe that there is a public for poetry, that it will grow, and that as it becomes more numerous and appreciative the work produced in this art will grow in power, in beauty, in significance. In this belief we have been encouraged by the generous enthusiasm of many subscribers to our fund, by the sympathy of other lovers of the art, and by the quick response of many prominent poets, both American and English, who have sent or promised contributions.

We hope to publish in *Poetry* some of the best work now being done in English verse. Within space limitations set at present by the small size of our monthly sheaf, we shall be able to print poems longer, and of more intimate and serious character, than the popular magazines can afford to use. The test, limited by ever-fallible human judgment, is to be quality alone; all forms, whether narrative, dramatic or lyric, will be acceptable. We hope to offer our subscribers a place of refuge, a green isle in the sea, where Beauty may plant her gardens, and Truth, austere revealer of joy and sorrow, of hidden delights and despairs, may follow her brave quest unafraid.

THE NEW BEAUTY

Of the countless offerings of verse which have reached us during the last half-year the greater number have been pathetically ingenuous in their intellectual attitude. Numerous books and more numerous manuscripts appeal importunately for time and space, whose eager authors seem as unaware of the twentieth century as if they had spent these recent years in an Elizabethan manor-house or a vine-clad Victorian cottage. This is true even of certain ones who assert their modernism by rhyming of slums and strikes, or by moralizing in choppy odes, or in choppier prose mistaken for *vers libre,* upon some social or political problem of the day.

It is not a question of subject, nor yet of form, this new beauty which must inspire every artist worthy of the age he lives in. The poet is not a follower, but a leader; he is a poet not because he can measure words or express patly current ideas, but because the new beauty is a vision in his eyes and a passion in his heart, and because he must strain every sinew of his spirit to reveal it to the world. He can not resign his ancient prophetic office; and the technique of its fulfilment—the style which he achieves with joyous ease or more or less painful labor, according to his temperament—necessarily can not satisfy him until it matches the beauty of the vision.

All this is so obvious as to be usually forgotten. Art in general, and poetry in particular, are regarded as a decoration of life, not as its very pulse and heart-beat, inevitable like a sunrise or a flower. Being a decoration, it becomes a side-issue, something extraneous, a matter of pleasing fancies and pretty patterns, which may be taken conveniently from the past and modified for modern uses. And so each generation imposes its opinion on the next, and the poet, who should be born and brought up to freedom, finds himself shut up in ready-made conventions and prejudices. If he is weakly inspired, his little gleam of the new beauty will be extinguished and forgotten, and he will go along imitating the masters and pottering with inessentials. And even though he is a giant in strength and an apostle in faith, whose vision of the new beauty would lead him through fire and sword, storm and shame, he must yet spend a heavy toll of his precious power in fighting the lords of things as they are, in destroying barriers and winning through to freedom.

If poetry is to have its share of that promised efflorescence which is to be "among the richest" this old world has known; if the signs do not fail, and it is indeed "good to live in this time of rude struggle for the capture of the new beauty," then our poets would seem to be in need of courage. They should pay less attention to old forms which have been worn thin by five centuries of English song. They should return rather to first principles, feel as if poetry were new, and they the first to forge rhythmic chains for the English language.

Poetry has given space, and will doubtless give more, to voices and fashions more or less reminiscent, convinced that it is only by such trial ventures that some men can discover their true place. A talent which seems authentic should be encouraged, even if it begins in a thin soprano or a rather raucous bass. The masterpiece is always a rarity, and it blooms not in a desert but in the midst of lesser growth. We have printed sonnets, but always with the *arriere pensée* that the sonnet is an exhausted form, whose every possible shade of cadence has been worked out and repeated until there are no more surprises left in it. Modern drama is waiting to be written, is part of that new beauty to be captured, but it will hardly be caught in classic or Elizabethan garments. Poetic narrative may have a future as great as its past, but it is rather late in the day for sea-dog epics like Mr. Noyes' *Drake*, and buccaneer ballads of blood and fire. Indeed, it may be questioned whether Mr. Masefield captures the new beauty in his tales of present-day squalor and struggle told in swinging Byronic verse; for his plots strike melodramatic attitudes and his lines have an old familiar stride.

It may be that alien hands will uncover the new treasure, that in this twentieth-century welter of nations the beauty of the English language must be rediscovered by some Russian immigrant or some traveler from Turkestan. Today it is not a poet of Anglo-Saxon race but a Hindoo with divinatory power in English, who has the keenest vision of the new beauty, and the richest modern message, not only for the millions who speak his mother-tongue but also for those far-scattered millions who carry Shakespeare's mother-tongue over the world. If the great achievement of the twentieth century is to be its making friends of East and

West, it may be that the one most important episode of England's rule over India will be the teaching of her language to Rabindranath Tagore.

It may be premature to express an opinion founded largely upon still unpublished translations from the Bengali. But this Hindoo shows us how provincial we are; England and America are little recently annexed corners of the ancient earth, and their poets should peer out over sea-walls and race-walls and pride-walls, and learn their own littleness and the bigness of the world.

General William Booth Enters Into Heaven
VACHEL LINDSAY

(*To be sung to the tune of* THE BLOOD OF THE LAMB *with indicated instruments.*)

Booth led boldly with his big bass drum.
    Are you washed in the blood of the Lamb?
The saints smiled gravely, and they said, "He's come."
    Are you washed in the blood of the Lamb?
Walking lepers followed, rank on rank,
Lurching bravos from the ditches dank,
Drabs from the alleyways and drug-fiends pale—
Minds still passion-ridden, soul-powers frail!
Vermin-eaten saints with mouldy breath,
Unwashed legions with the ways of death—
    Are you washed in the blood of the Lamb?

Every slum had sent its half-a-score
The round world over—Booth had groaned for more.
Every banner that the wide world flies
Bloomed with glory and transcendent dyes.

Nicholas Vachel Lindsay, "General William Booth Enters into Heaven," *Poetry*, 1 (Jan., 1913), 101–103.

Big-voiced lasses made their banjos bang!
Tranced, fanatical, they shrieked and sang,
    Are you washed in the blood of the Lamb?
Hallelujah! It was queer to see
Bull-necked convicts with that land make free!
Loons with bazoos blowing blare, blare, blare—
On, on, upward through the golden air.
    Are you washed in the blood of the Lamb?

Booth died blind, and still by faith he trod,
Eyes still dazzled by the ways of God.
Booth led boldly and he looked the chief:
Eagle countenance in sharp relief,
Beard a-flying, air of high command
Unabated in that holy land.

Jesus came from out the Court-House door,
Stretched his hands above the passing poor.
Booth saw not, but led his queer ones there
Round and round the mighty Court-House square.
Yet in an instant all that blear review
Marched on spotless, clad in raiment new.
The lame were straightened, withered limbs uncurled
And blind eyes opened on a new sweet world.

Drabs and vixens in a flash made whole!
Gone was the weasel-head, the snout, the jowl;
Sages and sibyls now, and athletes clean,
Rulers of empires, and of forests green!

The hosts were sandalled and their wings were fire—
    Are you washed in the blood of the Lamb?
But their noise played havoc with the angel-choir.
    Are you washed in the blood of the Lamb?
Oh, shout Salvation! it was good to see
Kings and princes by the Lamb set free.
The banjos rattled, and the tambourines
Jing-jing-jingled in the hands of queens!

And when Booth halted by the curb for prayer
He saw his Master through the flag-filled air.
Christ came gently with a robe and crown

For Booth the soldier while the throng knelt down.
He saw King Jesus—they were face to face,
And he knelt a-weeping in that holy place.
    Are you washed in the blood of the Lamb?

Chicago
CARL SANDBURG

    Hog Butcher for the World,
    Tool Maker, Stacker of Wheat,
    Player with Railroads and the Nation's Freight Handler;
    Stormy, husky, brawling,
    City of the Big Shoulders:

They tell me you are wicked and I believe them, for I have seen your
    painted women under the gas lamps luring the farm boys.
And they tell me you are crooked and I answer: Yes, it is true I have seen
    the gunman kill and go free to kill again.
And they tell me you are brutal and my reply is: On the faces of women
    and children I have seen the marks of wanton hunger.
And having answered so I turn once more to those who sneer at this my
    city, and I give them back the sneer and say to them:
Come and show me another city with lifted head singing so proud to be
    alive and coarse and strong and cunning.
Flinging magnetic curses amid the toil of piling job on job, here is a tall
    bold slugger set vivid against the little soft cities;
Fierce as a dog with tongue lapping for action, cunning as a savage pitted
    against the wilderness,
    Bareheaded,
    Shoveling,
    Wrecking,
    Planning,
    Building, breaking, rebuilding,
Under the smoke, dust all over his mouth, laughing with white teeth,

Carl Sandburg, "Chicago," *Poetry*, 3 (March, 1914), 191–192.

Under the terrible burden of destiny laughing as a young man laughs,
Laughing even as an ignorant fighter laughs who has never lost a battle,
Bragging and laughing that under his wrist is the pulse, and under his ribs
    the heart of the people,
              Laughing!
Laughing the stormy, husky, brawling laughter of Youth, half-naked,
    sweating, proud to be Hog Butcher, Tool Maker, Stacker of Wheat,
    Player with Railroads and Freight Handler to the Nation.

17. An Art Is Born: Motion Pictures

The achievements of Alfred Stieglitz and other pioneers suggested that photography could be an art. The motion picture opened a whole new dimension. Early films like "The Great Train Robbery" of 1903 and the popular serial, "Perils of Pauline," were comparatively crude. But the motion picture soon rose to higher levels thanks in large part to the work of David Wark Griffith and Charles Chaplin. As a director, Griffith experimented with new filming techniques to achieve realism and convey emotions. His first major production, "Birth of a Nation" (1915) featured "candid" sequences of action details. The film aroused a storm of controversy because of its allegedly prejudiced portrayal of Negroes in the Civil War and Reconstruction eras. Griffith sought to answer his critics with a film concerning the bitter fruits of prejudice through the ages—"Intolerance" (1916). A "spectacular" which began a Hollywood tradition, the film utilized 125,000 players and 7,500 horses! Versatile Charlie Chaplin made his name a household word in the character of a shuffling, outlandishly-dressed ragamuffin. He proved that comedy could be a serious and sensitive art form. By 1920 the film, silence and absence of color notwithstanding, had an immense following in the United States. Tom Mix demonstrated the box office appeal of the cowboy. The success of Elmo Lincoln as the first movie Tarzan in 1918 showed that popular taste ran to still more primitive heroes. Heroines fell into the spectrum between Mary Pickford, the demure maiden, and Theda Bara, the wild prototype of the sex queen.

150

1. THE POTENTIAL OF THE CAMERA: *"The Steerage, 1907" by Alfred Stieglitz.*

2. PRIMITIVE MELODRAMA: The Great Train Robbery (*1903*).

3. Perils of Pauline (*1914*).

4. THE DIRECTOR AS ARTIST: Birth of a Nation
(1915) *directed by David Wark Griffith.*

5. THE HOLLYWOOD TREATMENT: Intolerance (1916) directed by David Wark Griffith.

6. THE LITTLE GUY: *Charlie Chaplin in* The Tramp (*1915*).

7. THE COMIC ART: *Charlie Chaplin throttles a thug in* Easy Street (*1917*).

8. COWBOY AS HERO: *Tom Mix in a publicity still.*

9. PRIMITIVISM: *Elmo Lincoln, the first movie Tarzan, in* Tarzan of the Apes (*1918*).

10. THE SPECTRUM OF HEROINES: *Mary Pickford*

. . . *and Theda Bara.*

18. The Potential of Motion Pictures

For some observers of American culture the advent of motion pictures was a communication and aesthetic breakthrough of messianic significance. In 1915 Vachel Lindsay published a book about the potential of the new art. Emotional and uneven as it was, the volume suggests why the film aroused great excitement. In the process Lindsay touches on some of the nation's foremost cultural hopes and fears.

The Art of the Moving Picture
VACHEL LINDSAY

Local manager, why not an advertising campaign in your town that says: "Beginning Monday and henceforth, ours shall be known as the Conversational Theatre"? At the door let each person be handed the following card:—

"You are encouraged to discuss the picture with the friend who accompanies you to this place. Conversation, of course, must be sufficiently subdued not to disturb the stranger who did not come with you to the theatre. If you are so disposed, consider your answers to these questions: What play or part of a play given in this theatre did you like most to-day? What the least? What is the best picture you have ever seen anywhere? What pictures, seen here this month, shall we bring back?" Here give a list of the recent productions, with squares to mark by the

Vachel Lindsay, *The Art of the Moving Picture* (New York, Macmillan, 1915), 197–206, 217–223, 225–226, 261–263, 277–278, 281–289.

Australian ballot system: approved or disapproved. The cards with their answers could be slipped into the ballot-box at the door as the crowd goes out.

It may be these questions are for the exceptional audiences in residence districts. Perhaps with most crowds the last interrogation is the only one worth while. But by gathering habitually the answers to that alone the place would get the drift of its public, realize its genius, and become an art-gallery, the people bestowing the blue ribbons. The photoplay theatres have coupon contests and balloting already: the most popular young lady, money prizes to the best vote-getter in the audience, etc. Why not ballot on the matter in hand?

If the cards are sent out by the big producers, a referendum could be secured that would be invaluable in arguing down to rigid censorship, and enable them to make their own private censorship more intelligent. Various styles of experimental cards could be tried till the vital one is found.

There is growing up in this country a clan of half-formed moving picture critics. The present stage of their work is indicated by the eloquent notice describing Your Girl and Mine, in the chapter on Progress and Endowment. The metropolitan papers give their photoplay reporters as much space as the theatrical critics. Here in my home town the twelve moving picture places take one half a page of chaotic notices daily. The country is being badly led by professional photoplay newswriters who do not know where they are going, but are on the way.

But they aptly describe the habitual attendants as moving picture fans. The fan at the photoplay, as at the base-ball grounds, is neither a lowbrow nor a high-brow. He is an enthusiast who is as stirred by the charge of the photographic cavalry as by the home runs that he watches from the bleachers. In both places he has the privilege of comment while the game goes on. In the photoplay theatre it is not so vociferous, but as keenly felt. Each person roots by himself. He has his own judgment, and roasts the umpire: who is the keeper of the local theatre: or the producer, as the case may be. If these opinions of the fan can be collected and classified, an informal censorship is at once established. The photoplay reporters can then take the enthusiasts in hand and lead them to a realization of the finer points in awarding praise and blame. Even the sporting pages have their expert opinions with due influence on the betting odds. Out of the work of the photoplay reporters let a superstructure of art criticism be reared in periodicals like the Century, Harper's, Scribner's, The Atlantic, The Craftsman, and the architectural magazines. These are our natural custodians of art. They should reproduce the most exquisite tableaus, and be as fastidious in their selection of them as they are in the current examples of the other arts. Let them spread the news when photoplays keyed to the Rembrandt mood arrive. The reporters for the newspapers should get their ideas and refreshment in such places as the Ryerson Art Library of the Chicago Art Institute. They should begin with such books as Richard Muther's History of Modern Painting, John C. Van Dyke's Art for Art's Sake, Marquand and Frothingham's History of Sculpture, A. D. F. Hamlin's History of Architecture. They should take the business of guidance in this new world as a sacred trust, knowing they have the power to influence an enormous democracy.

The moving picture journals and the literati are in straits over the censorship question. The literati side with the managers, on the principles of free speech and a free press. But few of the aesthetically superwise are persistent fans. They rave for freedom, but are not, as a general thing, living back in the home town. They do not face the exigency of having their summer and winter amusement spoiled day after day.

Extremists among the pious are railing against the moving pictures as once they railed against novels. They have no notion that this institution is penetrating to the last backwoods of our civilization, where its presence is as hard to prevent as the rain. But some of us are destined to a reaction, almost as strong as the obsession. The religionists will think they lead it. They will be self-deceived. Moving picture nausea is already taking hold of numberless people, even when they are in the purely pagan mood. Forced by their limited purses, their inability to buy a Ford car, and the like, they go in their loneliness to film after film till the whole world seems to turn on a reel. When they are again at home, they see in the dark an imaginary screen with tremendous pictures, whirling by at a horribly accelerated pace, a photoplay delirium tremens. Faster and faster the reel turns in the back of their heads. When the moving picture sea-sickness is upon one, nothing satisfies but the quietest out of doors, the companionship of the gentlest of real people. The non-movie-life has charms such as one never before conceived. The worn citizen feels that the cranks and legislators can do what they please to the producers. He is through with them.

The moving picture business men do not realize that they have to face these nervous conditions in their erstwhile friends. They flatter themselves they are being pursued by some reincarnations of Anthony Comstock. There are several reasons why photoplay corporations are callous, along with the sufficient one that they are corporations.

First, they are engaged in a financial orgy. Fortunes are being found by actors and managers faster than they were dug up in 1849 and 1850 in California. Forty-niner lawlessness of soul prevails. They talk each other into a lordly state of mind. All is dash and experiment. Look at the advertisements in the leading moving picture magazines. They are like the praise of oil stock or Peruna. They bawl about films founded upon little classics. They howl about plots that are ostensibly from the soberest of novels, whose authors they blasphemously invoke. They boo and blow about twisted, callous scenarios that are bad imitations of the world's most beloved lyrics.

The producers do not realize the mass effect of the output of the business. It appears to many as a sea of unharnessed photography: sloppy conceptions set forth with sharp edges and irrelevant realism. The jumping, twitching, cold-blooded devices, day after day, create the aforesaid sea-sickness, that has nothing to do with the questionable subject. When on top of this we come to the picture that is actually insulting, we are up in arms indeed. It is supplied by a corporation magnate removed from his audience in location, fortune, interest, and mood: an absentee landlord. I was trying to convert a talented and noble friend to the films. The first time we went there was a prize-fight between a black and a white man, not advertised, used for a filler. I said it was queer, and would not happen again. The next time my noble friend was persuaded to go, there was a cock-fight, incidental to a Cuban romance. The third visit we beheld a lady who was dying for five minutes, rolling her eyes about in a way that was fearful to see. The convert was not made.

It is too easy to produce an unprovoked murder, an inexplicable arson, neither led up to nor followed by the ordinary human history of such acts, and therefore as arbitrary as the deeds of idiots or the insane. A villainous hate, an alleged love, a violent death, are flashed at us, without being in any sort of tableau logic. The public is ceaselessly played upon by tactless devices. Therefore it howls, just as children in the nursery do when the awkward governess tries the very thing the diplomatic governess, in reasonable time, may bring about.

The producer has the man in the audience who cares for the art peculiarly at his mercy. Compare him with the person who wants to read a magazine for an evening. He can look over all the periodicals in the local book store in fifteen minutes. He can select the one he wants, take this bit of printed matter home, go through the contents, find the three articles he prefers, get an evening of reading out of them, and be happy. Every day as many photoplays come to our town as magazines come to the book-store in a week or a month. There are good ones and bad ones buried in the list. There is no way to sample the films. One has to wait through the first third of a reel before he has an idea of the merits of a production, his ten cents is spent, and much of his time is gone. It would take five hours at least to find the best film in our town for one day. Meanwhile, nibbling and sampling, the seeker would run such a gauntlet of plot and dash and chase that his eyes and patience would be exhausted. Recently there returned to the city for a day one of Griffith's best Bio-graphs, The Last Drop of Water. It was good to see again. In order to watch this one reel twice I had to wait through five others of unutterable miscellany.

Since the producers and theatre-managers have us at their mercy, they are under every obligation to consider our delicate susceptibilities—granting the proposition that in an ideal world we will have no legal censorship. As to what to do in this actual nation, let the reader follow what John Collier has recently written in the Survey. Collier was the leading force in founding the National Board of Censorship. As a member of that volunteer extra-legal board which is independent and high minded, yet accepted by the leading picture companies, he is able to discuss legislation in a manner which the present writer cannot hope to match. Read John Collier. But I wish to suggest that the ideal censorship is that to which the daily press is subject, the elastic hand of public opinion, if the photoplay can be brought as near to newspaper conditions in this matter as it is in some others.

How does public opinion grip the journalist? The editor has a constant report from his constituency. A popular scoop sells an extra at once. An attack on the wrong idol cancels fifty subscriptions. People come to the office to do it, and say why. If there is a piece of real news on the second page, and fifty letters come in about it that night, next month when that character of news reappears it gets the front page. Some human pecu-liarities are not mentioned, some phrases not used. The total attribute of the blue-pencil man is diplomacy. But while the motion pictures come out every day, they get their discipline months afterwards in the legis-lation that insists on everything but tact. A tentative substitute for the letters that come to the editor, the personal call and cancelled sub-scription, and the rest, is the system of balloting on the picture, especially the answer to the question, "What picture seen here this month, or this week, shall we bring back?" Experience will teach how to put the queries. By the same system the public might dictate its own cut-outs. Let us have a democracy and a photoplay business working in daily rhythm. . . .

* * *

The moving picture captains of industry, like the California gold finders of 1849, making colossal fortunes in two or three years, have the same glorious irresponsibility and occasional need of the sheriff. They are Californians more literally than this. Around Los Angeles the greatest and most characteristic moving picture colonies are being built. Each photoplay magazine has its California letter, telling of the putting-up of new studios, and the transfer of actors, with much slap-you-on-the-back personal gossip. This is the outgrowth of the fact that every type of the photoplay but the intimate is founded on some phase of the out-of-doors. Being thus dependent, the plant can best be set up where there is no winter. Besides this, the Los Angeles region has the sea, the mountains, the desert, and many kinds of grove and field. Landscape and architecture are sub-tropical. But for a description of California, ask any traveller or study the background of most any photoplay.

If the photoplay is the consistent utterance of its scenes, if the actors are incarnations of the land they walk upon, as they should be, California indeed stands a chance to achieve through the films an utterance of her own. Will this land furthest west be the first to capture the inner spirit of this newest and most curious of the arts? It certainly has the opportunity that comes with the actors, producers, and equipment. . . . Already the California sort, in the commercial channels, has become the broadly accepted if mediocre national form. People who revere the Pilgrim Fathers of 1620 have often wished those gentlemen had moored their bark in the region of Los Angeles rather than Plymouth Rock, that Boston had been founded there. . . .

Patriotic art students have discussed with mingled irony and admiration the Boston domination of the only American culture of the nineteenth century, namely, literature. Indianapolis has had her day since then, Chicago is lifting her head. Nevertheless Boston still controls the textbook in English and dominates our high schools. Ironic feelings in this matter on the part of western men are based somewhat on envy and illegitimate cussedness, but are also grounded in the honest hope of a healthful rivalry. They want new romanticists and artists as indigenous to their soil as was Hawthorne to witch-haunted Salem or Longfellow to the chestnuts of his native heath. Whatever may be said of the patriarchs, from Oliver Wendell Holmes to Amos Bronson Alcott, they were true sons of the New England stone fences and meeting houses. They could not have been born or nurtured anywhere else on the face of the earth.

Some of us view with a peculiar thrill the prospect that Los Angeles may become the Boston of the photoplay. Perhaps it would be better to say the Florence, because California reminds one of colorful Italy more than of any part of the United States. Yet there is a difference.

The present-day man-in-the-street, man-about-town Californian has an obvious magnificence about him that is allied to the eucalyptus tree, the pomegranate. California is a gilded state. It has not the sordidness of gold, as has Wall Street, but it is the embodiment of the natural ore that the ragged prospector finds. The gold of California is the color of the orange, the glitter of dawn in the Yosemite, the hue of the golden gate that opens the sunset way to mystic and terrible Cathay and Hindustan.

The enemy of California says the state is magnificent but thin. He declares it is as though it were painted on a Brobdingnagian piece of gilt paper, and he who dampens his finger and thrusts it through finds an alkali valley on the other side, the lonely prickly pear, and a heap of ashes from a deserted campfire. He says the citizens of this state lack the richness of an aesthetic and religious tradition. He says there is no substitute for time. But even these things make for coincidence. This apparent thinness California has in common with the routine photoplay, which is at times as shallow in its thought as the shadow it throws upon the screen. This newness California has in common with all photoplays. It is thrillingly possible for the state and the art to acquire spiritual tradition and depth together.

Part of the thinness of California is not only its youth, but the result of the physical fact that the human race is there spread over so many acres of land. They try not only to count their mines and enumerate their palm trees, but they count the miles of their seacoast, and the acres under cultivation and the height of the peaks, and revel in large statistics and the bigness generally, and forget how a few men rattle around in a great deal of scenery. They shout their statistics across the Rockies and the deserts to New York. The Mississippi Valley is non-existent to the Californian. His fellow-feeling is for the opposite coast-line. Through the geographical accident of separation by mountain and desert from the rest of the country, he becomes a mere shouter, hurrahing so assiduously that all variety in the voice is lost. Then he tries gestures, and becomes flamboyant, rococo.

These are the defects of the motion picture qualities also. Its panoramic tendency runs wild. As an institution it advertises itself with the sweeping gesture. It has the same passion for coast-line. These are not the sins of New England. When, in the hands of masters, they become sources of strength, they will be a different set of virtues from those of New England.

There is no more natural place for the scattering of confetti than this state, except the moving picture scene itself. Both have a genius for gardens and dancing and carnival.

When the Californian relegates the dramatic to secondary scenes, both in his life and his photoplay, and turns to the genuinely epic and lyric, he and this instrument may find their immortality together as New England found its soul in the essays of Emerson. Tide upon tide of Spring comes into California through all four seasons. Fairy beauty overwhelms the lumbering grand-stand players. The tiniest garden is a jewelled pathway of wonder. But the Californian cannot shout "orange blossoms, orange blossoms; heliotrope, heliotrope!" He cannot boom forth "roseleaves, roseleaves" so that he does their beauties justice. Here is where the photoplay can begin to give him a more delicate utterance. And he can go on into stranger things and evolve all the Splendor Films into higher types, for the very name of California is splendor. The California photoplaywright can base his Crowd Picture upon the city-worshipping mobs of San Francisco. He can derive his Patriotic and Religious Splendors from something older and more magnificent than the aisles of the Romanesque, namely: the groves of the giant redwoods.

The campaign for a beautiful nation could very well emanate from the west coast, where with the slightest care grow up models for all the world of plant arrangement and tree-luxury. Our mechanical East is reproved, our tension is relaxed, our ugliness is challenged every time we look upon those garden paths and forests.

It is possible for Los Angeles to lay hold of the motion picture as our national text-book in Art as Boston appropriated to herself the guardianship of the national text-books of Literature. If California has a shining soul, and not merely a golden body, let her forget her seventeen-year-old melodramatics, and turn to her poets who understand the heart underneath the glory. . . .

❋　❋　❋

The moving picture goes almost as far as journalism into the social fabric in some ways, further in others. Soon, no doubt, many a little town will have its photographic newspress. We have already the weekly world-news films from the big centres.

With local journalism will come devices for advertising home enterprises. Some staple products will be made attractive by having film-actors show their uses. The motion pictures will be in the public schools to stay. Text-books in geography, history, zoölogy, botany, physiology, and other sciences will be illustrated by standardized films. Along with these changes, there will be available at certain centres collections of films equivalent to the Standard Dictionary and the Encyclopaedia Britannica.

And sooner or later we will have a straight out capture of a complete film expression by the serious forces of civilization. The merely impudent motion picture will be relegated to the leisure hours with yellow journalism. Photoplay libraries are inevitable, as active if not as multitudinous as the book-circulating libraries. The oncoming machinery and expense of the motion picture is immense. Where will the money come from? No one knows. What the people want they will get. The race of man cannot afford automobiles, but has them nevertheless. We cannot run away into non-automobile existence or non steam-engine or non-movie life long at a time. We must conquer this thing. While the more stately scientific and educational aspects just enumerated are slowly on their way, the artists must be up and about their ameliorative work.

Every considerable effort to develop a noble idiom will count in the final result, as the writers of early English made possible the language of the Bible, Shakespeare, and Milton. We are perfecting a medium to be used as long as Chinese ideographs have been. It will no doubt, like the Chinese language, record in the end massive and classical treatises, imperial chronicles, law-codes, traditions, and religious admonitions. . . .

❁   ❁   ❁

The whirlwind of cowboys and Indians with which the photoplay began, came about because this instrument, in asserting its genius, was feeling its way toward the most primitive forms of life it could find.

Now there is a tendency for even wilder things. We behold the half-draped figures living in tropical islands or our hairy forefathers acting out narratives of the stone age. The moving picture conventionality permits an abbreviation of drapery. If the primitive setting is convincing, the figure in the grassrobe or buffalo hide at once has its rights over the healthful imagination.

There is in this nation of moving-picture-goers a hunger for tales of fundamental life that are not yet told. The cave-man longs with an incurable homesickness for his ancient day. . . .

We face the exigency the world over of vast instruments like national armies being played against each other as idly and aimlessly as the checker-men on the cracker-barrels of corner groceries. And this invention, the kinetoscope, which affects or will affect as many people as the guns of Europe, is not yet understood in its powers, particularly those of bringing back the primitive in a big rich way. The primitive is always a new and higher beginning to the man who understand it. Not yet has the producer learned that the feeling of the crowd is patriarchal, splendid. He imagines the people want nothing but a silly lark.

All this apparatus and opportunity, and no immortal soul! Yet by faith and a study of the signs we proclaim that this lantern of wizard-drama is going to give us in time the visible things in the fulness of their primeval force, and some that have been for a long time invisible. . . . In this adolescence of Democracy the history of man is to be retraced, the same round on a higher spiral of life.

Our democratic dream has been a middle-class aspiration built on a bog of toil-soddened minds. The piles beneath the castle of our near-democratic arts were rotting for lack of folk-imagination. The Man with the Hoe had no spark in his brain. But now a light is blazing. We can build the American soul broad-based from the foundations. We can begin with dreams the veriest stone-club warrior can understand, and as far as an appeal to the eye can do it, lead him in fancy through every phase of life to the apocalyptic splendors. . . .

❊   ❊   ❊

Without airing my private theology I earnestly request the most sceptical reader of this book to assume that miracles in a Biblical sense have occurred. . . . Let him also assume [there] . . . will again occur, two thousand years in the future, events as wonderful as those others, twenty centuries back. Let us anticipate that many of these will be upon American soil. Particularly as sons and daughters of a new country it is a spiritual necessity for us to look forward to traditions, because we have so few from the past. . . .

Citizens of America, wise or foolish, when they look into the coming days, have the submarine mood of [Jules] Verne, the press-the-button complacency of [Edward] Bellamy, the wireless telegraph enthusiasm of [H. G.] Wells. If they express hopes that can be put into pictures with definite edges, they order machinery piled to the skies. They see the redeemed United States running deftly in its jewelled sockets, ticking like a watch.

This, their own chosen outlook, wearies the imaginations of our people, they do not know why. It gives no full-orbed apocalyptic joy. Only to the young mechanical engineer does such a hope express real Utopia. He can always keep ahead of the devices that herald its approach. No matter what day we attain and how busy we are adjusting ourselves, he can be moving on, inventing more to-morrows; ruling the age, not being ruled by it.

Because this Utopia is in the air, a goodly portion of the precocious boys turn to mechanical engineering. Youths with this bent are the most healthful and inspiring young citizens we have. They and their like will fulfil a multitude of the hopes of men like Verne, Bellamy, and Wells.

But if every mechanical inventor on earth voiced his dearest wish and lived to see it worked out, the real drama of prophecy and fulfilment, as written in the imagination of the human race, would remain uncompleted. . . .

It is my hope that the moving picture prophet-wizards will set before the world a new group of pictures of the future. . . . America will become a permanent World's Fair, she can be made so within the lives of men now living, if courageous architects have the campaign in hand. There are other hopes that look a long way further. They peer as far into the coming day as the Chinese historian looks into the past. And then they are but halfway to the millennium.

Any standard illustrator could give us Verne or Bellamy or Wells if he did his best. *But we want pictures beyond the skill of any delineator in the old mediums, yet within the power of the wizard photoplay producer.* Oh you who are coming to-morrow, show us everyday America as it will be when we are only halfway to the millennium yet thousands of years in the future! Tell what type of honors men will covet, what property they will still be apt to steal, what murders they will commit, what the law court and the jail will be or what will be the substitutes, how the newspaper will appear, the office, the busy street.

Picture to America the lovers in her half-millennium, when usage shall have become iron-handed once again, when noble sweethearts must break beautiful customs for the sake of their dreams. Show us the gauntlet of strange courtliness they must pass through before they reach one another, obstacles brought about by the immemorial distinctions of scholarship gowns or service badges.

Make a picture of a world where machinery is so highly developed it utterly disappeared long ago. Show us the antique United States, with ivy vines upon the popular socialist churches, and weather-beaten images of socialist saints in the niches of the doors. Show us the battered fountains, the brooding universities, the dusty libraries. Show us houses of administration with statues of heroes in front of them and gentle banners flowing from their pinnacles. Then paint pictures of the oldest trees of the time, and tree-revering ceremonies, with unique costumes and a special priesthood.

Show us the marriage procession, the christening, the consecration of the boy and girl to the state. Show us the political processions and election riots. Show us the people with their graceful games, their religious pantomimes. Show us impartially the memorial scenes to celebrate the great men and women, and the funerals of the poor. And then moving on toward the millennium itself, show America after her victories have been won, and she has grown old, as old as the Sphinx. Then give us the Dragon and Armageddon and the Lake of Fire.

Author-producer-photographer, who would prophesy, read the last book in the Bible, not to copy it in form and color, but that its power and grace and terror may enter into you. Delineate in your own way . . . the picture of our land redeemed. After fasting and prayer, let the Spirit conduct you till you see in definite line and form the throngs of the brotherhood of man, the colonnades where the arts are expounded, the gardens where the children dance.

That which man desires, that will man become. He largely fulfils his own prediction and vision. Let him therefore have a care how he prophesies and prays. We shall have a tin heaven and a tin earth, if the scientists are allowed exclusive command of our highest hours. . . .

I am moved to think Christ fulfilled that prophecy because he had read it from childhood. It is my entirely personal speculation, not brought forth dogmatically, that Scripture is not so much inspired as it is curiously and miraculously inspiring.

If the New Isaiahs of this time will write their forecastings in photoplay hieroglyphics, the children in times to come, having seen those films from infancy, or their later paraphrases in more perfect form, can rise and say, "This day is this Scripture fulfilled in your ears." But without prophecy there is no fulfilment, without Isaiah there is no Christ.

America is often shallow in her dreams because she has no past in the European and Asiatic sense. Our soil has no Roman coin or buried altar or Buddhist tope. For this reason multitudes of American artists have moved to Europe, and only the most universal of wars has driven them home. Year after year Europe drained us of our beauty-lovers, our highest painters and sculptors and the like. They have come pouring home, confused expatriates, trying to adjust themselves. It is time for the American craftsman and artist to grasp the fact that we must be men enough to construct a to-morrow that grows rich in forecastings in the same way that the past of Europe grows rich in sweet or terrible legends as men go back into it.

Scenario writers, producers, photoplay actors, endowers of exquisite films, sects using special motion pictures for a predetermined end, all you who are taking the work as a sacred trust, I bid you God-speed. Let us resolve that whatever America's to-morrow may be, she shall have a day that is beautiful and not crass, spiritual, not material. Let us resolve that she shall dream dreams deeper than the sea and higher than the clouds of heaven, that she shall come forth crowned and transfigured with her statesmen and wizards and saints and sages about her, with magic behind her and miracle before her.

Pray that you be delivered from the temptation to cynicism and the timidities of orthodoxy. Pray that the workers in this your glorious new art be delivered from the mere lust of the flesh and pride of life. Let your spirits outflame your burning bodies.

Consider what it will do to your souls, if you are true to your trust. Every year, despite earthly sorrow and the punishment of your mortal sins, despite all weakness and all of Time's revenges upon you, despite Nature's reproofs and the whips of the angels, new visions will come, new prophecies will come. You will be seasoned spirits in the eyes of the wise. The record of your ripeness will be found in your craftsmanship. You will be God's thoroughbreds.

It has come then, this new weapon of men, and the face of the whole earth changes. In after centuries its beginning will be indeed remembered.

It has come, this new weapon of men, and by faith and a study of the signs we proclaim that it will go on and on in immemorial wonder.

19. The Response to "Modern" Art

The Armory Show of 1913 afforded an opportunity for the exponents of and detractors from "modern" art to air their opinions. In the following selections Kenyon Cox, an artist, and Royal Cortissoz, a professional art critic, obviously represent the adverse position. In fact Cortissoz was a bulwark of artistic conservatism and used his editorial post on the *New York Tribune* to defend time-honored "fundamental laws" of art. At one point he went so far as to equate the influence of "modernism" on American art with that of immigration on American society and government. In his opinion both imperiled the health of the nation by introducing insidious, alien elements. W. D. MacColl, on the other hand, defends the insurgent artists and dismisses Cortissoz as hopelessly reactionary. Finally Theodore Roosevelt, in the unaccustomed role of art critic, expresses the nonprofessional's opinion of the Armory Show.

The "Modern" Spirit in Art
KENYON COX

It is proper to begin an account of the extraordinary exhibition of modern art recently held in New York with an acknowledgment that it is well such an exhibition should be held and that, therefore, the thanks of the public are due to the gentlemen who got it together. We have heard a great deal about the Post-Impressionists and the Cubists; we have read expositions of their ideas and methods which have had a plausible sound in the absence of the works to be explained; we have had some denunci-

Kenyon Cox, "The 'Modern' Spirit in Art," *Harper's Weekly,* 57 (March 15, 1913), 10.

ation and ridicule, some enthusiastic praise, and a great deal of half-frightened and wholly puzzled effort to understand what it was taken for granted, must have some real significance; but we have not heretofore had an opportunity of seeing the things themselves—the paintings and sculpture actually produced by these men. Now the things are quite indescribable and unbelievable. Neither the praises of their admirers, the ridicule of their opponents, nor the soberest attempt at impartial description can give any idea of them. No reproduction can approach them. They must be seen to be believed possible, and therefore it is well that they should have been seen. From this point of view my only regret is that the Association of American Painters and Sculptors did not see fit to include some representation of the Futurists in their exhibition, that the whole thing might be done once for all. In a case of necessity one may be willing to take a drastic emetic and may even humbly thank the medical man for the efficacy of the dose. The more thorough it is the less chance is there that it may have to be repeated.

Of course I cannot pretend to have approached the exhibition entirely without prejudice. One cannot have studied and practised an art for forty years without the formation of some opinions—even of some convictions. But I remembered the condemnation of Corot and Millet by Gérôme and Cabanel; I remembered the natural conservatism of middle age; I took to heart the admonition of the preface to the catalogue, that "to be afraid of what is different or unfamiliar is to be afraid of life." I meant to make a genuine effort to sort out these people, to distinguish their different aims and doctrines, to take notes and to analyze, to treat them seriously if disapprovingly. I cannot do it. Nor can I laugh. This thing is not amusing; it is heartrending and sickening. I was quoted the other day as having said that the human race is rapidly approaching insanity. I never said it, but if I were convinced that this is really "modern art" and that these men are representative of our time, I should be constrained to believe it.

In recollecting the appalling morning I spent in this place certain personalities do, however, define themselves and certain tendencies make themselves clear. It is no time for squeamishness or for standing upon "professional courtesy," and such persons as I may mention I shall treat quite frankly—in that respect, at least, I may follow their own example. Fortunately there is little necessity of dwelling upon the American part of the show. It contains some good work by artists who must wonder at the galley aboard which they find themselves, some work with real merit by men who have aided in the launching of the galley, and a great deal of bad work which, however, seldom reaches the depths of badness attainable by Frenchmen and Germans. But this work, good, bad, and indifferent, is either perfectly well known or is so paled by comparison that it needs no mention. Some of it is silly, but little of it is dangerous. There is one American, however, who must be spoken of because he has pushed the new doctrines to a conclusion in some respects more logical and complete than have any of the foreigners. In the wildest productions of Picabia or Picasso there is usually discernible, upon sufficiently painstaking investigation, some faint trace of the natural objects which are supposed to have inspired them; and even when this disappears the title remains to show that such objects have existed. It has remained for Mr. Marsden Hartley to take the final step and to arrange his lines and spots purely for their own sake, abandoning all pretense of representation or even of suggestion. He exhibits certain rectangles of paper covered with a maze of charcoal lines which are catalogued simply as Drawing No. 1, Drawing No. 2, etc.

This, I say, is the logical end, for the real meaning of this Cubist movement is nothing else than the total destruction of the art of painting—that art of which the dictionary definition is "the art of representing, by means of figures and colors applied on a surface, objects presented to the eye or to the imagination." Two years ago I wrote: "We have reached the edge of the cliff and must turn back or fall into the abyss." Deliberately and determinedly these men have stepped over the edge. Now the total destruction of painting as a representative art is a thing which a lover of painting could hardly envisage with entire equanimity, yet one may admit that such a thing might take place and yet an art remain that should have its own value. A Turkish rug or a tile from the Alhambra is nearly without representative purpose, but it has intrinsic beauty and some conceivable human use. The important question is what it is proposed to substitute for this art of painting which the world has cherished since there were men definitely differentiated from beasts. They have abolished the representation of nature and all forms of recognized and traditional decoration; what will they give us instead? And here is the difference between Mr. Hartley and his Parisian brothers. His "drawings" are purely nugatory. If one finds it impossible to imagine the kind of human being that could take any pleasure in them one is free to admit that there is nothing especially disgusting about them. But one cannot say as much for the works of the Frenchmen. In some strange way they have made their work revolting and defiling. To have looked at it is to have passed through a pathological museum where the layman has no right to go. One feels that one has seen not an exhibition, but an exposure.

Of course the work of these artistic anarchists formed only a part of the exhibition. A serious attempt was made to get together a representative showing of the artists whom they consider their forerunners, and a number of the smaller galleries contained what might be considered a series of illustrations of Meier-Graefe. A good many critics who find the latest manifestations of the "modern" spirit quite intolerable are yet able to maintain a complacent satisfaction in these earlier exemplifications of it and even, by contrast, to increase their pleasure in work which seems relatively sane and wholesome. I wish I could feel, as they do, that there is a sudden dislocation with the appearance of Matisse and that everything before him falls naturally into its place as a continuation of the great tradition. I wish I were not forced to see that the easy slope to Avernus began as far back as the sixties of the last century. The lack of discipline and the exaltation of the individual have been the destructive forces of modern art, and they began their work long ago. For a time the persistence of earlier ideals and the possession by the revolutionaries of the very training which they attacked as unnecessary saved the art from entire dissolution. Now all discipline has disappeared, all training is proclaimed useless, and individualism has reached the pitch of sheer insanity or triumphant charlatanism. . . .

Believing, as I do, that there are still commandments in art as in morals, and still laws in art as in physics, I have no fear that this kind of art will prevail, or even that it can long endure. But it may do a good deal of harm while it lasts. It may dazzle the young students of art with the prospect of an easily attained notoriety which they cannot distinguish from fame, and prevent their acquiring any serious training during the years when, if ever, such training must be acquired; it may so debauch criticism that it shall lose what little authority or usefulness it still retains; it may corrupt public taste and stimulate an appetite for excitement that is as dangerous as the appetite for any other poisonous drug; finally, it may juggle out of the pockets of the gullible a few dollars that will be far more wasted than if they were thrown into the sea. To the critics it is useless to speak. How shall we instruct our self-appointed instructors? The students and the public may possibly listen, and for them I have a few words of earnest advice.

To the student I would say: Distrust all short cuts to art or to glory. No work worth doing was ever done without long preparation and continuous endeavor. The success that is attained in a month will be forgotten in a year. To the public I would say: Do not allow yourselves to be blinded by the sophistries of the foolish dupes or the self-interested exploiters of all this charlatanry. Remember that it is for you that art is created, and judge honestly for yourselves whether this which calls itself art is useful to you or to the world. You are not infallible, but your instincts are right in the main, and you are, after all, the final judges. If your stomach revolts against this rubbish it is because it is not fit for human food. Let no man persuade you to stuff yourselves with it.

The Post-Impressionist Illusion
ROYAL CORTISSOZ

It is said that when the former President of the French Republic, M. Fallières, went to the opening of the autumn Salon of 1912, he looked long at the paintings of the Cubists and Futurists. "Charming!" he murmured to the Under-Secretary for Fine Arts, who stood at his elbow, and then he added anxiously, "But you won't have to buy any for the state galleries, will you?" I know perfectly well how that anecdote must have been received whenever it was repeated in Post-Impressionist circles. "Oh, Fallières! But he was always a bourgeois, anyway." It so happened, however, that the solicitude of the French functionary has been shared by all kinds of people, including some quite competent artists; and I note this fact at the outset because the confusion in which the whole subject of Post-Impressionism has been enveloped has been rendered worse confounded by much foolish recrimination.

The Post-Impressionists themselves have not made most of the noise. This has been developed largely in print, and hierophants of the "movement," which as I shall presently endeavor to show, is not, strictly speaking, a movement at all, have made tremendous play with one of the favorite devices of those who traffic in the freakish things of art and letters. "Behold this masterpiece!" they say. "What! you see nothing in it? You find it ugly? Well, well, what a besotted idea of beauty you must have! Repose yourself before this canvas. It is saturated in beauty. You do not see it because you have the Philistine eye; but with patience and reverent study you may hope to unlock the secret of our great man." And so on,

Royal Cortissoz, "The Post-Impressionist Illusion," *Century*, 85 (April, 1913), 805–810, 812, 814, 815.

with many a delicate suggestion of compasionate good will. It is an old trick. The playgoer who does not like dirty plays is denounced as a prude; the music-lover who resents cacophony is told he is a pedant; and in all these matters the final crushing blow administered to the man of discrimination is the ascription to him of a hidebound prejudice against things that are new because they are new. If he declines to be convinced of this, he is reminded triumphantly that all revolutionaries in the domain of thought, from Galileo and Columbus to Wagner and Manet, have been for a time persecuted and derided. *Ergo,* since the Post-Impressionists have provoked a vast amount of scornful mirth, they are necessarily great men.

It is not my purpose to laugh at them, nor do I wish to swell the flood of recrimination of which I have spoken. In the foregoing remarks I have sought merely to clear the ground of the cant which often encumbers it. Let us look at Post-Impressionism for what it is, regardless alike of its acolytes and its equally furious opponents. I said just now that it was not a movement at all. A movement, I take it, represents in art, at all events, what men do when they are pretty closely allied by strong sympathies and by fidelity to a body of principles susceptible of some sort of definition. Such a group need not be wedded to a formula, but it cannot well avoid subscribing to a fairly definable scheme of ideas. . . . I must take the risk and state what, after careful study, I have gathered to be the Post-Impressionist aim. It is to eschew such approximately accurate representation of things seen as has been hitherto pursued by painters of all schools, and to cover the canvas with an arrangement of line and color symbolizing the very essence of the object or scene attacked. For some occult reason it is assumed that a portrait or picture painted according to the familiar grammar of art, understood of all men, is clogged with irrelevant matter. The great masters of the past, to be sure, are not invalidated, and they need not be sent to the lumber-room; but their day is done, and with the Post-Impressionists we must slough off a quantity of played-out conventions before we can enter the promised land.

The temptation to go deeper into the metaphysics of the subject is not, I admit, very strong, for I do not like to chew sawdust, nor do I enjoy going down into a cellar at midnight without a candle to look for a black cat that isn't there. . . . The cat, I maintain, is not there. That is the nubbin of the whole argument. Post-Impressionism as a movement, as a ponderable theory, is, like the cat, an illusion. The portentous things we hear about it are not the adumbrations of an intelligible and precious truth, but are mere ex-parte assertions. . . .

These are the days of impossible beliefs, but not of lost causes, and the first belief engendered in the Post-Impressionist is an immeasurable belief in himself. What chiefly impresses me about him as a type is his conviction that what he chooses to do in art is right because he chooses to do it. This egotism is doubtless compatible with some engaging qualities. I have read the volume of letters written by Van Gogh to his friend Bernard, and I have read the latter's introductory pages. It is plain that these two were full of a candid enthusiasm for painting, keenly interested in the masters, ancient and modern, and ardently desirous of solving technical problems. But of each it may also be said that he had "too much ego in his cosmos," and in the case of Van Gogh, the result was disastrous. . . . Passionately in love with color, and groping toward an effective use of it in the expression of truth, he gives you occasionally in his thick impasto a gleam of sensuously beautiful tone. But as he grew more and more absorbed in himself, which is to say more and more indifferent to the artistic lessons of the centuries, his pictures receded further and further from the representation of nature, and fulfilled instead an arbitrary, capricious conception of art. The laws of perspective are strained. Landscape and other natural forms are set awry. So simple an object as a jug containing some flowers is drawn with the uncouthness of the immature, even childish, executant. From the point of view of the Post-Impressionist prophet, all this may be referred to inventive genius beating out a new artistic language. I submit that it is explained rather by incompetence suffused with egotism. The man was unbalanced. Once, when he was staying at Arles, a girl of his acquaintance received from him a packet which she opened, expecting it to reveal a welcome present. She found that it contained one of the painter's ears, which he had that morning cut off with his razor. The incident is too horrible, intrinsically and in its suggestion of the most tragic of human ills, to be lightly employed for purposes of argument. Nevertheless, it is legitimate to affirm that the hero of this anecdote, who spent some time in an asylum and ultimately committed suicide, was unlikely to think straight. That has been the trouble with all the Post-Impressionists. They have not thought straight.

The thinking they have done, and they have done much, has been invertebrate and confusing. Steadily, too, it has led them to produce work not only incompetent, but grotesque. It has led them from complacency to what I can only describe as insolence. If these seem hard words, let me recall an incident of the Post-Impressionist exhibition in London two years ago. Mr. Roger Fry, writing in defense of the project, cited various persons who were in sympathy with it, and named among them Mr. John

S. Sargent. In the course of a letter to the London "Nation" that distinguished painter said: "Mr. Fry may have been told—and have believed —that the sight of those paintings had made me a convert to his faith in them. The fact is that *I am absolutely skeptical as to their having any claim whatever to being works of art,* with the exception of some of the pictures by Gauguin that strike me as admirable in color, and in color only." The italics are mine, and I hope I may be pardoned for using them, for it is important, I think, that the testimony in this case of a master like Sargent should not be overlooked. . . . If Matisse were the demigod he is assumed to be, there would be at least some hints of an Olympian quality breathed through his *gauche* puerilities. Picasso, too, the great panjandrum of the Cubist tabernacle, is credited with profound gifts. Why does he not use them? And why must we sit patient, if not with awe-struck and grateful submissiveness, before a portrait or a picture seemingly representing a grotesque object made of children's blocks cut up and fitted together? This is not a movement, a principle. It is unadulterated "cheek." . . .

I make no excuse for ignoring a multitude of names in this brief survey. Why dwell upon names that mean nothing?

It is the dull sterility of this so-called "movement" that offers the chief point of attack for those who resent its intrusion into the field of art. Let the Post-Impressionists and their loquacious friends wax eloquent among themselves as to what constitutes beauty and what they may mean by the theories through which they assume to develop its secret. Their debatings are worthless so long as they go on producing flatly impossible pictures and statues. The oracular assertion that the statues and the pictures are beautiful and great is merely so much impudence and "bounce."

It is, after all, a little cool for ill-equipped experimenters to take themselves so seriously. The dabster in music or the drama or literature is usually expected to acquire some proficiency in his medium before he undertakes to speak out. By some mysterious dispensation, which no one yet has accounted for, the artist, and especially the painter, is early let loose upon the world, whether he has acquired a decent training or not.

Here, from the incomplete, halting methods of Cézanne, there has flowed out of Paris into Germany, Russia, England, and to some slight extent the United States, a gospel of stupid license and self-assertion which would have been swept into the rubbish-heap were it not for the timidity of our mental habit. When the stuff is rebuked as it should be, the Post-Impressionist impresarios and fuglemen insolently proffer us a farrago of super-subtle rhetoric. The farce will end when people look at

Post-Impressionist pictures as Mr. Sargent looked at those shown in London, "absolutely skeptical as to their having any claim whatever to being works of art."

The International Exhibition of Modern Art
W. D. MacCOLL

I do not propose to answer Mr. Cortissoz's critique in detail, but to contrast with it quite frankly my own impression of what I would call the Post-Impressionist *reality* as it was brought before us in the International Exhibition of Modern Art.

My own impression, and that of an increasing number of persons, is that among modern painters a certain number, including certain of the so-called Post-Impressionists, achieve the first place by the force of a pure native power that is in them. But that is not all. It is not simply their power, but a certain charm also which is in their work that attracts us. The quality of greatness in them, we feel, is not strained. They lead us with ease into great subjects; and they enter as unaffectedly into our consciousness of what is beautiful as any of those revelations which come to us only through our instincts. We feel, in fact, that we have nothing to compare with them at the moment of their making their effect upon us. Or, to adopt another way of speaking, the appeal which they make is so direct and so personal that it removes life to another court by referring it not to any past experience of life, but exactly to a sense, a recognition of new life, new art. They give us something that was not in our life, that was not in the art of painting before, and it appeals to us with all the power and the charm of a quickened consciousness of the value and meaning of life itself.

For after all what is art to us if it is only a Name, if it is only a formula or a precedent? or art criticism if it is only an analysis, the fight over a name? Art we feel is a symbol, however impoverished, of life, and life is

W. D. MacColl, "The International Exhibition of Modern Art," *Forum*, 50 (July, 1913), 24–27, 28, 29, 32, 34, 35.

more than any analysis. It is also instinct and a gift; an infinite procession of facts, analyzable or not; an elixir which first manifests itself in our affection (in our being affected by it), and from there spreads and delivers its message through the whole harmony or otherwise of our existence. The critic is called in only after the event; and the critic who rests in an "absolute scepticism" of the meaning or value of life, in whatever guise it appears, is as valueless surely as a doctor who refuses to take up the case of a patient.

There is another way of regarding the qualities of power and charm which the work of these men symbolizes. Their power lies in a spontaneity of action that does disrupt and change for us the former aspect of the world, together with a spiritual grace, a harmony, that links all things together again. The world has remained the same yet not the same: we have changed. There is no more beauty now than there was before; but there has been a quickening. It is this *quickening*, this sense of change into something rich and strange, which we feel as beauty, as life; and whenever any object whether it be Named good or bad (according to the consciousness of the ugly or of the beautiful in other persons) becomes expressive to *us* of that, it is probable that we may and that we will act out all our spiritual desire toward it. That doubtless is what Mr. Cortissoz too means when he speaks of arousing himself from a "timidity of mental habit." But he is aroused by the consciousness of something that, as his whole essay is intended to portray, is "coarse and unlovely" to him. With such a starting-point the resultant can be guessed at. By comparison, however, with the works of such men, our real "fuglemen," ancient or modern, all later or "lesser" paintings suffer, because they will seem to us to imitate the style (the manner and not the spirit) or to refresh the memory (the reason and not the basic affection) of the effect first made upon us, and afterwards sustained, by such earliest, such purest and most spontaneous impressions. All others are like echo, which is fainter than the voice, or like remembrance, which is paler than passion.

Now this is exactly what I experienced in the International Exhibition of Modern Art when I turned from the works of Gaugin hanging on one wall to the work of Augustus John on the opposite wall with his large canvas *Going Down to the Sea*. Beautiful, suave, rhythmic as John's picture was, for me it awakened only memory, not passion, the orderly processes of reason without the spontaneous gift or symbol of life. The style or manner of John's painting reminded me of Ary Scheffer, of Puvis de Chavannes, of a dozen other painters, all fine too, and that in itself is an artistic achievement; but beyond that I was not sure what John's picture meant to me, or what sensation of life it was intended to give me. My emotion therefore was distracted; my thoughts were not carried on the wings of any rich or strange change. There was nothing new in my life through having seen this picture. It had not for me the force of a more direct, more personal appeal to life: *more* love and more life. It is probable, however, that others might feel that for them it had been a new experience, an *Erklärung*, and would feel grateful for it in consequence. Everything in the world doubtless has its basis in somebody's affection.

In turning, however, to Matisse's portrait close by, called *Le Madras Rouge*, before I had made any analysis of its color, style, or composition, I found the rhythms of my brain and heart themselves phrasing the words upon my lips: "How terse, how vigorous, how——!" (Where do such words come from?) Or in passing into the next room, behold! Cézanne's pictures are hanging on the walls. How quickly, how easily he takes possession of me. Such rich and deep poetical affection for his subject conquers me. I fall at once into a reverie of musical dreams. And he is without the slightest affectation. Why should I have any? There is none in my gratitude. His color (I say, with all due apology to Mr. Cortissoz) is like a well-tuned instrument playing itself. There are no mock heroics here.

And yet, as judged by these pictures in the International Exhibition, Cézanne's intensity, his great force and unchangeableness of purpose as a man and as a painter, are not so apparent. I receive a far profounder impression of those very qualities in a *Still Life* by Manet, whom, nevertheless, we all accept to-day. When the subject is tragic Cézanne seems merely to suggest it to you and leaves it there. I feel a note of sadness, of meditation in his work. But in the swaying rhythms of his trees and plains in the dreaming landscape he seems to me what I had not realized so clearly before, so far from being strange, uncouth or "eccentric" that he fits quite simply and naturally into a splendid vision of the progress of art which he himself projects before me. It is almost as if he were saying: You see I am nothing but a Barbizon of a later day, loving the same country, yet holding myself to a certain classic simplicity in my appreciation of it.

That is the classic tradition which we believe Cézanne has found, and it comes to us with the scent and freshness of the wind, outvoicing all those fetichistic mumblings of the leaves among the trees. It is the reassurance of what so "drearily" had been forgotten and neglected:
"the never-ending audacity of elected persons"
that Whitman speaks of, "masters" this and that in painting or in aught else. For a moment the machinery of art has melted away, the sorcery of

spotted light and broken color has been set aside, and lo! Intuition, the strange shy goddess, has been found again in a new raiment, smiling but not mincing, admiring herself in a new landscape of the world. It is a return to nature, a return especially to something of that Arcadian simplicity which is always in the morning of the world's loves. *"Je reste,"* Cézanne said, not the master, but, exactly, *"le primitif de la voie que j'ai découverte."* "O queen that lovest Golgi, and Idalium, and the steep of Eryx, O Aphrodite, that playest with gold, lo, from the stream eternal of Acheron they have brought back to thee Adonis—even in the twelfth month they have brought him, the dainty-footed hours."

In the whole exhibition, however, none was lovelier to me than Gaugin. He too spreads with ease again his splendid fruitfulness over his whole canvas. He has the force and romantic passion of a painter like Courbet; and how carefully guarded and exalted it is. His pictures are not unlike his descriptions in Noa-Noa. The fire, the sombre beauty, the passion of the Tahitian forest are there. In *Sous les Palmiers* we get its full deep solitude; in *Faa Iheihe* it has become a decorative panel worthy of a dog's palace; in two other large canvases it is a *Still Life* beyond comparison rich, removed, final. All the wealth of the great Venetians, I feel, is here without any lowering of their temper and with how much more of our present day humanity. His art is subtle in a manner which appeals to us more to-day,—with less of visual, more of tangible or tactual reality: it is more plastic. He gives us actual portraiture; he is a traveller in those real lands of the mind's eye. And finally, you do not know till you have looked into it what glowing deeps his passion has led you safely past.

Matisse does the same. His range simply is not so large. He loves in silence. He, too, leaves it to you. All life and art does that, save "lawyer-craft and soldiercraft."

The Van Gogh collection of pictures was disappointing like the rest, not on account of the pictures themselves, but because their range and selection was so limited. One would have to see some of his wonderful human portraiture,—the *Le Berceuse,* for instance,—to know the best that he is capable of; and in the life of an artist from an artist's viewpoint, the strength of a man's whole chain of life is measurable not by its weaker links (that is for the life of the world), but by its strongest, by bringing all the others to the test of the most excellent in him. And yet what cataracts of color lay there, like sounds swept from the storm of his emotion in the face of life and of nature. He recalls to me the spirit of Rembrandt. Indeed he is as thoroughly and typically Dutch as Rembrandt or as Ruysdael were, and far more passionately so than Mauve or

Maris is to-day. And he too like Naaman, captain of the host of the king of Syria, though a mighty man of valor, was yet—a leper! Mr. Cortissoz reminded me of that terrible story in the Second Book of Kings by reminding his reader that Van Gogh cut off his ear with a razor and sent it in a letter, and then *died insane!* If we can,—if we will,—if our sense of duty to humanity and to the art of painting will allow us, we may, I think, imagine him instead intoxicating himself with the extraordinary, the revolutionary and revolutionizing joy of color that throbbed like wine in his veins. Even the gowns and bonnets of our womenkind to-day are embellished with the colors to which these men, Cézanne, Van Gogh, Gaugin gave life. How is it that, with the living evidences of their influence on every hand and flowing "out of Paris into Germany, Russia, England, and to some slight extent the United States," our critics are unable to discern any part of humanity in their art?

Color is everywhere. We do not need to look for it on the walls of an exhibition. And everywhere, perhaps, it is subserving different ends, clothing with life the different forms and aspects of life. And that perhaps is why we do look and also why we distinguish according to our bent or our necessity. If we turn to our own painters we cannot fail to notice that Prendergast possesses an almost unexampled use of it. That is his distinction. Another painter like George Bellows uses it, when I have analyzed my emotion before it, for the sake of a brief word, an exclamation. "God! it was fine!" he seems to me to say of a polo match; and as a result we get a first hand note, a fleeting glimpse of but one incident in a whole game which is itself but one incident in the whole of life. . . .

This "new" sculpture like this "new" painting has for a moment infused a "new" life,—I mean simply, as before, a more present and personal meaning into art. It compels us to recognize "new" and living personalities in the world about us. Is that not enough distinction for any art? I find moreover that, like everything "new" perhaps, while it may not personify a perfectly recognizable abstraction of somebody else's mind (after the approved manner of all schools and tribunes) yet it does apparently abstract a personification of something in the artist's own mind. The artist has dared to have an opinion of his own. But as we are already supposed to value that priceless possession, his crime, I can only think, must lie in the fact that his opinion involves a certain amount of disturbance, or the fear of disturbance, to those who, like Mr. Cortissoz, can neither receive it nor let it alone. *That is,* perhaps, what this new art is doing for us. But it is also what life is always doing for us, is it not? In any case, it is ours, it is of to-day. There ought to be some way of understanding it, of discovering what it is saying to us, of what is real as well as what is illusionary in it. . . .

"They are a joke," I hear some one remark in the gaping throng. But why so distressed about it? I feel inclined to answer. Would it really be the first joke you had seen in painting? and these are at least a good joke, are they not? Why not discriminate even in "jokes"? His pictures have a very refined beauty of color, if you can forget that the destiny of color is not simply to make a piece of paint look like a piece of fish, or like a piece of flesh, or like a piece of fashion; like a boxing match, or like a snow-scene, or like a lady caught without her clothes or showing herself off in furs. His color is simply instrumental to the design which *he* has in mind; and I find in it something fluid and rhythmical, a kind of musical mechanism almost, and in a measure eclectic—the invention perhaps of an ascetic mind. Yet on the other hand a little *Still Life* by him is very broadly and plastically conceived; and there is the portrait of his wife!

His mannerisms in any case are not mere affectation: they are *his* style, his meaning. If he hasn't quite the warmth or passion of invention which a more dramatic instinct would have provided, he has unquestionably at all events grace, dignity and repose. I feel that we get some measure of his reaction to life by noting this, that he is always at ease with himself and with his subject, careful, never flustered. And there is nothing petty or snobbish about his work. What a relief that is! It may at times lean to pedantry; it is an intellectual art, and that of course is the strange thing to find in art to-day.

A Layman's View of an Art Exhibition
THEODORE ROOSEVELT

The recent "International Exhibition of Modern Art" in New York was really noteworthy. Messrs. Davies, Kuhn, Gregg, and their fellow-members of the Association of American Painters and Sculptors have done a

Theodore Roosevelt, "A Layman's Views of an Art Exhibition," *Outlook*, 103 (March 29, 1913), 718–720.

work of very real value in securing such an exhibition of the works of both foreign and native painters and sculptors. Primarily their purpose was to give the public a chance to see what has recently been going on abroad. No similar collection of the works of European "moderns" has ever been exhibited in this country. The exhibitors are quite right as to the need of showing to our people in this manner the art forces which of late have been at work in Europe, forces which cannot be ignored.

This does not mean that I in the least accept the view that these men take of the European extremists whose pictures are here exhibited. It is true, as the champions of these extremists say, that there can be no life without change, no development without change, and that to be afraid of what is different or unfamiliar is to be afraid of life. It is no less true, however, that change may mean death and not life, and retrogression instead of development. Probably we err in treating most of these pictures seriously. It is likely that many of them represent in the painters the astute appreciation of the powers to make folly lucrative which the late P. T. Barnum showed with his faked mermaid. There are thousands of people who will pay small sums to look at a faked mermaid; and now and then one of this kind with enough money will buy a Cubist picture, or a picture of a misshapen nude woman, repellent from every standpoint.

In some ways it is the work of the American painters and sculptors which is of most interest in this collection, and a glance at this work must convince any one of the real good that is coming out of the new movements, fantastic though many of the developments of these new movements are. There was one note entirely absent from the exhibition, and that was the note of the commonplace. There was not a touch of simpering, self-satisfied conventionality anywhere in the exhibition. Any sculptor or painter who had in him something to express and the power of expressing it found the field open to him. He did not have to be afraid because his work was not along ordinary lines. There was no stunting or dwarfing, no requirement that a man whose gift lay in new directions should measure up or down to stereotyped and fossilized standards.

For all of this there can be only hearty praise. But this does not in the least mean that the extremists whose paintings and pictures were represented are entitled to any praise, save, perhaps, that they have helped to break fetters. Probably in any reform movement, any progressive movement, in any field of life, the penalty for avoiding the commonplace is a liability to extravagance. It is vitally necessary to move forward and to shake off the dead hand, often the fossilized dead hand, of the reactionaries; and yet we have to face the fact that there is apt to be a lunatic fringe among the votaries of any forward movement. In this recent art exhibition the lunatic fringe was fully in evidence, especially in the rooms devoted to the Cubists and the Futurists, or Near-Impressionists. I am not entirely certain which of the two latter terms should be used in connection with some of the various pictures and representations of plastic art— and, frankly, it is not of the least consequence. The Cubists are entitled to the serious attention of all who find enjoyment in the colored puzzle pictures of the Sunday newspapers. Of course there is no reason for choosing the cube as a symbol, except that it is probably less fitted than any other mathematical expression for any but the most formal decorative art. There is no reason why people should not call themselves Cubists, or Octagonists, or Parallelopipedonists, or Knights of the Isosceles Triangle, or Brothers of the Cosine, if they so desire; as expressing anything serious and permanent, one term is as fatuous as another. Take the picture which for some reason is called "A naked man going down stairs." There is in my bath-room a really good Navajo rug which, on any proper interpretation of the Cubist theory, is a far more satisfactory and decorative picture. Now if, for some inscrutable reason, it suited somebody to call this rug a picture of, say, "A well-dressed man going up a ladder," the name would fit the facts just about as well as in the case of the Cubist picture of the "Naked man going down stairs." From the standpoint of terminology, each name would have whatever merit inheres in a rather cheap straining after effect; and from the standpoint of decorative value, of sincerity, and of artistic merit, the Navajo rug is infinitely ahead of the picture.

As for many of the human figures in the pictures of the Futurists, they show that the school would be better entitled to the name of the "Past-ists." I was interested to find that a man of scientific attainments who had likewise looked at the pictures had been struck, as I was, by their resemblance to the later work of the paleolithic artists of the French and Spanish caves. There are interesting samples of the strivings for the representation of the human form among artists of many different countries and times, all in the same stage of paleolithic culture, to be found in a recent number of the "Revue d'Ethnographie." The paleolithic artist was able to portray the bison, the mammoth, the reindeer, and the horse with spirit and success, while he still stumbled painfully in the effort to portray man. This stumbling effort in his case represented progress, and he was entitled to great credit for it. Forty thousand years later, when entered into artificially and deliberately, it represents only a smirking pose of retrogression, and is not praiseworthy. So with much of the sculpture. A family group of precisely the merit that inheres in a structure made of the wooden blocks in a nursery is not entitled to be reproduced in marble. Admirers speak of the kneeling female figure by Lehmbruck—I use "female" advisedly, for although obviously mammalian it is not especially human—as "full of lyric grace," as "tremendously sincere," and "of a jewel-like precious-ness." I am not competent to say whether these words themselves repre-sent sincerity or merely a conventional jargon; it is just as easy to be conventional about the fantastic as about the commonplace. In any event one might as well speak of the "lyric grace" of a praying mantis, which adopts much the same attitude; and why a deformed pelvis should be called "sincere," or a tibia of giraffe-like lengths "precious," is a question of pathological rather than artistic significance. This figure and the absurd portrait head of some young lady have the merit that inheres in extrava-gant caricature. It is a merit, but it is not a high merit. It entitles these pieces to stand in sculpture where nonsense rhymes stand in literature and the sketches of Aubrey Beardsley in pictorial art. These modern sculp-tured caricatures in no way approach the gargoyles of Gothic cathedrals, probably because the modern artists are too self-conscious and make themselves ridiculous by pretentiousness. The makers of the gargoyles knew very well that the gargoyles did not represent what was most impor-tant in the Gothic cathedrals. They stood for just a little point of gro-tesque reaction against, and relief from, the tremendous elemental vast-ness and grandeur of the Houses of God. They were imps, sinister and comic, grim and yet futile, and they fitted admirably into the framework of the theology that found its expression in the towering and wonderful piles which they ornamented.

Very little of the work of the extremists among the European "mod-erns" seems to be good in and for itself; nevertheless it has certainly helped any number of American artists to do work that is original and serious; and this not only in painting but in sculpture. I wish the exhibi-tion had contained some of the work of the late Marcius Symonds; very few people knew or cared for it while he lived; but not since Turner has there been another man on whose canvas glowed so much of that unearthly "light that never was on land or sea." But the exhibition con-tained so much of extraordinary merit that it is ungrateful even to men-tion an omission. To name the pictures one would like to possess—and the bronzes and tanagras and plasters—would mean to make a catalogue of indefinite length. One of the most striking pictures was the "Terminal Yards"—the seeing eye was there, and the cunning hand. I should like to mention all the pictures of the President of the association, Arthur B. Davies. As first-class decorative work of an entirely new type, the very unexpected pictures of Sheriff Bob Chandler have a merit all their own. The "Arizona Desert," the "Canadian Night," the group of girls on the roof of a New York tenement-house, the studies in the Bronx Zoo, the "Heracles," the studies for the Utah monument, the little group called "Gossip," which has something of the quality of the famous Fifteenth Idyl of Theocritus, the "Pelf," with its grim suggestiveness—these, and a hundred others, are worthy of study, each of them; I am naming at random those which at the moment I happen to recall. I am not speaking of the acknowledged masters, of Whistler, Puvis de Chavannes, Monet; nor of John's children; nor of Cézanne's old woman with a rosary; nor of Redon's marvelous color pieces—a worthy critic should speak of these. All I am trying to do is to point out why a layman is grateful to those who arranged this exhibition.

20. Rebellion in Painting

For American painting the early twentieth century was a time of seething discontent beating against and finally bursting old bounds. The conservative style with its painstaking attention to detail resulted in canvases of near-photographic fidelity such as those of John Singer Sargent and William Merritt Chase. The insurgents dispensed with such restraints, seeking instead an expression of the artist's emotions in confrontation with his subject. Subject matter changed. The traditional emphasis on portraiture and formal landscapes gave way to an interest in everyday reality. Leading the new school of realists was the former newspaper illustrator John Sloan whose "McSorley's Bar" of 1912 appeared in the Armory Show. Sloan delighted in capturing the commonplace—as it might appear, for instance, from a rear window in Greenwich Village. George Bellows loved the primitiveness of the prizefight and the rawness of a city street in winter.

The inspiration for part of the revolt in painting came from the Cubists and Futurists of Europe. No single work in the Armory Show excited more attention, pro and con, than Marcel Duchamp's "Nude Descending A Staircase." Among the American artists who practiced nonrepresentational techniques were Max Weber and Arthur G. Dove. John Marin's street scenes, compared for instance to Bellows', represent a progression toward expressionism. It remained for the Italian-born but fervently American Joseph Stella to combine the "modern" style with an ability to discern order and beauty beneath the rush of the twentieth century.

1. THE TRADITIONAL: *John Singer Sargent,*
   "Mrs. William Crowninshield Endicott" (1910).

2. THE TRADITIONAL: *William Merritt Chase, "Blue Kimono" (1902).*

3. SALOONS IN ART: *John Sloan, "McSorley's Bar" (1912).*

4. THE CITY SCENE: *John Sloan, "Backyards, Greenwich Village" (1914).*

5. RAW POWER: *George Bellows, "Stag at Sharkey's" (1909).*

6. ASH CAN REALISM: *George Bellows, "The Steaming Streets" (1908).*

7. CUBISM: *Marcel Duchamp, "Nude Descending a Staircase" (1912).*

8. ABSTRACTION: *Max Weber, "Chinese Restaurant" (1915).*

9. ABSTRACTION: *Arthur G. Dove, "Plant Forms" (1915).*

10. ADVANCED EXPRESSIONISM: *John Marin, "Movement, Fifth Avenue" (1912).*

11. THE DISCOVERY OF ORDER AND BEAUTY IN MODERN CIVILIZATION:
Joseph Stella, "Battle of Lights, Coney Island" (1913).

12. *Stella, "Brooklyn Bridge" (1917–1918).*

200

13. *Stella, "New York Interpreted—The Bridge" (1922).*

PART THREE

WORK AND PLAY

21. The "New" Humor

Humor is one of the best indicators of popular thought. To ask what strikes a period as funny is to probe its deepest values and tastes. Like other forms of cultural expression in the early twentieth century, humor became the subject of sharp altercation. Aaron Hoffman, a leading vaudeville comedian, represents the "new" humor. His monologue, below, was the most famous of its time. Designed to be extemporaneously updated with current material, the piece enjoyed a long life on the stage. The present version dates to 1914. Katherine Roof's essay about American taste in humor indicates that she would have disapproved of almost everything in the Hoffman monologue.

The German Senator
AARON HOFFMAN

My dear friends and falling citizens:

My heart fills up with vaccination to be disabled to come out here before such an intelligence massage of people and have the chance to undress such a large conglomerated aggravation.

I do not come before you like other political speakers, with false pride in one hand and the Star Strangled Banana in the other.

I come before you as a true, sterilized citizen, a man who is for the public and against the people, and I want to tell you, my 'steemed friends, when I look back on the early hysterics of our country, and think

Aaron Hoffman, "The German Senator: A Monologue" in *Writing for Vaudeville* (Springfield, Mass., The Home Correspondence School, 1915), 435–443.

how our forefathers strangled to make this country voss iss is it; when you think of the lives that was loosed and the blood that was shredded, we got to feel a feeling of patriotic symptoms—we got to feel a patriotic symp—symps—you got to feel the patri—you can't help it, you got to feel it.

I tell you, our hearts must fill up with indigestion when we look out to see the Statue of Liberty, the way she stands, all alone, dressed up in nothing, with a light in her hand, showing her freedom.

And what a fine place they picked out for Liberty to stand.

With Coney Island on one side and Blackwell's Island on the other.

And when she stands there now, looking on the country the way it is and what she has to stand for, I tell you tears and tears must drop from her eyes. Well, to prove it—look at the ocean she filled up.

And no wonder she's crying. Read the nuisance papers. See what is going on.

Look what the country owes.

According to the last report of the Secretary of the Pleasury, the United States owes five billion dollars.

Nobody knows what we owe it for;

And nobody ever sees what we have got for it;

And if you go to Washington, the Capsule of the United States, and ask them, THEY don't even know THEMSELVES.

Then they say, what keeps the country broke is the Pay-no-more Canal.

It cost the Government nine thousand dollars an hour to dig the canal. THINK OF THAT!

Nine thousand dollars an hour for digging, and the worst of it is, they ain't digging.

Up to date, it has cost a hundred and seventy million dollars to dig a hole—they've been at it for over nine years—and the only hole they've dug is in the United States Treasury.

Every six months, the Chief Engineer, he comes up with a report;

He says: "Mr. Congress, the canal is getting better every day, a million dollars MORE please."

He gets the money, goes out, buys a couple of shovels, then sends back a telegram: HOORAY—The digging is very good, the two oceans will soon be one.

Can you beat that?

Before they started the canal it didn't cost us nothing, and we had two oceans.

And by the time they get through, it'll cost us three hundred million and we'll only have one.

And now that the canal is nearly finished, it looks like it was going to get us into trouble.

Japan is against it on one side and England don't like it on the other.

And that's why we've got to have a navy.

Of course, we've got a navy.

But everybody is kicking about it.

Why should they kick?

All we appropriated for the navy last year was four million dollars.

And there's eighty million people in this country.

And that figures a nickel apiece.

And what the hell kind of a navy do you expect for a nickel?

Still they are crying that the country is in destitution circumstances. That is inconsis—inconsis—you can't deny it.

Our country has got a superabum, a superabum—a superabum—we've got a lot of money.

There's money lying in the treasury that never was touched. And the first fellow that will touch it will get six months.

The whole trouble is the trusts.

Look what the cold storage trust have done with the eggs. Sixty cents a dozen—for the good ones. And the good ones are rotten.

Then they say the reason prices are going up is because wages are getting higher.

But why should they raise the price of eggs?

The chickens ain't getting any more wages.

And if meat goes up any higher, it will be worth more than money.

Then there won't be any money.

Instead of carrying money in your pocket, you'll carry meat around.

A sirloin steak will be worth a thousand dollar bill.

When you go down to the bank to make a deposit, instead of giving the cashier a thousand dollar bill, you'll slip him a sirloin steak.

If you ask him for change, he'll give you a hunk of bologny.

If they keep on, we won't be able to live at all.

Statistics prove that the average wages of the workingman is one dollar a day.

Out of that, he's got to spend fifty cents a day for food; fifty-five cents for rent; ten cents for car fare.

And at the end of a hard day's work—he owes himself fifteen cents.

Yet the rich people say that the poor people are getting prosperous.

They say, look at our streets. You see nothing but automobiles. You don't see half the poor people now that you used to.

Certainly you don't.

Half of them have already been run over and the other half is afraid to come out.

Why, between the automobiles and the trusts the poor man hasn't got a chance to live.

And if only the gas trust gets a little stronger, the price of gas will go up so high a poor man won't even be able to commit suicide.

They'll have him both ways. He can't live and he can't die.

And that's why I am with the socialists.

They say, "Down with the trusts! Do away with money. Make everything equal."

Imagine a fellow going into a jewelry store and saying:

"Give me a diamond ring, here's a lemon."

But the socialists have got some good ideas for the working people. And my heart and soul is with the labor class of people. I am for labor unions.

But what help are the labor unions to the working man?

Look at it in the right light.

A man pays twenty-five dollars to join a union. He gets a job in a shop for two dollars a day, works two weeks, the union gets out on a strike and he owes himself a dollar.

The unions are crying the days are too long.

They want the days shorter. They want the days should be eight hours long.

But think of the fellows out in the North Pole where the days are six months long.

That's the place for the poor man to live.

When the landlord comes around and says, "Rent," all you have to do is to tell him to come around the day after tomorrow.

Then Andrew Carnigger, he comes out and tells us you should save money and put it in the bank.

What's the use of putting your money in the bank?

It's easy enough to put it in, but it ain't easy to get it out. When you want to take your money out, you got to give the cashier sixty days notice.

And did you ever figure out how far a cashier can go in sixty days?

Then they say, as the world goes on, we are improving.

It's ridiculum.

We were better off years ago than we are now.

Look at Adam in the Garden of Eat-ing.

Life to him was a pleasure;

There was a fellow that had nothing to worry about.

Anything he wanted he could get.

But the darn fool had to get lonesome.

And that's the guy that started all our troubles.

We would be all right today, if it wasn't for Adam and Evil.

Then they say that Adam fell for an apple.

It just shows how men have improved.

No man would fall for an apple today.

It would have to be a peach.

And I tell you, it's no wonder that women feel stuck up. They say they can do more than men can do.

That's very true, when you go back to the first woman, Eve.

She was only one little woman, all by herself, and she put the whole human race on the bum.

Could a man do that?

And yet she was only a rib out of Adam's side.

It just goes to show you what a cheap proposition woman was.

Nowadays, when you want to marry a woman, you got to buy a diamond ring, take her to the theatres, buy her taxicheaters, and what's left of your wages you got to spend on candy and tango trots and turkey teas. There's where Adam had it on all of us.

All Eve cost him was one bone.

It all goes to show you how much better off man was in those days than today, and while John D. Rottenfeller, the great Philosopede, he comes out and says, nobody has a right to be poor; he says, anybody can live on eighteen dollars a week.

He don't have to tell us that.

Let him tell us how to get the eighteen.

And still that great statesment, William Chinning Bryan, he comes out and says, we are living in a great country. He says we are living in a country of excitement, intelligence and education.

That's very true.

Look at our public school system.

A child can go to school for nothing, and when he grows up to be a man he is thoroughly educated, he can go into the public school and be a teacher and get fifty dollars a month.

And the janitor gets ninety-five.

That shows you how education is coming to the front.

Wouldn't it better, instead of sending a child to school, to learn him to clean out a cellar?

And what's the cause of all the trouble?

The House of Representatives.

We send them to Washington to look out for the people and the only time they look out for the people is when they look out the window and see them coming.

Then they get $7,500 a year. They spend $10,000 a year, and at the end of the year they have $100,000 saved.

No wonder they are careless with our money.

That's all they got to do. Sit around Washington and touch the treasury.

Every couple of days a fellow comes into Congress and says:

"Good morning, Congress, let me have $4,000,000."

That's all they do, is make touches for millions.

You never heard of those suckers making a touch for a quarter, or a half a dollar.

To show you what they do with our money, look at our Weather Bureau Department.

We pay a fellow $10,000 a year. For what?

To tell us when it's going to rain.

And he don't know himself.

But he don't want to know.

He knows that if he ever guesses it right, he is going to lose his job. But believe me, it's a soft job.

Nothing to do.

He gets up in the morning, eats a nice breakfast, smokes a good fat cigar; then he looks out of the window and says, "Fine weather to-day."

Then he takes his umbrella and goes out for a walk.

I tell you, my dear friends, the way the country stands now, the country stands on the brink of a preci—the country stands on the brink of a precip—and if somebody shoves it, it is going over.

And the cause of all the trouble in the country is the crooked politics.

And that's why the women suffering gents have gotten together and are fighting for their rights.

And you can't blame them.

Now I see where one married woman has hit on a great idea.

She says there's only one protection for the wives.

And that's a wives' union.

Imagine a union for wives.

A couple gets married.

And as soon as they get settled, along comes the walking delegate and orders a strike.

Then imagine thousands and thousands of wives walking up and down the streets on strike, and scabs taking their places.

The American Sense of Humor
KATHERINE ROOF

The American sense of humor has been as characteristic, in a way, of the comments of the New England sea captain or the Yankee shop-keeper as of the sayings of Lowell, Holmes, or Mark Twain. It is of a quality subtle and unanalyzable; a thing that can play upon the surface of depths, that can assert itself in the face of disaster and apparent defeat. There is something fine and courageous in it aside from its charm as a mental quality. But how much of it will survive another generation of de-Americanization? How much of it do we find in the humor of the theater or newspaper, or in the utterances of the American citizen of to-day? On the other hand, we seem to have acquired a class of indi-viduals whose so-called sense of humor takes the form of an uncouth flippancy, a type of mind that stares blankly in the face of the real arti-cle, and laughs noisily at the things that should command respect.

True American humor, while it may deal lightly with some ceremony or grave superstition in which the question of real veneration is not involved, contains no real irreverence. It is neither self-conscious nor flippant. Yet this brainless outgrowth of our National mental habit is quite opposite from the original quality in intention and effect. Because it is only the imitation of the mental attitude in a class of individuals of a cruder type and without the psychologic make-up that created it in the beginning, it has resulted in this clownish habit of laughter at things that should be seriously or reverently regarded.

The cause for this apparent change in the quality of the American mind lies in the fact that the type of the average citizen of to-day is different from that of a generation or two ago—more forceful perhaps in certain ways, but of coarser grain. The whole tendency in our country at present is toward abnormal growth and superficial development. Our civilization is upon a false basis, for material prosperity is easily achieved

Katherine Roof, "The American Sense of Humor," *Outlook*, 96 (Oct. 8, 1910), 311–316.

by only two classes among honest people—the man with business per-spicacity and the manual laborer in needed industries. As to fraudulent schemes, America is probably more conducive to their success than any other country in the world. The rapid pace of things, the possibility of swift advancement to the uncultivated, combined with the theoretic ideal of equality, tend to induce superficiality. No one must feel inferior to his neighbor no matter how recent his sophistication, therefore the general desire is for effect, a surface grasp of a subject. Many magazines and newspapers pander to this desire, producing articles that will make people feel that they know about a subject upon which they could not possibly be informed without serious study or technical knowledge.

I once received the following instructions from the editor of a popular magazine who wanted an article upon a certain opera. "Do the story," he wrote, "so that the man or woman who never heard a grand opera or never heard of one before will read the story and leave it with a feeling that he knows *all about it!*" With this complacent and certainly far from honest mental condition receiving every encouragement, the ability to think is atrophied and the finer attributes, including humor—which can exist in the most uneducated mind provided it does its own thinking—must cease to exist.

Also the tremendous influx of Continental foreigners—the raw and often the waste material of the countries they come from—into a democracy, English-speaking and founded upon Anglo-Saxon morality, is a powerful factor in the creation of a new type. This second-generation product, evolved from our polyglot population, is actually a very different being mentally from the native American—inevitably with so different an inheritance and home environment. And among other changes a perversion of the idea of humor occurs when the American mental habit is grafted upon minds of a different color. Yet these second-generation citizens (a weed-like growth essentially un-American), owing to their adaptability to the needs of the country, are provided with a liberal amount of spending money considered relatively to their requirements, and are all literate, thanks to our public schools. They assist to support public amusements therefore, and so have come to affect the character of popular entertainments of the kind where supply and demand were formerly regulated by a more enlightened class.

We judge a people's taste in humor by its amusements—that is, the theaters they patronize, the magazines and newspapers they read—especially the Sunday editions. The newspapers, in their editorials, their comic supplements, their selected anecdotes, their manner of serving up the news, are enormously important factors in the development of this undesirable flippancy which has no relation to real humor; certain newspapers have acquired a reputation for wit which they endeavor to live up to, but they only succeed—save for an exceptional editorial now and then—in producing a labored and heavy flippancy. On the whole, the effect of the papers upon the uncultured and unthinking classes who are influenced by them would seem to be to induce and exaggerate two equally undermining qualities—a sickly false sentiment and a flippant attitude toward the real issues of life. It is upon his manipulation of these two elements that the lawyer of a certain class depends to affect his jury.

It is a well-known fact that New York taste controls the character of the theatrical entertainment for the country. The quality of the New York theater audience, then, becomes a matter of moment. Of what is it composed? There is our friend, the Tired Business Man, who, we are told, only wants to be amused, and is anxious, therefore, for a laugh in or out of season when he goes to the theater. It is undeniable that the tremendous condensation of New York life, with its tendency to focus and concentrate this man's mind upon business at the expense of all else, tends to make him less open to other impressions than his predecessor, the American of the last generation. Also a large percentage of the business men of New York are not native Americans, or even of Anglo-Saxon extraction, so that their sense of humor, if they have one, is certainly not American. The intelligent class is, of course, in the minority in any country. But, admitting that fact, it is discouraging to realize that the majority of individuals supporting public entertainments in the large American cities are of this imperfectly evolved type, of no distinctive nationality, born of the forcing-house conditions of American life. Indeed, one is sometimes tempted to feel that our brave democracy is becoming primarily a forcing-house for weeds.

To put the matter in a nutshell, in New York individuals with a moving-picture-show intelligence can afford the price of orchestra chairs in a Broadway theater. They do not constitute the entire audience, but their class is so large numerically that they affect, if they do not control, the success or failure of a play as well as the circulation of a Sunday paper and of a large class of magazines. For all these things are a question of supply and demand, are what is known as a "business proposition." The theatrical manager aims to fill his house; the majority of magazines and newspapers, bent upon circulation, avoid publishing matter that would displease uncultivated readers through being incomprehensible to them.

Therefore the standard has become both lowered and cheapened. Probably in no other country in the world are the representative theaters run upon the basis of pleasing the lowest intellectual grade of their patrons.

Of all the various forms of deterioration resulting from the substitution of the business basis for other standards, none is more lamentable than this peculiar form of demoralization that has occurred in the realm of humor.

This condition is most noticeable in the theater when the play is one designed to appeal to a more mature taste than the average production caters to. In the vaudeville entertainments and farces the jokes have become almost as physical in character as those of the Continental theaters where the height of humor is represented by some accident to or attack upon the person. But it is in the inept, mistaken mirth of the New York audience that the lowest ebb of intelligence is betrayed, and it is disconcerting to the veritable American to see these clownish misconceptions pass as illustrations of the American sense of humor.

It is not possible to attend a play where some neighbor is not audibly following the movements of the players—"He looks out of the window," "She sees him," etc., etc.—or slyly anticipating the obvious *dénouement*. It is not surprising, therefore, that the really humorous point should escape recognition or that situations of serious meaning should be received with irrelevant and irreverent laughter.

The manner in which Eugene Walter's play "The Easiest Way" was received was inexpressibly shocking. This drama makes an attempt to treat frankly certain unpleasant conditions existing in New York, and especially in the theatrical world. The situation, by the way, of a theater making capital out of its own depravity is sufficiently curious. But more depressing to the thoughtful observer than the play itself was the spectacle of the audience receiving the painful revelations of the inner workings of these things with peals of laughter. The truth of the matter probably is that minds trained in the grooves of vaudeville and melodrama do not work upon the material offered them, with the result that any striking line or situation not labeled in large type as a noble sentiment or a tearful appeal jars a laugh from them. Melodrama leads them to expect the whitewashing of wedlock as the logical end of "The Easiest Way." This will legitimize the naughty jokes (that is to say, lines full of sickening and sordid tragedy), so meantime, with a conscience at rest, they feel at liberty to enjoy what they conceive to be the comedy passages. When, however, the young man repudiates the weakly vicious girl in the end, and she puts on a picture hat and starts for "Rector's," puzzled looks are to be observed upon many features. Applause was faint when the curtain dropped; the mental state was evidently that of confusion; for to this class of mind the actors exist as so many real people, "horrid" or "lovely," to be hated or admired. What kind of girl (this naïve mind may be conceived as asking itself) was this, anyway? She had seemed to be the heroine. Was she the villainess, after all? Yet, confusing as it proved, it was still sufficiently amusing and harrowing to be set down as a "good show."

Does this mean that the individuals who make up the audience have no standards, no ideals, that they can laugh at revelations of degradation and vice? So far as the majority is concerned, that is unlikely. It is rather that they go to the theater to laugh or to weep and not to think, and that, in short, not thinking, they fail to apply their life standards to the mimic world of the playhouse.

To the mind educated in vaudeville certain things are an invariable cue for laughter: drunkenness (either in life or in the theater), the desperate spinster, the woman who lies about her age, the gay deceiver husband, the mother-in-law, the perception that some one has "got left," but most of all, the predicament. All of these mirth-provoking subjects are equally present in the funny papers. Many of them are common to all countries. Marital infidelity is, however, much more heavily coated with sugar in the American than in the French farce, and the happy ending is invariably conceded to Anglo-Saxon standards. But the conception of a joke that is peculiarly characteristic of this perverted form of American humor is the predicament! No matter how tragic the issue, the sight of any one driven to the wall, oppressed by the situation, is something that, to the common mind, can have been devised for no other purpose than that of amusement. This state of mind may be observed in an idle New York crowd watching a minor accident, but in general in a theater it may be set down to the application of vaudeville standards to all things seen in a playhouse. . . .

If these things only signified a deterioration in the art of the theater it would be serious enough; but unfortunately there is much evidence to prove that it indicates among a fairly large class of people a deterioration of the standards that regulate life. It is an undeniable fact that the country contains a class of individuals who have acquired false standards founded upon this very combination of false sentiment and flippancy encouraged by the theaters and newspapers. The case is the same whether they are inattentive shop-girls, indifferent waiters, incompetent plumbers, or rich idlers of the class that live in hotels and shoot around in motors from one restaurant, one "show," to another, with apparently no homes, no roots, anywhere. These people not only regard lightly and coarsely most of the facts of life, but even that of death itself. Seriously considered, how shocking a thing it was to have such a phrase as "Remember the Maine" converted into popular slang!

The casual and indifferent attitude of a large class of chauffeurs and other case-hardened motorists toward loss of life is a very grave illustration of the case in point. Indeed, the whole condition of irresponsibility in the matter of accidents is allied to this perverted development of the idea of humor.

"That's one on me," remarked a switch-tender when, through his criminal inattentiveness to duty, one train was sent crashing into another, a number of lives were lost and a score of people maimed. This particular switch-tender evaded arrest and punishment and was the life of a firemen's ball, according to report, less than a year later. No doubt he is making similar jokes still.

It is noticeable among a large class of the employed that their own blunders are regarded either as entertaining social material or as an excellent joke upon the recipient of the incompetent service. It is also evident that the amusing little blunder is never supposed to have any effect upon the size of the tip expected.

No doubt much of the carelessness characteristic of personal service in America, the universal slipshod indifference to obligation on the part of those holding responsible positions, might be laid at the door of this infection of flippancy which is in the air, and which is a degraded, immoral offshoot of the original American sense of humor.

It is an attitude that has come about understandably enough through our illogically achieved prosperity, a condition the very opposite of the oppressed poverty of the Russian peasant, which is reflected in their stolidity and seriousness. This abnormal prosperity of ours has its varying effect upon all classes—the native American, the immigrant, and the second-generation product that is neither American nor foreign. The result, a confusion of ideals, is the natural outcome of a situation where people are placed in an economic condition to which they are as yet unadapted.

We can only hope that this unhappy tendency is one of the inevitable defects of the transition stage, and that in another generation it will have been eradicated, whatever modifications the native type may have undergone by that time.

22. Comic Strips and Cartoon Art

The United States led the world in developing the comic strip. Richard F. Outcault created the first important strip, "The Yellow Kid," for the *New York World* in 1896. Six years later he transferred his talents to the *New York Herald* and began "Buster Brown." Buster and his dog Tige soon became American institutions, better known than the best of the best-selling novel heroes. Rivaling Outcault as king of the early comic strips was George Herriman and his "Krazy Kat." The innocent, sentimental, all-loving Krazy, and his cohorts Ignatz Mouse and Officer Pupp, first appeared in 1910 and were soon featured in dozens of newspapers across the country. Moving with unceasing optimism in a fantasy world full of maliciousness, Krazy Kat seemed to appeal to people whose own dreams were continually frustrated. In the opinion of Gilbert Seldes, the Herriman strip was "the most amusing and fantastic and satisfactory work of art produced in America." Cartoons also provided a way of discussing the human situation. The bite existed just beneath the humor. The eternal theme of sexual attraction was the special province of Charles Dana Gibson whose "Gibson girl" not only dominated art but set a style of female charm which American women strove to copy.

1. A REVERSAL OF ROLES AND A MORAL:
Richard F. Outcault, "Buster Brown."

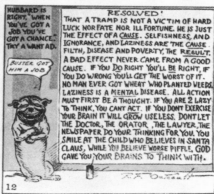

2. A FANTASY WORLD: *George Herriman, "Krazy Kat."*

3. THE ETERNAL OPTIMIST: *George Herriman, "Krazy Kat."*

4. CARTOONS AND SOCIAL ISSUES: *W. O. Wilson in* Judge (*1904*) *and Robert Minor in* The Masses (*1915*).

"Your Honor, this woman gave birth to a naked child!"

5. THE GIBSON GIRL: *Charles Dana Gibson in Collier's (1903).*

23. The Searchlight of Satire

Under the guise of laughter Ringgold Wilmer Lardner lashed the aspirations of middle class Americans. A baseball umpire and sportswriter before he turned humorist, Lardner's first stories concerned the bush-league minds of ballplayers. Brushing aside the sentimentality that cloaked sports heroes, Lardner called a spade a spade. In 1916 he created Gullible, a harbinger of Sinclair Lewis' Babbitt. While Lardner and his audience were obviously amused by Gullible and his wife, the humor rested on the recognition that the portrait rang at least partially true for many Americans.

Gullible's Travels
RING LARDNER

I promised the Wife that if anybody ast me what kind of a time did I have at Palm Beach I'd say I had a swell time. And if they ast me who did we meet I'd tell 'em everybody that was worth meetin'. And if they ast me didn't the trip cost a lot I'd say Yes; but it was worth the money. I promised her I wouldn't spill none o' the real details. But if you can't break a promise you made to your own wife what kind of a promise can you break? Answer me that, Edgar.

I'm not one o' these kind o' people that'd keep a joke to themself just because the joke was on them. But they's plenty of our friends that I wouldn't have 'em hear about it for the world. I wouldn't tell you, only

Ring W. Lardner, "Gullible's Travels," *Saturday Evening Post,* 189 (Aug. 19, 1916), 3–5, 31, 34, 35, 38.

I know you're not the village gossip and won't crack it to anybody. Not even to your own Missus, see? I don't trust no women.

It was along last January when I and the Wife was both hit by the *society bacillus*. I think it was at the opera. You remember me tellin' you about us and the Hatches goin' to *Carmen* and then me takin' my Missus and her sister, Bess, and four of one suit named Bishop to see *The Three Kings?* Well, I'll own up that I enjoyed wearin' the soup and fish and minglin' amongst the *high polloi* and pretendin' we really was somebody. And I know my wife enjoyed it, too, though they was nothin' said between us at the time.

The next stage was where our friends wasn't good enough for us no more. We used to be tickled to death to spend an evenin' playin' rummy with the Hatches. But all of a sudden they didn't seem to be no fun in it and when Hatch'd call up we'd stall out of it. From the number o' times I told him that I or the Missus was tired out and goin' right to bed, he must of thought we'd got jobs as telephone linemen.

We quit attendin' pitcher shows because the rest o' the audience wasn't the kind o' people you'd care to mix with. We didn't go over to Ben's and dance because they wasn't no class to the crowd there. About once a week we'd beat it to one o' the good hotels down-town, all dressed up like a horse, and have our dinner with the rest o' the E-light. They wasn't nobody talked to us only the waiters, but we could look as much as we liked and it was sport tryin' to guess the names o' the gang at the next table.

Then we took to readin' the society news at breakfast. It used to be that I didn't waste time on nothin' but the market and sportin' pages, but now I pass 'em up and listen w'ile the Missus rattled off what was doin' on the Lake Shore Drive.

Every little w'ile we'd see where So-and-So was at Palm Beach or just goin' there or just comin' back. We got to kiddin' about it.

"Well," I'd say, "we'd better be startin' pretty soon or we'll miss the best part o' the season."

"Yes," the Wife'd say back, "we'd go right now if it wasn't for all them engagements next week."

We kidded and kidded till finally, one night, she forgot we was just kiddin'.

"You didn't take no vacation last summer," she says.

"No," says I. "They wasn't no chance to get away."

"But you promised me," she says, "that you'd take one this winter to make up for it."

"I know I did," I says; "but it'd be a sucker play to take a vacation in weather like this."

"The weather ain't like this everywheres," she says.

"You must of been goin' to night school," I says.

"Another thing you promised me," says she, "was that when you could afford it you'd take me on a real honeymoon trip to make up for the dinky one we had."

"That still goes," I says, "when I can afford it."

"You can afford it now," says she. "We don't owe nothin' and we got money in the bank."

"Yes," I says. "Pretty close to three hundred bucks."

"You forgot somethin'," she says. "You forgot them war babies."

Did I tell you about that? Last fall I done a little dabblin' in Crucial Steel and at this time I'm tellin' you about I still had a hold of it, but stood to pull down six hundred. Not bad, eh?

"It'd be a mistake to let loose now," I says.

"All right," she says. "Hold on, and I hope you lose every cent. You never did care nothin' for me."

Then we done a little spoonin' and then I ast her what was the big idear.

"We ain't swelled on ourself," she says; "but I know and you know that the friends we been associatin' with ain't in our class. They don't know how to dress and they can't talk about nothin' but their goldfish and their meat bills. They don't try to get nowheres, but all they do is play rummy and take in the Majestic. I and you like nice people and good music and things that's worth w'ile. It's a crime for us to be wastin' our time with riff and raff that'd run around barefooted if it wasn't for the police."

"I wouldn't say we'd wasted much time on 'em lately," I says.

"No," says she, "and I've had a better time these last three weeks than I ever had in my life."

"And you can keep right on havin' it," I says.

"I could have a whole lot better time, and you could, too," she says, "if we could get acquainted with some congenial people to go round with; people that's tastes is the same as ourn."

"If any o' them people calls up on the phone," I says, "I'll be as pleasant to 'em as I can."

"You're always too smart," says the Wife. "You don't never pay attention to no schemes o' mine."

"What's the scheme now?"

"You'll find fault with it because I thought it up," she says. "If it was your scheme you'd think it was grand."

"If it really was good you wouldn't be scared to spring it," I says.

"Will you promise to go through with it?" says she.

"If it ain't too ridic'lous," I told her.

"See! I knowed that'd be the way," she says.

"Don't talk crazy," I says. "Where'd we be if we'd went through with every plan you ever sprang?"

"Will you promise to listen to my side of it without actin' cute?" she says.

So I didn't see no harm in goin' that far.

"I want you to take me to Palm Beach," says she. "I want you to take a vacation, and that's where we'll spend it."

"And that ain't all we'd spend," I says.

"Remember your promise," says she.

So I shut up and listened.

The dope she give me was along these lines: We could get special round-trip rate on any o' the railroads and that part of it wouldn't cost nowheres near as much as a man'd naturally think. The hotel rates was pretty steep, but the meals was throwed in, and just imagine what them meals would be! And we'd be stayin' under the same roof with the Vanderbilts and Goulds, and eatin' at the same table, and probably, before we was there a week, callin' 'em Steve and Gus. They was dancin' every night and all the guests danced with each other, and how would it feel fox-trottin' with the president o' the B. & O., or the Delmonico girls from New York! And all Chicago society was down there, and when we met 'em we'd know 'em for life and have some real friends amongst 'em when we got back home.

That's how she had it figured and she must of been practisin' her speech, because it certainly did sound good to me. To make it short, I fell, and dated her up to meet me down-town the next day and call on the railroad bandits. The first one we seen admitted that his was the best route and that he wouldn't only soak us one hundred and forty-seven dollars and seventy cents to and from Palm Beach and back, includin' an apartment from here to Jacksonville and as many stop-overs as we wanted to make. He told us we wouldn't have to write for no hotel accommodations because the hotels had an agent right over on Madison Street that'd be glad to do everything to us.

So we says we'd be back later and then we beat it over to the Florida East Coast's local studio.

"How much for a double room by the week?" I ast the man.

"They ain't no weekly rates," he says. "By the day it'd be twelve dollars and up for two at the Breakers, and fourteen dollars and up at the Poinciana."

"I like the Breakers better," says I.

"You can't get in there," he says. "They're full for the season."

"That's a long spree," I says.

"Can we get in the other hotel?" ast the Wife.

"I can find out," says the man.

"We want a room with bath," says she.

"That'd be more," says he. "That'd be fifteen dollars or sixteen dollars and up."

"What do we want of a bath," I says, "with the whole Atlantic Ocean in the front yard?"

"I'm afraid you'd have trouble gettin' a bath," says the man. "The hotels is both o' them pretty well filled up on account o' the war in Europe."

"What's that got to do with it?" I ast him.

"A whole lot," he says. "The people that usually goes abroad is all down to Palm Beach this winter."

"I don't see why," I says. "If one o' them U-boats hit 'em they'd at least be gettin' their bath for nothin'."

We left him with the understandin' that he was to wire down there and find out what was the best they could give us. We called him up in a couple o' days and he told us we could have a double room, without no bath, at the Poinciana, beginnin' the fifteenth o' February. He didn't know just what the price would be.

Well, I fixed it up to take my vacation startin' the tenth, and sold out my Crucial Steel, and divided the spoils with the railroad company. We decided we'd stop off in St. Augustine two days, because the Missus found out somewheres that they might be two or three o' the Four Hundred lingerin' there, and we didn't want to miss nobody.

"Now," I says, "all we got to do is set round and wait for the tenth o' the month."

"Is that so!" says the Wife. "I suppose you're perfectly satisfied with your clo'es."

"I've got to be," I says, "unless the Salvation Army has somethin' that'll fit me."

"What's the matter with our charge account?" she says.

"I don't like to charge nothin'," I says, "when I know they ain't no chance of ever payin' for it."

"All right," she says, "then we're not goin' to Palm Beach. I'd rather stay home than go down there lookin' like general housework."

"Do you need clo'es yourself?" I ast her.

"I certainly do," she says. "About two hundred dollars' worth. But I got one hundred and fifty dollars o' my own."

"All right," I says. "I'll stand for the other fifty and then we're all set."

"No, we're not," she says. "That just fixes me. But I want you to look as good as I do."

"Nature'll see to that," I says.

But they was no arguin' with her. Our trip, she says, was an investment; it was goin' to get us in right with people worth w'ile. And we wouldn't have a chance in the world unless we looked the part.

So before the tenth come round, we was long two new evenin' gowns, two female sport suits, four or five pairs o' shoes, all colors, one Tuxedo dinner coat, three dress shirts, half a dozen other kinds o' shirts, two pairs o' transparent white trousers, one new business suit and Lord knows how much underwear and how many hats and stockin's. And I had till the fifteenth o' March to pay off the mortgage on the old homestead.

Just as we was gettin' ready to leave for the train the phone rung. It was Mrs. Hatch and she wanted us to come over for a little rummy. I was shavin' and the Missus done the talkin'.

"What did you tell her?" I ast.

"I told her we was goin' away," says the Wife.

"I bet you forgot to mention where we was goin'," I says.

"Pay me," says she.

The Poinciana station's a couple hundred yards from one end o' the hotel, and that means it's close to five miles from the clerk's desk. By the time we'd registered and been gave our key and marathoned another five miles or so to where our room was located at, I was about ready for the inquest. But the Missus was full o' pep and wild to get down to breakfast and look over our stable mates. She says we would eat without changin' our clo'es; people'd forgive us for not dressin' up on account o' just gettin' there. W'ile she was lookin' out the window at the royal palms and buzzards, I moseyed round the room inspectin' where the different doors led to. Pretty near the first one I opened went into a private bath.

"Here," I says; "they've give us the wrong room."

Then my wife seen it and begin to squeal.

"Goody!" she says. "We've got a bath! We've got a bath!"

"But," says I, "they promised we wouldn't have none. It must be a mistake."

"Never you mind about a mistake," she says. "This is our room and they can't chase us out of it."

"We'll chase ourself out," says I. "Rooms with a bath is fifteen and sixteen dollars and up. Rooms without no bath is bad enough."

"We'll keep this room or I won't stay here," she says.

"All right, you win," I says; but I didn't mean it.

I made her set in the lobby down-stairs w'ile I went to the clerk pretendin' that I had to see about our trunk.

"Say," I says to him, "you've made a bad mistake. You told your man in Chicago that we couldn't have no room with a bath, and now you've give us one."

"You're lucky," he says. "A party who had a bath ordered for these two weeks canceled their reservation and now you've got it."

"Lucky, am I?" I says. "And how much is the luck goin' to cost me?"

"It'll be seventeen dollars per day for that room," he says, and turned away to hide a blush.

I went back to my Wife.

"Do you know what we're payin' for that room?" I says. "We're payin' seventeen dollars."

"Well," she says, "our meals is throwed in."

"Yes," says I, "and the hotel furnishes a key."

"You promised in St. Augustine," she says, "that you wouldn't worry no more about expenses."

Well, rather than make a scene in front o' the bellhops and the few millionaires that was able to be about at that hour o' the mornin', I just says "All right!" and led her into the dinin'-room.

The head waiter met us at the door and turned us over to his assistant. Then some more assistants took hold of us one at a time and we was relayed to a beautiful spot next door to the kitchen and bounded on all sides by posts and pillars. It was all right for me, but a whole lot too private for the Missus; so I had to call the fella that had been our pacemaker on the last lap.

"We don't like this table," I says.

"It's the only one I can give you," he says.

I slipped him half a buck.

"Come to think of it," he says, "I believe they's one I forgot all about."

And he moved us way up near the middle o' the place.

Say, you ought to seen that dinin'-room! From one end of it to the other is a toll call, and if a man that was settin' at the table farthest from the kitchen ordered roast lamb he'd get mutton. At that, they was crowded for fair and it kept the head waiters hustlin' to find trough space for one and all.

It was round nine o'clock when we put in our modest order for orange juice, oatmeal, liver and bacon, and cakes and coffee, and a quarter to ten or so when our waiter returned from the nearest orange grove with Exhibit A. We amused ourself meanw'ile by givin' our neighbors the once over and wonderin' which o' them was goin' to pal with us. As far as I could tell from the glances we received, they wasn't no immediate danger of us bein' annoyed by attentions.

They was only a few womenfolks on deck and they was dressed pretty quiet; so quiet that the Missus was scared she'd shock 'em with the sport skirt she'd bought in Chi. Later on in the day, when the girls come out for their dress parade, the Missus' costume made about as much noise as eatin' marshmallows in a foundry.

After breakfast we went to the room for a change o' raiment. I put on my white trousers and wished to heaven that the sun'd go under a cloud till I got used to tellin' people without words just where my linen began and I left off. The rest o' my outfit was white shoes that hurt, and white sox, and a two-dollar silk shirt that showed up a zebra, and a red tie and a soft collar and a blue coat. The Missus wore a sport suit that I won't try and describe—you'll probably see it on her sometime in the next five years.

We went down-stairs again and out on the porch, where some o' the old birds was takin' a sun bath.

"Where now?" I says.

"The beach, o' course," says the Missus.

"Where is it at?" I ast her.

"I suppose," she says, "that we'll find it somewheres near the ocean."

"I don't believe you can stand this climate," says I.

"The ocean," she says, "must be down at the end o' that avenue, where most everybody seems to be headed."

"Havin' went to our room and back twice, I don't feel like another five-mile hike," I says.

"It ain't no five miles," she says; "but let's ride, anyway."

"Come on," says I, pointin' to a street-car that was standin' in the middle o' the avenue.

"Oh, no," she says. "I've watched and found out that the real people takes them funny-lookin' wheel chairs."

I was wonderin' what she meant when one o' them pretty near run over us. It was part bicycle, part go-cart and part African. In the one we dodged they was room for one passenger, but some o' them carried two.

"I wonder what they'd soak us for the trip," I says.

"Not more'n a dime, I don't believe," says the Missus.

But when we'd hired one and been w'isked down under the palms and past the golf field to the bath-house, we was obliged to part with fifty cents legal and tender.

"I feel much refreshed," I says. "I believe when it comes time to go back I'll be able to walk."

The bath-house is acrost the street from the other hotel, the Breakers, that the man had told us was full for the season. Both buildin's fronts on the ocean; and boy, it's some ocean! I bet they's fish in there that never seen each other!

"Oh, let's go bathin' right away!" says the Missus.

"Our suits is up to the other beanery," says I, and I was glad of it. They wasn't nothin' temptin' to me about them man-eatin' waves.

But the Wife's a persistent cuss.

"We won't go to-day," she says, "but we'll go in the bath-house and get some rooms for to-morrow."

The bath-house porch was a ringer for the *Follies*. Here and down on the beach was where you seen the costumes at this time o' day. I was so busy rubberin' that I passed the entrance door three times without noticin' it. From the top o' their heads to the bottom o' their feet the girls was a mess o' colors. They wasn't no two dressed alike and if any one o' them had of walked down State Street we'd of had an epidemic o' stiff neck to contend with in Chi. Finally the Missus grabbed me and hauled me into the office.

"Two private rooms," she says to the clerk. "One lady and one gent."

"Five dollars a week apiece," he says. "But we're all filled up."

"You ought to be all locked up!" I says.

"Will you have anything open to-morrow?" ast the Missus.

"I think I can fix you then," he says.

"What do we get for the five?" I ast him.

"Private room and we take care o' your bathin' suit," says he.

"How much if you don't take care o' the suit?" I ast him. "My suit's been gettin' along fine with very little care."

"Five dollars a week apiece," he says, "and if you want the rooms you better take 'em, because they're in big demand."

By the time we'd closed this grand bargain, everybody'd moved offen the porch and down to the water, where a couple dozen o' them went in for a swim and the rest set and watched. They was a long row o' chairs on the beach for spectators and we was just goin' to flop into two o' them when another bandit come up and told us it'd cost a dime apiece per hour.

"We're goin' to be here two weeks," I says. "Will you sell us two chairs?"

He wasn't in no comical mood, so we sunk down on the sand and seen the show from there. We had plenty o' company that preferred these kind o' seats free to the chairs at ten cents a whack.

Besides the people that was in the water gettin' knocked down by the waves and pretendin' like they enjoyed it, about half o' the gang on the sand was wearin' bathin' suits just to be clubby. You could tell by lookin' at the suits that they hadn't never been wet and wasn't intended for no such ridic'lous purpose. I wisht I could describe 'em to you, but it'd take a female to do it right.

One little girl, either fourteen or twenty-four, had white silk slippers and sox that come pretty near up to her ankles, and from there to her knees it was just plain Nature. Northbound from her knees was pair of bicycle trousers that disappeared when they come to the bottom of her Mother Hubbard. This here garment was a thing without no neck or sleeves that begin bulgin' at the top and spread out gradual all the way down, like a croquette. To top her off, she had a jockey cap; and—believe me—I'd of played her mount acrost the board. They was plenty o' class in the field with her, but nothin' that approached her speed. Later on I seen her several times round the hotel, wearin' somethin' near the same outfit, without the jockey cap and with longer croquettes.

We set there in the sand till people begun to get up and leave. Then we trailed along back o' them to the Breakers' porch, where they was music to dance and stuff to inhale.

"We'll grab a table," I says to the Missus. "I'm dyin' o' thirst."

But I was allowed to keep on dyin'.

"I can serve you somethin' soft," says the waiter.

"I'll bet you can't!" I says.

"You ain't got no locker here?" he says.

"What do you mean—locker?" I ast him.

"It's the locker liquor law," he says. "We can serve you a drink if you own your own bottles."

"I'd just as soon own a bottle," I says. "I'll become the proprietor of a bottle o' beer."

"It'll take three or four hours to get it for you," he says, "and you'd have to order it through the order desk. If you're stoppin' at one o' the hotels and want a drink once in a w'ile, you better get busy and put in an order."

So I had to watch the Missus put away a glass of orange juice that cost forty cents and was just the same size as they give us for breakfast free for nothin'. And, not havin' had nothin' to make me forget that my feet hurt, I was obliged to pay another four bits for an Afromobile to cart us back to our own boardin' house.

"Well," says the Missus when we got there, "it's time to wash up and go to lunch."

"Wash up and go to lunch, then," I says; "but I'm goin' to investigate this here locker liquor or liquor locker law."

So she got her key and beat it, and I limped to the bar.

"I want a highball," I says to the boy.

"What's your number?" says he.

"It varies," I says. "Sometimes I can hold twenty and sometimes four or five makes me sing."

"I mean, have you got a locker here?" he says.

"No; but I want to get one," says I.

"The gent over there to the desk will fix you," says he.

So over to the desk I went and ast for a locker.

"What do you drink?" ast the gent.

"I'm from Chicago," I says. "I drink bourbon."

"What's your name and room number?" he says, and I told him.

Then he ast me how often did I shave and what did I think o' the Kaiser and what my name was before I got married, and if I had any intentions of ever running an elevator. Finally he says I was all right.

"I'll order you some bourbon," he says. "Anything else?"

I was goin' to say no, but I happened to remember that the Wife generally always wants a bronix before dinner. So I had to also put in a bid for a bottle o' gin and bottles o' the Vermouth brothers, Tony and Pierre. It wasn't till later that I appreciated what a grand law this here law was. When I got my drinks I paid ten cents apiece for 'em for service, besides payin' for the bottles o' stuff to drink. And, besides that, about every third highball or bronix I ordered, the waiter'd bring back word that I was just out of ingredients and then they'd be another delay w'ile they sent to the garage for more. If they had that law all over the country they'd soon be an end o' drinkin', because everybody'd get so mad they'd kill each other.

My cross-examination had took quite a long time, but when I got to my room the Wife wasn't back from lunch yet and I had to cover the Marathon route all over again and look her up. We only had the one key to the room, and o' course couldn't expect no more'n that at the price.

The Missus had brought one o' the daily programs they get out and she knowed just what we had to do the rest o' the day.

"For the next couple hours," she says, "we can suit ourself."

"All right," says I. "It suits me to take off my shoes and lay down."

"I'll rest, too," she says; "but at half past four we have to be in the Cocoanut Grove for tea and dancin'. And then we come back to the room and dress for dinner. Then we eat and then we set around till the evenin' dance starts. Then we dance till we're ready for bed."

"Who do we dance all these dances with?" I ast her.

"With whoever we get acquainted with," she says.

"All right," says I; "but let's be careful."

Well, we took our nap and then we followed schedule and had our tea in the Cocoanut Grove. You know how I love tea! My feet was still achin' and the Missus couldn't talk me into no dance.

When we'd set there an hour and was saturated with tea, the Wife says it was time to go up and change into our Tuxedos. I was all in when we reached the room and willin' to even pass up supper and nestle in the hay, but I was informed that the biggest part o' the day's doin's was yet to come. So from six o'clock till after seven I wrestled with studs, and hooks and eyes that didn't act like they'd ever met before and wasn't anxious to get acquainted, and then down we went again to the dinin'-room.

"How about a little bronix before the feed?" I says.

"It would taste good," says the Missus.

So I called Eph and give him the order. In somethin' less than half an hour he come back empty-handed.

"You ain't got no cocktail stuff," he says.

"I certainly have," says I. "I ordered it early this afternoon."

"Where at?" he ast me.

"Over in the bar," I says.

"Oh, the regular bar!" he says. "That don't count. You got to have stuff at the service bar to get it served in here."

"I ain't as thirsty as I thought I was," says I.

"Me, neither," says the Missus.

So we went ahead and ordered our meal, and w'ile we was waitin' for it a young couple come and took the other two chairs at our table. They didn't have to announce through a megaphone that they was honeymooners. It was wrote all over 'em. They was reachin' under the table for each other's hand every other minute, and when they wasn't doin' that they was smilin' at each other or gigglin' at nothin'. You couldn't feel that good and be payin' seventeen dollars a day for room and board unless you was just married or somethin'.

I thought at first their company'd be fun, but after a few meals it got like the southern cookin' and begun to undermine the health.

The conversation between they and us was what you could call limited. It took place the next day at lunch. The young husband thought he was about to take a bite o' the entry, which happened to be roast mutton with sirup; but he couldn't help from lookin' at her at the same time and his empty fork started for his face prongs up.

"Look out for your eye," I says.

He dropped the fork and they both blushed till you could see it right through the sunburn. Then they give me a Mexican look and our acquaintance was at an end.

This first night, when we was through eatin', we wandered out in the lobby and took seats where we could watch the passin' show. The men was all dressed like me, except I was up to date and had on a mushroom shirt, w'ile they was sportin' the old-fashioned concrete bosom. The women's dresses begun at the top with a belt, and some o' them stopped at the mezzanine floor, w'ile others went clear down to the basement and helped keep the rugs clean. They was one that must of thought it was the Fourth o' July. From the top of her head to where the top of her bathin' suit had left off, she was a red, red rose. From there to the top of her gown was white, and her gown, what they was of it—was blue.

"My!" says the Missus. "What stunnin' gowns!"

"Yes," I says, "and you could have one just like 'em if you'd take the shade offen the piano lamp at home and cut it down to the right size."

Round ten o'clock we wandered in the Palm Garden, where the dancin' had been renewed. The Wife wanted to plunge right in the mazes o' the foxy trot.

"I'll take some courage first," says I. And then was when I found out that it cost you ten cents extra besides the tip to pay for a drink that you already owned in fee simple.

Well, I guess we must of danced about six dances together and had that many quarrels before she was ready to go to bed. And oh, how grand that old hay-pile felt when I finally bounced into it!

The next day we went to the ocean at the legal hour—half past eleven. I never had so much fun in my life. The surf was runnin' high, I heard 'em say; and I don't know which I'd rather do, go bathin' in the ocean at Palm Beach when the surf is runnin' high, or have a dentist get one o' my molars ready for a big inlay at a big outlay. Once in a w'ile I managed to not get throwed on my head when a wave hit me. As for swimmin', you had just as much chance as if you was at State and Madison at the noon

hour. And before I'd been in a minute they was enough salt in my different features to keep the Blackstone hotel runnin' all through the onion
season.

The Missus enjoyed it just as much as me. She tried to pretend at first,
and when she got floored she'd give a squeal that was supposed to mean
heavenly bliss. But after she'd been bruised from head to feet and her
hair looked and felt like spinach with French dressin', and she'd drank
all she could hold o' the Gulf Stream, she didn't resist none when I drug
her in to shore and staggered with her up to our private rooms at five a
week per each.

Without consultin' her, I went to the desk at the Casino and told 'em
they could have them rooms back.

"All right," says the clerk, and turned our keys over to the next in line.

"How about a refund?"I ast him; but he was waitin' on somebody else.

After that we done our bathin' in the tub. But we was down to the
beach every morning at eleven-thirty to watch the rest o' them get batted
round.

And at half past twelve every day we'd follow the crowd to the
Breakers' porch and dance together, the Missus and I. Then it'd be back
to the other hostelry, sometimes limpin' and sometimes in an Afromobile,
and a drink or two in the Palm Garden before lunch. And after lunch
we'd lay down; or we'd pay some Eph two or three dollars to pedal us
through the windin' jungle trail, that was every bit as wild as the Art
Institute; or we'd ferry acrost Lake Worth to West Palm Beach and take
in a movie, or we'd stand in front o' the portable Fifth Avenue stores
w'ile the Missus wished she could have this dress or that hat, or somethin'
else that she wouldn't of looked at if she'd been home and in her right
mind. But always at half past four we had to live up to the rules and be
in the Cocoanut Grove for tea and some more foxy trottin'. And then it
was dress for dinner, eat dinner, watch the parade and wind up the
glorious day with more dancin'.

I bet you any amount you name that the Castles in their whole life
haven't danced together as much as I and the Missus did at Palm Beach.
I'd of gave five dollars if even one o' the waiters had took her offen my
hands for one dance. But I knowed that if I made the offer public they'd
of been a really serious quarrel between us instead o' just the minor
brawls occasioned by steppin' on each other's feet.

She made a discovery one night. She found out that they was a place
called the Beach Club where most o' the real people disappeared to
every evenin' after dinner. She says we would have to go there too.

"But I ain't a member," I says.

"Then find out how you get to be one," she says.

So to the Beach Club I went and made inquiries.

"You'll have to be introduced by a guy that already belongs," says the man at the door.

"Who belongs?" I ast him.

"Hundreds o' people," he says. "Who do you know?"

"Two waiters, two barkeepers and one elevator boy," I says.

He laughed, but his laugh didn't get me no membership card and I had to dance three or four extra times the next day to square myself with the Missus.

She made another discovery and it cost me six bucks. She found out that, though the meals in the regular dinin'-room was included in the triflin' rates per day, the real people had at least two o' their meals in the garden grill and paid extra for 'em. We tried it for one meal and I must say I enjoyed it—all but the check.

"We can't keep up that clip," I says to her.

"We could," says she, "if you wasn't spendin' so much on your locker."

"The locker's a matter o' life and death," I says. "They ain't no man in the world that could dance as much with their own wife as I do and live without liquid stimulus."

When we'd been there four days she got to be on speakin' terms with the ladies' maid that hung round the lobby and helped put the costumes back on when they slipped off. From this here maid the Missus learned who was who, and the information was relayed to me as soon as they was a chance. We'd be settin' on the porch when I'd feel an elbow in my ribs all of a sudden. I'd look up at who was passin' and then try and pretend I was excited.

"Who is it?" I'd whisper.

"That's Mrs. Vandeventer," the Wife'd say. "Her husband's the biggest street-car conductor in Philadelphia."

Or somebody'd set beside us at the beach or in the Palm Garden and my ribs would be all battered up before the Missus was calm enough to tip me off.

"The Vincents," she'd say; "the canned prune people."

It was a little bit thrillin' at first to be rubbin' elbows with all them celeb's; but it got so finally that I could walk out o' the dinin'-room right behind Scotti, the opera singer, without forgettin' that my feet hurt.

The Washington's Birthday Ball brought 'em all together at once, and the Missus pointed out eight and nine at a time and got me so mixed up that I didn't know Pat Vanderbilt from Maggie Rockefeller. The only one you couldn't make no mistake about was a Russian count that you couldn't pronounce. He was buyin' bay mules or somethin' for the Russian government, and he was in ambush.

"They say he can't hardly speak a word of English," says the Missus.

"If I knowed the word for barber shop in Russia," says I, "I'd tell him they was one in this hotel."

In our mail box the next mornin' they was a notice that our first week was up and all we owed was one hundred and forty-six dollars and fifty cents. The bill for room and meals was one hundred and nineteen dollars. The rest was for gettin' clo'es pressed and keepin' the locker damp.

I didn't have no appetite for breakfast. I told the Wife I'd wait up in the room and for her to come when she got through. When she blew in I had my speech prepared.

"Look here," I says; "this is our eighth day in Palm Beach society. You're on speakin' terms with a maid and I've got acquainted with half a dozen o' the male hired help. It's cost us about a hundred and sixty-five dollars, includin' them private rooms down to the Casino and our Afro-mobile trips, and this and that. You know a whole lot o' swell people by sight, but you can't talk to 'em. It'd be just as much satisfaction and hundreds o' dollars cheaper to look up their names in the telephone directory at home; then phone to 'em and, when you got 'em, tell 'em it was the wrong number. That way, you'd get 'em to speak to you at least.

"As for sport," I says, "we don't play golf and we don't play tennis and we don't swim. We go through the same program o' doin' nothin' every day. We dance, but we don't never change partners. For twelve dollars I could buy a phonograph up home and I and you could trot round the livin'-room all evenin' without no danger o' havin' some o' them fancy birds cave our shins in. And we could have twice as much liquid refreshments up there at about a twentieth the cost.

"That Gould I met on the train comin' down," I says, "was a even bigger liar than I give him credit for. He says that when he was here people pestered him to death by comin' up and speakin' to him. We ain't had to dodge nobody or hide behind a cocoanut tree to remain exclusive. He says Palm Beach was too common for him. What he should of said was that it was too lonesome. If they was just one white man here that'd listen to my stuff I wouldn't have no kick. But it ain't no pleasure tellin' stories to the Ephs. They laugh whether it's good or not, and then want a dime for laughin'.

"As for our clo'es," I says, "they would be all right for a couple o' days' stay. But the dames round here, and the men, too, has somethin' different to put on for every mornin', afternoon and night. You've wore your two evenin' gowns so much that I just have to snap my finger at the hooks and they go and grab the right eyes.

"The meals would be grand," I says, "if the cook didn't keep gettin' mixed up and puttin' puddin' sauce on the meat and gravy on the pie.

"I'm glad we've been to Palm Beach," I says. "I wouldn't of missed it for nothin'. But the ocean won't be no different to-morrow than it was yesterday, and the same for the daily program. It don't even rain here, to give us a little variety.

"Now what do you say," I says, "to us just settlin' this bill, and whatever we owe since then, and beatin' it out o' here just as fast as we can go?"

The Missus didn't say nothin' for a w'ile. She was too busy cryin'. She knowed that what I'd said was the truth, but she wouldn't give up without a struggle.

"Just three more days," she says finally. "If we don't meet somebody worth meetin' in the next three days I'll go wherever you want to take me."

"All right," I says; "three more days it is. What's a little matter o' sixty dollars?"

Well, in them next two days and a half she done some desperate flirtin', but as it was all with women I didn't get jealous. She picked out some o' the E-light o' Chicago and tried every trick she could think up. She told 'em their noses was shiny and offered 'em her powder. She stepped on their white shoes just so's to get a chance to beg their pardon. She told 'em their clo'es was unhooked, and then unhooked 'em so's she could hook 'em up again. She tried to loan 'em her finger-nail tools. When she seen one fannin' herself she'd say: "Excuse me, Mrs. So-and-So; but we got the coolest room in the hotel, and I'd be glad to have you go up there and quit perspirin'." But not a rise did she get.

Not till the afternoon o' the third day o' grace. And I don't know if I ought to tell you this or not—only I'm sure you won't spill it nowheres.

We'd went up in our room after lunch. I was tired out and she was discouraged. We'd set round for over an hour, not sayin' or doin' nothin'.

I wanted to talk about the chance of us gettin' away the next mornin', but I didn't dast bring up the subject.

The Missus complained of it bein' hot and opened the door to leave the breeze go through. She was settin' in a chair near the doorway, pretendin' to read the *Palm Beach News*. All of a sudden she jumped up and kind o' hissed at me.

"What's the matter?" I says, springin' from the lounge.

"Come here!" she says, and went out the door into the hall.

I got there as fast as I could, thinkin' it was a rat or a fire. But the Missus just pointed to a lady walkin' away from us, six or seven doors down.

"It's Mrs. Potter," she says; "*the* Mrs. Potter from Chicago!"

"Oh!" I says, puttin' all the excitement I could into my voice.

And I was just startin' back into the room when I seen Mrs. Potter stop and turn round and come to'rd us. She stopped again maybe twenty feet from where the Missus was standin'.

"Are you on this floor?" she says.

The Missus shook like a leaf.

"Yes," says she, so low you couldn't hardly hear her.

"Please see that they's some towels put in 559," says *the* Mrs. Potter from Chicago.

24. Heroes of Popular Fiction

It would be difficult to find three more popular books in any era than Owen Wister's *The Virginian* (1902), Burt L. Standish's *Frank Merriwell at Yale* (1903), and Edgar Rice Burrough's *Tarzan of the Apes* (1914). Although generally scorned by the custodians of culture, these works nonetheless won wide approval. Like folktales in any culture, they succeeded because they expressed popular hopes and fears.

Wister's book was the first "western," launching a genre that played a leading role in twentieth century popular fiction. *The Virginian,* dedicated to Theodore Roosevelt, appeared in April 1902. Its surprised publisher was obliged to reprint fifteen times before the following January. A dramatization ran four months in New York and eight years on the road. In the following selection Wister's narrator first sees the Virginian and then observes him in confrontation with an archtypical "badman," Trampas.

Burt L. Standish, whose real name was Gilbert Patten, had already published more than a score of Frank Merriwell tales when *Frank Merriwell at Yale* appeared. Merriwell was the classic dime novel hero, an infallible all-American whose chronic successes thrilled millions of readers in the pulp journals.

Until he conceived of Tarzan as a protagonist, Edgar Rice Burroughs was a struggling hack. After Tarzan he became the best-selling American author of all time and a millionaire. Thirty-six million copies of the Tarzan stories were distributed and beginning in 1918 the motion pictures took up the theme with astonishing success. The reason is related less to Burroughs' ability as a writer than to the mood of the American people at the time he wrote. In the excerpt below Tarzan receives his first taste of civilization after a life lived in the jungle with apes.

The Virginian
OWEN WISTER

Lounging there at ease against the wall was a slim young giant, more beautiful than pictures. His broad, soft hat was pushed back; a loose-knotted, dull-scarlet handkerchief sagged from his throat; and one casual thumb was hooked in the cartridge-belt that slanted across his hips. He had plainly come many miles from somewhere across the vast horizon, as the dust upon him showed. His boots were white with it. His overalls were gray with it. The weather-beaten bloom of his face shone through it duskily, as the ripe peaches look upon their trees in a dry season. But no dinginess of travel or shabbiness of attire could tarnish the splendor that radiated from his youth and strength. The old man upon whose temper his remarks were doing such deadly work was combed and curried to a finish, a bridegroom swept and garnished; but alas for age! Had I been the bride, I should have taken the giant, dust and all. . . .

The saloon . . . was very quiet and orderly. Beer in quart bottles at a dollar I had never met before; but saving its price, I found no complaint to make of it. Through folding doors I passed from the bar proper with its bottles and elk head back to the hall with its various tables. I saw a man sliding cards from a case, and across the table from him another man laying counters down. Near by was a second dealer pulling cards from the bottom of a pack, and opposite him a solemn old rustic piling and changing coins upon the cards which lay already exposed.

But now I heard a voice that drew my eyes to the far corner of the room.

"Why didn't you stay in Arizona?"

Harmless looking words as I write them down here. Yet at the sound of them I noticed the eyes of the others directed to that corner. What answer was given to them I did not hear, nor did I see who spoke. Then came another remark.

"Well, Arizona's no place for amatures."

This time the two card dealers that I stood near began to give a part of their attention to the group that sat in the corner. There was in me a

Owen Wister, *The Virginian* (New York, Macmillan Co., 1902), 4–5, 26–30.

desire to leave this room. So far my hours at Medicine Bow had seemed to glide beneath a sunshine of merriment, of easy-going jocularity. This was suddenly gone, like the wind changing to north in the middle of a warm day. But I stayed, being ashamed to go.

Five or six players sat over in the corner at a round table where counters were piled. Their eyes were close upon their cards, and one seemed to be dealing a card at a time to each, with pauses and betting between. Steve was there, and the Virginian; the others were new faces.

"No place for amatures," repeated the voice; and now I saw that it was the dealer's. There was in his countenance the same ugliness that his words conveyed.

"Who's that talkin'?" said one of the men near me, in a low voice.

"Trampas."

"What's he?"

"Cow-puncher, bronco-buster, tin-horn, most anything."

"Who's he talkin' at?"

"Think it's the black-headed guy he's talking at."

"That ain't supposed to be safe, is it?"

"Guess we're all goin' to find out in a few minutes."

"Been trouble between 'em?"

"They've not met before. Trampas don't enjoy losin' to a stranger."

"Fello's from Arizona, yu' say?"

"No. Virginia. He's recently back from havin' a look at Arizona. Went down there last year for a change. Works for the Sunk Creek outfit." And then the dealer lowered his voice still further and said something in the other man's ear, causing him to grin. After which both of them looked at me.

There had been silence over in the corner; but now the man Trampas spoke again.

"*And* ten," said he, sliding out some chips from before him. Very strange it was to hear him, how he contrived to make those words a personal taunt. The Virginian was looking at his cards. He might have been deaf.

"*And* twenty," said the next player, easily.

The next threw his cards down.

It was now the Virginian's turn to bet, or leave the game, and he did not speak at once.

Therefore Trampas spoke. "Your bet, you son-of-a-bitch."

The Virginian's pistol came out, and his hand lay on the table holding it unaimed. And with a voice as gentle as ever, the voice that sounded almost like a caress, but drawling a very little more than usual, so that there was almost a space between each word, he issued his orders to the man Trampas:—

"When you call me that, *smile!*" And he looked at Trampas across the table.

Yes, the voice was gentle. But in my ears it seemed as if somewhere the bell of death was ringing; and silence, like a stroke, fell on the large room. All men present, as if by some magnetic current, had become aware of this crisis. In my ignorance, and the total stoppage of my thoughts, I stood stock-still, and noticed various people crouching, or shifting their positions.

"Sit quiet," said the dealer, scornfully to the man near me. "Can't you see he don't want to push trouble? He has handed Trampas the choice to back down or draw his steel."

Then, with equal suddenness and ease, the room came out of its strangeness. Voices and cards, the click of chips, the puff of tobacco, glasses lifted to drink,—this level of smooth relaxation hinted no more plainly of what lay beneath than does the surface tell the depth of the sea.

For Trampas had made his choice. And that choice was not to "draw his steel." If it was knowledge that he sought he had found it, and no mistake! We heard no further reference to what he had been pleased to style "amatures." In no company would the black-headed man who had visited Arizona be rated a novice at the cool art of self-preservation.

One doubt remained: what kind of a man was Trampas? A public back-down is an unfinished thing,—for some natures at least. I looked at his face, and thought it sullen, but tricky rather than courageous.

Something had been added to my knowledge also. Once again I had heard applied to the Virginian that epithet which Steve so freely used. The same words, identical to the letter. But this time they had produced a pistol. "When you call me that, *smile!*" So I perceived a new example of the old truth, that the letter means nothing until the spirit gives it life.

Frank Merriwell at Yale
BURT L. STANDISH

Frank went to his room with his head in a whirl. He had dreamed of working hard to secure a place on the freshman team, but he had not dreamed there was a possibility that he would be given a trial in the regular Yale nine during his first year in college.

Merriwell knew well enough that Phillips men * were given the preference in everything at Yale as a rule, for they had friends to pull them through, while the fellows who had been prepared by private tutors lacked such an advantage.

But Frank had likewise discovered that in most cases a man was judged fairly at Yale, and he could become whatever he chose to make himself, in case he had the ability.

The Phillips man might have the advantage at the start, but he could not hold the advantage unless he proved himself worthy. If the unknown student had nerve and determination he could win his way for all of the wire pulling of the friends of some rival who was not so capable.

Frank had heard the cry which had been raised at that time that the old spirit of democracy was dying out at Yale, and that great changes had taken place there. He had heard that Yale was getting to be more like another college, where the swell set are strongly in evidence and the senior likely to be very exclusive, having but a small circle of speaking acquaintances.

It was said that in the old days the Yale junior or senior knew everybody worth knowing. But this had changed. The blue-blooded aristocrat had appeared at Yale, and he had chosen his circle of acquaintances with great care. To all outward appearances, this man believed that outside his limited circle there was nobody at Yale worth knowing.

Professor Scotch, Frank's guardian, had read this in certain newspaper articles relating to Yale, and had expressed his regret that such should be the case.

After coming to Yale Frank kept his eyes open to see to what extent such a state of affairs obtained. At first it had seemed that the newspapers

* Phillips Academy was a private, Eastern, preparatory school which sent many of its graduates to Yale. [Ed.]

Burt L. Standish, Frank Merriwell at Yale (Philadelphia, David McKay, 1903), 257–262, 372–383.

were right, but he came to see that his position as freshman did not give him the proper opportunity to judge.

In the course of time Frank came to believe that the old spirit was still powerful at Yale. There were a limited number of young gentlemen who plainly considered themselves superior beings, and who positively refused to make acquaintances outside a certain limit; but those men held no positions in athletics, were seldom of prominence in the societies, and were regarded as cads by the men most worth knowing. They were to be pitied, not envied. . . .

The democratic spirit at Yale came mainly from athletics, as Frank soon discovered. . . . In athletics strength and skill win, regardles of money or family; so it happened that the poorest man in the university stood a show of becoming the lion and idol of the whole body of young men. . . .

Frank had proven that it was not necessary for a man to drink at Yale in order to be esteemed as a good fellow. Frank was a total abstainer, and his friends had found that nothing would induce him to drink or smoke. At first they ridiculed him, but they came to secretly admire him, and it is certain that his example was productive of no small amount of good.

Frank's acquaintances declared he had a mighty nerve, for he was able to travel with a crowd that drank and smoked, and still refrained from doing either. That was something difficult for them to understand.

It was apparent to everybody that Merriwell's popularity did not depend on his ability to absorb beer or his generosity in opening fizz. It came from his sterling qualities, his ability as an athlete, his natural magnetism, and his genial, sunny nature. Although he was refined and gentlemanly, there was not the least suggestion of anything soft or effeminate about him. . . .

A monster crowd had gathered to witness the deciding game. Blue and crimson were the prevailing colors. On the bleachers at one side of the grandstand sat hundreds upon hundreds of Harvard men, cheering all together and being answered by the hundreds of Yale men on the other side of the grand stand. There were plenty of ladies and citizens present and the scene was inspiring. A band of music served to quicken the blood in the veins which were already throbbing.

There was short preliminary practice, and then at exactly three o'clock the umpire walked down behind the home plate and called: "Play ball!" . . .

✿　✿　✿

Yale took the field, and as the boys in blue trotted out, the familiar Yale yell broke from hundreds of throats. Blue pennants were wildly fluttering, the band was playing a lively air, and for the moment it seemed as if the sympathy of the majority of the spectators was with Yale.

But when Hinkley, Harvard's great single hitter, who always headed the batting list, walked out with his pet "wagon tongue," a different sound swept over the multitude, and the air seemed filled with crimson pennants.

Merriwell went into the box, and the umpire broke open a pasteboard box, brought out a ball that was wrapped in tin foil, removed the covering, and tossed the snowy sphere to the freshman pitcher Yale had so audaciously stacked up against Harvard.

Frank looked the box over, examined the rubber plate, and seemed to make himself familiar with every inch of the ground in his vicinity. Then he faced Hinkley, and a moment later delivered the first ball.

Hinkley smashed it on the nose, and it was past Merriwell in a second, skipping along the ground and passing over second base just beyond the baseman's reach, although he made a good run for it.

The center fielder secured the ball and returned it to second, but Hinkley had made a safe single off the very first ball delivered.

Harvard roared, while the Yale crowd was silent.

A great mob of freshmen was up from New Haven to see the game and watch Merriwell's work, and some of them immediately expressed disappointment and dismay.

"Here is where Merriwell meets his Waterloo," said Sport Harris. "He'll be batted out before the game is fairly begun."

That was quite enough to arouse Rattleton, who heard the remark.

"I'll bet you ten dollars he isn't batted out at all," spluttered Harry, fiercely. "Here's my money, too!"

"Make it twenty-five and I will go you," drawled Harris.

"All right, I'll make it twenty-five."

The money was staked.

Derry, also a heavy hitter, was second on Harvard's list. Derry had a bat that was as long and as large as the regulations would permit, and as heavy as lead; yet, despite the weight of the stick, the strapping Vermonter handled it as if it were a feather.

Frank sent up a coaxer, but Derry refused to be coaxed. The second ball was high, but Derry cracked it for two bags, and Hinkley got around to third.

It began to seem as if Merriwell would be batted out in the first inning, and the Yale crowd looked weary and disgusted at the start.

The next batter fouled out, however, and the next one sent a red-hot liner directly at Merriwell. There was no time to get out of the way, so

Frank caught it, snapped the ball to third, found Hinkley off the bag, and retired the side without a score.

This termination of the first half of the inning was so swift and unexpected that it took some seconds for the spectators to realize what had happened. When they did, however, Yale was wildly cheered.

"What do you think about it now, Harris?" demanded Harry, exultantly.

"I think Merriwell saved his neck by a dead lucky catch," was the answer. "If he had missed that ball he would have been removed within five minutes."

Pierson, who was sitting on the bench, was looking doubtful, and he held a consultation with Costigan, captain of the team, as soon as the latter came in from third base.

Costigan asked Frank how he felt, and Merriwell replied that he had never felt better in his life, so it was decided to let him see what he could do in the box the next inning.

Yedding, who was in the box for Harvard, could not have been in better condition, and the first three Yale men to face him went out in one-two-three order, making the first inning a whitewash for both sides.

As Merriwell went into the box the second time there were cries for Heffiner, who was on the bench, ready to pitch if forced to do so, for all of the fact that it might ruin his arm forever, so far as ball playing was concerned.

In trying to deceive the first man up Merriwell gave him three balls in succession. Then he was forced to put them over. He knew the batter would take one or two, and so he sent two straight, swift ones directly over, and two strikes were called.

Then came the critical moment, for the next ball pitched would settle the matter. Frank sent in a rise and the batter struck at it, missed it, and was declared out, the ball having landed with a "plunk" in the hands of the catcher.

The next batter got first on a single, but the third man sent an easy one to Frank, who gathered it in, threw the runner out at second, and the second baseman sent the ball to first in time to retire the side on a double play.

"You are all right, Merriwell, old man," enthusiastically declared Heffiner, as Frank came in to the bench. "They haven't been able to score off you yet, and they won't be able to touch you at all after you get into gear."

Pierson was relieved, and Costigan looked well satisfied.

"Now we must have some scores, boys," said the captain.

But Yedding showed that he was out for blood, for he allowed but one safe hit, and again retired Yale without a score.

Surely it was a hot game, and excitement was running high. Would Harvard be able to score the next time? That was the question everybody was asking.

Yedding came to the bat in this inning, and Merriwell struck him out with ease, while not another man got a safe hit, although one got first on the shortstop's error.

The Yale crowd cheered like Indians when Harvard was shut out for the third time, the freshmen seeming to yell louder than all the others. They originated a cry which was like this:

"He is doing very well! Who? Why, Merriwell!"

Merriwell was the first man up, and Yedding did his best to get square by striking the freshman out. In this he was successful, much to his satisfaction.

But no man got a hit, and the third inning ended as had the others, neither side having made a run.

The fourth opened in breathless suspense, but it was quickly over, neither side getting a man beyond second.

It did not seem possible that this thing could continue much longer, but the fifth inning brought the same result, although Yale succeeded in getting a man to third with only one out. An attempt to sacrifice him home failed, and a double play was made, retiring the side.

Harvard opened the sixth by batting a ball straight at Yale's shortstop, who played tag with it, chasing it around his feet long enough to allow the batter to reach first. It was not a hit, but an error for short.

This seemed to break the Yale team up somewhat. The runner tried for second on the first ball pitched, and Yale's catcher overthrew, although he had plenty of time to catch the man. The runner kept on to third and got it on a slide.

Now Harvard rejoiced. Although he had not obtained a hit, the man had reached third on two errors, and there was every prospect of scoring.

Merriwell did not seem to lose his temper or his coolness. He took plenty of time to let everybody get quieted down, and then he quickly struck out the next man. The third man, however, managed to hit the ball fairly and knocked a fly into left field. It was gathered in easily, but the man on third held the bag till the fly was caught and made a desperate dash for home.

The left fielder threw well, and the ball struck in the catcher's mitt. It did not stick, however, and the catcher lost the only opportunity to stop the score.

Harvard had scored at last!

The Harvard cheer rent the air, and crimson fluttered on all sides.

Frank struck out the next man, and then Yale came to bat, resolved to do or die. But they did not do much. Yedding was as good as ever, and the fielders gathered in anything that came their way.

At the end of the eighth inning the score remained one to nothing in Harvard's favor. It looked as if Yale would receive a shut out, and that was something awful to contemplate. The "sons of Old Eli" were ready to do anything to win a score or two.

In the first half of the ninth Harvard went at it to make some more runs. One man got a hit, stole second, and went to third on an error that allowed the batter to reach first.

Sport Harris had been disappointed when Merriwell continued to remain in the box, but now he said:

"He's rattled. Here's where they kill him."

But Frank proved that he was not rattled. He tricked the man on third into getting off the bag and then threw him out in a way that brought a yell of delight from Yale men. That fixed it so the next batter could not sacrifice with the object of letting the man on third home. Then he got down to business, and Harvard was whitewashed for the last time.

"Oh, if Yale can score now!" muttered hundreds.

The first man up flied out to center, and the next man was thrown out at first. That seemed to settle it. The spectators were making preparations to leave. The Yale bat-tender, with his face long and doleful, was gathering up the sticks.

What's that? The next man got a safe hit, a single that placed him on first. Then Frank Merriwell was seen carefully selecting a bat.

"Oh, if he were a heavy hitter!" groaned many voices.

Yedding was confident—much too confident. He laughed in Frank's face. He did not think it necessary to watch the man on first closely, and so that man found an opportunity to steal second.

Two strikes and two balls had been called. Then Yedding sent in a swift one to cut the inside corner. Merriwell swung at it.

Crack! Bat and ball met fairly, and away sailed the sphere over the head of the shortstop.

"Run!"

That word was a roar. No need to tell Frank to run. In a moment he was scudding down to first, while the left fielder was going back for the ball which had passed beyond his reach. Frank kept on for second. There was so much noise he could not hear the coachers, but he saw the fielder had not secured the ball. He made third, and the excited coacher sent him home with a furious gesture.

Every man, woman and child was standing. It seemed as if every one was shouting and waving flags, hats, or handkerchiefs. It was a moment of such thrilling, nerve-tingling excitement as is seldom experienced. If Merriwell reached home Yale won; if he failed, the score was tied, for the man in advance had scored.

The fielder had secured the ball, he drove it to the shortstop, and shortstop whirled and sent it whistling home. The catcher was ready to stop Merriwell.

"Slide!"

That word Frank heard above all the commotion. He did slide. Forward he scooted in a cloud of dust. The catcher got the ball and put it onto Frank—an instant too late!

A sudden silence.

"Safe home!" rang the voice of the umpire.

Then another roar, louder, wilder, full of unbounded joy! The Yale cheer! The band drowned by all the uproar! The sight of sturdy lads in blue, delirious with delight, hugging a dust-covered youth, lifting him to their shoulders, and bearing him away in triumph. Merriwell had won his own game, and his record was made. It was a glorious finish!

"Never saw anything better," declared Harry. "Frank, you are a wonder!"

"He is that!" declared several others. "Old Yale can't get along without him."

Tarzan of the Apes
EDGAR RICE BURROUGHS

Another month brought them to a little group of buildings at the mouth of a wide river, and there Tarzan saw many boats, and was filled with the old timidity of the wild thing by the sight of many men.

Gradually he became accustomed to the strange noises and the odd ways of civilization, so that presently none might know that, two short months before, this handsome Frenchman in immaculate white ducks, who laughed and chatted with the gayest of them, had been swinging

Edgar Rice Burroughs, *Tarzan of the Apes* (New York, McClurg, 1914), 196–201.

naked through primeval forests to pounce upon some unwary victim, which, raw, was to fill his savage belly.

The knife and fork, so contemptuously flung aside a month before, Tarzan now manipulated as exquisitely as did the polished D'Arnot.

So apt a pupil had he been that the young Frenchman had laboured assiduously to make of Tarzan of the Apes a polished gentleman in so far as nicety of manners and speech were concerned.

"God made you a gentleman at heart, my friend," D'Arnot had said; "but we want His works to show upon the exterior also."

As soon as they had reached the little port D'Arnot had cabled his Government of his safety, and requested a three months' leave, which had been granted.

He had also cabled his bankers for funds, and the enforced wait of a month, under which both chafed, was due to their inability to charter a vessel for the return to Tarzan's jungle after the treasure.

During their stay at the coast town "Monsieur Tarzan" became the wonder of both whites and blacks because of several occurrences which to Tarzan seemed the merest of nothings.

Once a huge black, crazed by drink, had run amuck and terrorized the town, until his evil star had led him to where the black-haired French giant lolled upon the veranda of the hotel.

Mounting the broad steps, with brandishing knife, the negro made straight for a party of four men sitting at a table sipping the inevitable absinthe.

Shouting in alarm, the four took to their heels, and then the black spied Tarzan.

With a roar he charged the ape-man, while half a hundred heads peered from sheltering windows and doorways to witness the butchering of the poor Frenchman by the giant black.

Tarzan met the rush with the fighting smile that the joy of battle always brought to his lips.

As the negro closed upon him, steel muscles gripped the black wrist of the uplifted knife-hand, and a single swift wrench left the hand dangling below a broken bone.

With the pain and surprise, the madness left the black man, and as Tarzan dropped back into his chair the fellow turned, crying with agony, and dashed wildly toward the native village.

On another occasion, as Tarzan and D'Arnot sat at dinner with a number of other whites, the talk fell upon lions and lion-hunting.

Opinion was divided as to the bravery of the king of beasts—some maintaining that he was an arrant coward, but all agreeing that it was with a feeling of greater security that they gripped their express rifles when the monarch of the jungle roared about a camp at night.

D'Arnot and Tarzan had agreed that his past be kept secret, and so none other than the French officer knew of the ape-man's familiarity with the beasts of the jungle.

"Monsieur Tarzan has not expressed himself," said one of the party. "A man of his prowess who has spent some time in Africa, as I understand Monsieur Tarzan has, must have had experiences with lions—yes?"

"Some," replied Tarzan dryly. "Enough to know that each of you are right in your judgment of the characteristics of the lions—you have met. But one might as well judge all blacks by the fellow who ran amuck last week, or decide that all whites are cowards because one has met a cowardly white.

"There is as much individuality among the lower orders, gentlemen, as there is among ourselves.

"To-day we may go out and stumble upon a lion which is over-timid— he runs away from us. To-morrow we may meet his uncle or his twin-brother, and our friends wonder why we do not return from the jungle.

"For myself, I always assume that a lion is ferocious, and so I am never caught off my guard."

"There would be little pleasure in hunting," retorted the first speaker, "if one is afraid of the thing he hunts."

D'Arnot smiled. Tarzan afraid!

"I do not exactly understand what you mean by fear," said Tarzan. "Like lions, fear is a different thing in different men, but to me the only pleasure in the hunt is the knowledge that the hunted thing has power to harm me as much as I have to harm him.

"If I went out with a couple of rifles and a gun-bearer, and twenty or thirty beaters, to hunt a lion, I should not feel that the lion had much chance, and so the pleasure of the hunt would be lessened in proportion to the increased safety which I felt."

"Then I am to take it that Monsieur Tarzan would prefer to go naked into the jungle, armed only with a jack-knife, to kill the king of beasts?" laughed the other good-naturedly, but with the merest touch of sarcasm in his tone.

"And a piece of rope," added Tarzan.

Just then the deep roar of a lion sounded from the distant jungle, as though to challenge whoever dared enter the lists with him.

"There is your opportunity, Monsieur Tarzan," bantered the Frenchman.

"I am not hungry," said Tarzan simply.

The men laughed, all but D'Arnot. He alone knew that a savage beast had spoken its simple reason through the lips of the ape-man.

"But you are afraid, just as any of us would be, to go out there naked, armed only with a knife and a piece of rope," said the banterer. "Is it not so?"

"No," replied Tarzan. "Only a fool performs any act without reason."

"Five thousand francs is a reason," said the other. "I wager you that amount you cannot bring back a lion from the jungle under the conditions we have named—naked and armed only with a knife and a piece of rope."

Tarzan glanced toward D'Arnot and nodded his head.

"Make it ten thousand," said D'Arnot.

"Done," replied the other.

Tarzan arose.

"I shall have to leave my clothes at the edge of the settlement, so that if I do not return before daylight I shall have something to wear through the streets."

"You are not going now," exclaimed the wagerer—"at night?"

"Why not?" asked Tarzan. "Numa walks abroad at night—it will be easier to find him."

"No," said the other, "I do not want your blood upon my hands. It will be foolhardy enough if you go forth by day."

"I shall go now," replied Tarzan, and went to his room for his knife and rope.

The men accompanied him to the edge of the jungle, where he left his clothes in a small storehouse.

But when he would have entered the blackness of the undergrowth they tried to dissuade him; and the wagerer was most insistent of all that he abandon his foolhardy venture.

"I will accede that you have won," he said, "and the ten thousand francs are yours if you will give up this foolish attempt, which can only end in your death."

Tarzan laughed, and in another moment the jungle had swallowed him.

The men stood silent for some moments and then slowly turned and walked back to the hotel veranda.

Tarzan had no sooner entered the jungle than he took to the trees, and it was with a feeling of exultant freedom that he swung once more through the forest branches.

This was life! ah, how he loved it. Civilization held nothing like this in its narrow and circumscribed sphere, hemmed in by restrictions and conventionalities. Even clothes were a hindrance and a nuisance.

At last he was free. He had not realized what a prisoner he had been.

How easy it would be to circle back to the coast, and then make toward the south and his own jungle and cabin.

Now he caught the scent of Numa, for he was travelling up wind. Presently his quick ears detected the familiar sound of padded feet and the brushing of a huge, fur-clad body through the undergrowth.

Tarzan came quietly above the unsuspecting beast, and silently stalked him until he came into a little patch of moonlight.

Then the quick noose settled and tightened about the tawny throat, and, as he had done it a hundred times in the past, Tarzan made fast the end to a strong branch and, while the beast fought and clawed for freedom, dropped to the ground behind him, and leaping upon the great back, plunged his long thin blade a dozen times into the fierce heart.

Then with his foot upon the carcass of Numa, he raised his voice in the awesome victory cry of his savage tribe.

For a moment Tarzan stood irresolute, swayed by conflicting emotions of loyalty to D'Arnot and a mighty lust for the freedom of his own jungle. At last the vision of a beautiful face, and the memory of warm lips crushed to his, dissolved the fascinating picture he had been drawing of his old life.

The ape-man threw the warm carcass of Numa across his shoulders and took to the trees once more.

The men upon the veranda had sat for an hour, almost in silence.

They had tried ineffectually to converse on various subjects, and always the thing uppermost in the mind of each had caused the conversation to lapse.

"*Mon Dieu!*" said the wagerer at length, "I can endure it no longer. I am going into the jungle with my express and bring back that mad man."

"I will go with you," said one.

"And I"—"And I"—"And I," chorused the others.

As though the suggestion had broken the spell of some horrid nightmare they hastened to their various quarters, and presently were headed toward the jungle—each man heavily armed.

"God! What was that?" suddenly cried one of the party, an Englishman, as Tarzan's savage cry came faintly to their ears.

"I heard the same thing once before," said a Belgian, "when I was in the gorilla country. My carriers said it was the cry of a great bull ape who has made a kill."

D'Arnot remembered Clayton's description of the awful roar with which Tarzan had announced his kills, and he half smiled in spite of the horror which filled him to think that the uncanny sound could have issued from a human throat—from the lips of his friend.

As the party stood finally near the edge of the jungle, debating as to the best distribution of their forces, they were startled by a low laugh near them, and turning, beheld advancing toward them a giant figure bearing a dead lion upon its broad shoulders.

Even D'Arnot was thunderstruck, for it seemed impossible that the man could have so quickly dispatched a lion with the pitiful weapons he had taken, or that alone he could have borne the huge carcass through the tangled jungle.

The men crowded about Tarzan with many questions, but his only answer was a laughing deprecation of his feat.

To Tarzan it was as though one should eulogize a butcher for his heroism in killing a cow, for Tarzan had killed so often for food and for self-preservation that the act seemed anything but remarkable to him. But he was indeed a hero in the eyes of these men—men accustomed to hunting big game.

25. The Showgirl

The age in which the Ziegfeld Follies were synonymous with "revues" was just emerging from the cloak Victorian morality threw over women in particular, and sex in general. Flamboyant Florenz Ziegfeld helped make sex respectable. As the nation's leading impresario of female beauty, Ziegfeld elevated sex appeal to an art form. He knew, however, that most Americans were not prepared for too much of the new freedom, and consequently was cautious. His "product" was a mixture of schoolgirl and siren. Thus Marilyn Miller, the star of many Follies, was photographed with a daringly low neckline but described as "a burst of sunshine" so young "her mother still has to sign her contracts." In 1919 *American Magazine* asked Ziegfeld to describe his criteria for pretty girls.

Picking Out Pretty Girls for the Stage
FLORENZ ZIEGFELD, JR.

There are more types of pretty girls in America than in any other country in the world. I don't offer this as a piece of news. Everyone that has given the subject any thought, and who has not? realizes that in the United States there are all the nationalities ever discovered; and that each one of them has its own special type of beauty.

But I doubt if anyone has had a more striking proof of this fact than I

Florenz Ziegfeld, Jr., "Picking Out Pretty Girls for the Stage," *American Magazine*, 88 (Dec., 1919), 34, 119–122, 125, 126, 129.

have; for, as manager of two musical shows, I get a demonstration of it almost every day in the year.

There is not a section of the country that does not furnish its quota of pretty girls to the Ziegfeld Follies and the Midnight Frolic. Mr. Wayburn and I choose the successful applicants from among hundreds who come to us. So we ought to know something about beauty—and we think we do.

No part of the country has a monopoly in this matter, but the South is one of the best sources of supply, and California is another. Among cities, perhaps New York, Philadelphia, Baltimore, and San Francisco are in the lead.

The Southern type usually has dark hair and eyes, is graceful, and has charm of manner. The California type—in fact, the Western type in general—is more likely to have blue or gray eyes, fair or brown hair, and a free, athletic carriage that suggests outdoor life.

The New York type is less natural, has more assurance, and is more conscious. Not conscious in the sense of being awkward, but conscious of its power to attract.

You see, this question of beauty is a very complex one, especially when it comes to choosing girls for a musical show. A pretty face is the first essential; there are very few parts for a girl who hasn't also a good figure, and who cannot dance, or at least carry herself gracefully.

This is not so important off the stage. But if you think it does not count a great deal even there, just go to a dancing party and watch the "wall flowers." You may find the prettiest girl in the room sitting among them. If anybody does happen to ask her for a dance, or even if she merely walks across the room, you will see *why* she is neglected.

In trying out girls for our companies, the first thing we do is to weed out those who are not pretty in face and form. The next test is so simple that it probably will surprise you. It is merely to have them *walk* across the stage in time to music.

The outsider may be interested in knowing just how these try-outs are conducted, so I will describe one of them further on. But as the question of beauty itself must be settled before an applicant takes any other test, we may as well follow that order here and now.

The most interesting thing in this connection is that a girl must have something besides beauty, if she is to create more than a passing impression.

You may think that a chorus girl can make a great hit, just because she has a pretty face and figure. But if beauty is *all* she has, she will not get beyond the chorus or some small part.

The ones who make the really big successes have beauty—*plus person-ality*. And they can even be shy on beauty, if they have enough per-sonality. Beauty is something you *see*. Personality is something you *feel*.

Now suppose that to those two possessions, beauty and personality, you add a third—the ability to do at least some one thing supremely well. Believe *me!* that is the combination that wins!

On the stage, it may be the ability to act, or dance, or sing, or mimic others, or even just to wear beautiful clothes as they should be worn. And off the stage the same thing holds true: the beautiful and charming girl, or woman, who can *do* something well is sure of all the popularity she wants. If she sings, or talks, or rides, or dances, or plays tennis, or enter-tains, or does *something* better than the common run of people do it, she will be pushed to the front, whether she cares about it or not.

But a girl may have a lovely face, so far as coloring and features go; and if there is "nobody home" behind that face, people will soon get bored.

In the theatre we sometimes make a place for a girl without brains, if she is so lovely to look at that we simply cannot pass her by. But we never give her an important part. Because the more she has to do, the more she will betray her stupidity. It is the girl with less perfect features, but with a vivid personality and some talent which she has worked hard to develop, who walks away with the honors.

There is Marilyn Miller, for example, who has the principal rôle in the Follies this year. If all the girls in the company were simply lined up in a row, you might perhaps pick out several whom you thought prettier than Miss Miller.

Then how does she happen to be the headliner? Because she is very pretty in face and has a beautiful figure; she dances exquisitely; and she has a wonderful personality. She is the incarnation of freshness, of youth, of vitality.

Probably you have noticed that dancers always smile. That is as much a part of their "job" as the steps are. They are *taught* to smile, because smiling is part of the game. The idea is that dancing is an expression of joy. So the professional dancer smiles in order to convey the idea of happiness.

But comparatively few of them do convey it. Often a dancer drops her smile with her final bow, and walks off as if the rent collector were wait-ing for her just off stage.

But Marilyn Miller is like a burst of sunshine. If she hadn't that quality, she would still be a pretty girl, of course, but she would not make any particular dent in your consciousness.

The public taste changes in regard to beauty, just as it does in other things. Some years ago the popular stage type was the tall, handsome one. The sextet in "Floradora" started that furore. It also started the phrase, "show girls," which has become common now. That was just what these tall, beautiful creatures were. They did not dance; they simply paraded around, showing off beautiful costumes.

Every possible change was rung on this fad, until the inevitable reaction came and the popular taste swung around to the small girl, full of "pep" and action. That was when Mr. Wayburn's pony ballets began to make a sensation. To-day we include all the types. For that reason, it would be impossible to pick out one girl as absolutely the prettiest in the entire company.

Still, there is a popular type at present. It is the girl of medium height, who is slender, but not too slender. A few years ago, the popular type was the small girl who was rather plump. To-day, she should be a couple of inches taller, but should weigh just about the same.

The little girl has her place, however, and a very important one. Many people seem to regard size as an indication of age. A very small girl seems young to them just because she is small. And as we all like youth, the small girl is popular.

If she has a touch of impudence—well, we don't enjoy her any the less. We feel a good deal like a big dog playing with a kitten. If the dog could laugh, I'm sure he would when the kitten cuffs him. That is the way a man feels about the pretty impudence of a little girl. It amuses him immensely.

As for the tall, beautiful girl, we couldn't put on our shows without her. She provides the gorgeous effects because she can wear the most stunning costumes. The small girls do most of the dancing and frolicking. But the tall girls have distinction and their own special kind of grace.

They must have better features, too. A small girl can have a "snub" nose; but if she has a lot of curls, dancing eyes, and an irresistible little smile, she will make a good impression. But imagine a very tall girl with a snub nose! It would take a lot of personality to get over that.

About as perfect a type of the tall girl as you could find anywhere is Dolores, of this year's Follies. She has lovely gray eyes, a finely chiseled nose, and quite a wonderful mouth. Add to that a beautiful figure, a fine carriage which enables her to wear stunning costumes with superb effect, and a personality so striking that when she comes on stage you see no one else.

As a rule, the small girl is a type which is popular with men. Women are "crazy" about the tall girls. Men admire them, too; but they seem to like the others better.

Small girls, by the way, are prettier if they have curly hair. But the tall girls do not seem to need it. They are just as effective with smooth, straight hair, or only slightly wavy.

Jewish girls are not, as a rule, above medium height. In fact, many of them are below it. There are a great many very pretty girls among Jewish people; but they mature early and lose their youthful slenderness. For that reason they do not last long as chorus girls.

If you are a manager in search of "show" material, there is one nationality you cannot afford to overlook, and that is the Irish. A great many very pretty girls have more or less Irish blood in their veins. They usually have nice eyes, a good nose, pretty hair, and an expressive mouth. Also, they generally have plenty of temperament. Occasionally they drop the last two syllables, to be sure; but even then they are at least interesting.

English girls have a beauty of their own and those that come to us are valuable recruits, because they are trained dancers. But most of the pretty girls in our companies are Americans. By that I mean that not only are they native-born, but that their parents and grandparents and remoter ancestors were also natives of this country. There are more types of beauty, more *varieties* of charm, among strictly American girls than among those of any other nationality.

Blondes seem to be fewer to-day than they used to be. At least, they are fewer in the ranks of the show girls. As for the artificial blonde she is becoming less and less common. And I think you will find that this is true off the stage as well as on.

In fact, I think there is a decided trend toward naturalness. Women and girls, not only in the theatre but also in private life, have been going through a period of exaggerated make-up. It has been so extreme that there is bound to be a reaction; and I, for one, will welcome it.

A certain amount of make-up is necessary on the stage, because the footlights "kill" the natural color. The delicate tints of even a good complexion are lost behind the footlights, and the person looks pale, even ghastly.

But I am always trying to impress on our girls that it is a mistake to make up heavily. Too much is as bad as none at all. As for the exaggerated make-up one sees on the street these days, it is often positively repulsive. As I said before, a reaction is bound to come; and I know that I am one of a vast majority that will be glad of it.

In the Midnight Frolic, on the New Amsterdam Roof, the performers are so close to the audience that they have to be especially careful about this. Most of them do not make up as much as the women who are in the spectators' seats.

We have to study this matter of make-up scientifically because Urban, who designs our stage effects, is fond of using blue lights. And, by the way, the effect of different colored lights is a subject which women off the stage might do well to study for their own advantage.

When make-up is used, blue lights cause the pink on the cheeks to look like a crude patch of color with sharply defined edges. Pink lights have almost the same effect; and so do white ones. The most becoming lighting is obtained by using pale straw-colored globes, really a deep cream color. I believe this is true off the stage as well; although, if no makeup at all is used and a person is pale or sallow, a soft pink light would probably be better than the straw-colored one.

When it comes to the color of a costume, pink is the most universally becoming and also the most effective on the stage. There are exceptions, of course. A certain type of red-haired girl should not wear pink. Gold-browns will bring out the brown in her hair—if there is any. A vivid red will kill the less vivid color of the hair; while a contrasting color, like blue or green, will accentuate it.

To the red-haired girl who is pretty the color of her hair should be an asset. For some reason unknown to science, most red-haired people have a decided personality. So here is a pretty girl with the highly desirable quality of personality, and nature has given her in the color of her hair something which at once attracts attention. With that kind of an advantage over other girls, she ought to be thankful. But instead of that she does not *play* up, but tries to *cover* up, the very thing she ought to use. We always have several red-haired girls in our companies, and they are very attractive.

There is one thing which is a great factor in beauty off the stage, but which has almost no importance in the theatre. That is a good complexion. A lovely pink and white skin, smooth and fine in texture, is a wonderful asset to the girl in private life. But on the stage a delicate complexion cannot "get across" the footlights. We have to resort to a certain amount of make-up. And as a poor complexion can be successfully camouflaged by make-up, this factor does not have any real importance in the theatre.

What does count is beauty of feature, pretty hair, and charm of expression. There is a rather prevalent idea that dark eyes are desirable on the stage; and it is true that they are more or less effective. But some of the most strikingly pretty girls in our companies have blue or gray eyes. Marilyn Miller has blue eyes, Dolores has gray; so have Diana Allen, Martha Mansfield, Corone Paynter, Jessie Reed, and others of the Follies.

The color does not count so much as size, brilliance, line, and expression. The most beautiful eyes are those which are very clear and limpid, no matter what their color may be, and which are full of warmth and feeling.

A pretty mouth is almost an essential of beauty. When I come to think of it, I realize that at least three fourths of our girls have a decidedly short upper lip. I won't say that this is indispensable to beauty, for I know it is not. But at least it seems to accompany it very often.

A certain very well-known young actress, one of the most popular girls on the stage, was rehearsing with one of our companies a few years ago and somebody started joking her about her long upper lip. She had a keen sense of humor and immediately began making very funny attempts to overcome this drawback. Amid shrieks of laughter from the onlookers, she finally gave up in mock despair. But she is a girl who does not have to worry about not being a great beauty; for she is so clever and has so much personality that she "puts it all over" the merely pretty girls.

Of course good teeth are an almost necessary adjunct to a pretty mouth. There is something very attractive about clean and regular teeth, just as there is about anything that is wholesome and seems to indicate health. Even though a girl is not pretty, people will like to look at her if her skin is smooth, her eyes clear, her teeth white and regular, her hair well kept, and her cheeks rosy. If girls realized this, they would eat, sleep, and exercise in a way to improve their teeth—simply to make themselves more attractive, if for no other reason.

Somebody asked me the other day if the "wholesome" type of girl was liked on the stage, meaning by that the girl who looks sort of genuine and natural and "nice."

Yes, she is. Of course for the stage she must be pretty, too. But if she is both pretty *and* nice, she will arouse plenty of admiration. A lot of girls make the mistake of trying to imitate the vampire type. Most of them are not vampires by nature, any more than a kitten is a hyena. But for some reason an astonishing number of modern young girls seem to be trying to look that part. My advice to them is to forget it! The vampire is not a popular household pet.

That remark suggests what may be an interesting bit of information as to what becomes of most of the pretty girls of the stage. They marry. So far as age goes, our chorus girls and show girls are bounded on the south by sixteen, and on the north by twenty-three. In other words, almost all of them are from seventeen to twenty-two years old. We have very few older than that, for the simple reason that Cupid and Hymen claim them.

One girl in our companies has been with us seven years. Her record with us is longer than any of the others. The oldest chorus girl I know of, in musical shows like ours, is thirty-six years old and has a grown daughter. She is still attractive and a good dancer, too; but she is unique in her record.

The first signs of departing youth come in the eyes, the cheeks, and the neck line just below the chin. The eyes grow a little less clear, the cheeks sag just a trifle, and the chin shows a fatal inclination to become a pair! Later, the condition known as a "turkey neck" puts in an appearance, and that is a sign that middle age is inexorably approaching.

But these things do not happen to the average girl of twenty-three. It all depends on whether she takes care of herself. If a chorus girl burns the candle at both ends, her beauty is of short duration. But the majority of them don't.

That is one thing about which the public has a wrong idea. The average conception of the life of a chorus girl is—well, it isn't fit to print. I imagine it will surprise most readers when I tell them that last year, when the Follies went on the road, almost fifty girls in the company took their mothers along.

I said I would tell how we try out the girls who apply. First, Mr. Wayburn talks with each one individually. Those who are entirely unsuited, either because they are not pretty, or because they are too stout, or too thin, or are conspicuously awkward, he lets go. The others are told to report at a certain time for a try-out. If they have had experience, they are told to bring their practice clothes.

"Practice clothes" is the professional term for a wide variety of costumes which the girls wear at rehearsals. They generally consist of high-heeled slippers, long silk stockings or tights, and above these a medley of short garments. Sometimes a girl wears light-colored cotton bloomers —pink is a favorite color—which reach only part way to the knees. Then there is a pink smock, or jumper, or blouse of some sort, low-necked and short-sleeved. Other girls dress all in black; black slippers, black stockings, a very short black skirt, and a low-necked black waist. Often they wear a bright sash with these black costumes. Others wear half hose, with bare knees. In fact, they consult their own wishes and taste about their practice clothes, the only requirement being that they shall wear something that gives them freedom of motion and that will enable the director to see whether they are doing the steps correctly.

Perhaps forty or fifty girls are tried out at a time. Some of them are in practice clothes, others in their street costumes. Suppose it is on the Roof, at the New Amsterdam Theatre. The floor is cleared for a space about forty feet square and a row of chairs placed on two opposite sides facing each other. On the third side is a piano and a pianist. Across from him, on the fourth side, sits Mr. Wayburn, at a small table, where I join him later.

The girls are ranged according to height. Mr. Wayburn then explains, for the benefit of the newcomers, what they are to do. It is very simple: The pianist plays something in march time, and they are to walk in time with the music, with occasional "hesitation" steps at certain points.

He takes them in groups of six or eight, lines them up opposite him, has them walk toward him, turn and walk back, turn again and come toward him, and so on until he says, "That will do. Seats!"

There is no talking, no foolishness. Not only then, but at rehearsals later on, there is absolutely no nonsense. Mr. Wayburn often rehearses a hundred girls at a time. That is, they are all present, seated on benches or chairs around three sides of the hall, or on the stage, if the rehearsal is on a large stage like that of the Century Theatre. He may have only twenty girls on the floor at once; but the rest are expected to stay quietly in their places. If there is any talking, even among the girls who are simply waiting their turn, he stops it instantly.

They are there for serious work. He expects them to give their whole attention to it. You will not find a schoolroom, with a hundred pupils in it, that is more quiet than one of our rehearsals.

The try-out is conducted in the same way. Scarcely a word is spoken, except for the brief orders by the director. He never makes any comment on a particular girl, never says anything that will call attention to her awkwardness, if she is awkward. And the girls themselves take their cue from him. There are no smiles, or giggles, if some girl makes a poor showing. I doubt if there would be, anyway. It is a trying ordeal for them all, and I imagine that they have a fellow feeling for one another. At any rate, as they watch each group on the floor their faces are as serious as if they were at a prayer meeting.

The names and telephone numbers of the girls are taken as soon as they have been seated in order. When they have gone through their walking test, Mr. Wayburn writes opposite each girl's name what is to be done in her case. Some are to report again. They are considered promising enough to have their voices tried. Others are good material; but perhaps we don't need them, so they are sent to some other manager who is making up a company. Others are worth keeping in touch with, so we file their names. And some are hopeless.

When all of the groups have gone through the try-out, Mr. Wayburn's assistant takes the list, calls each girl to him separately, and explains to her just what the decision is in her case. This is done in a low tone, so that only the girl herself can hear. And from the expression of his face no one can tell whether she is accepted or not. He asks those who are told to report again not to say anything to the others.

In this way we try to save the rejected ones from any embarrassment, or feeling of humiliation.

That is the way girls are tried out for the Follies and the Frolic. It is a serious, businesslike proceeding. The rehearsals are conducted the same way. And when the show is finally put on, we carry the same methods into that. I do not permit anybody, even my personal friends, to go behind the scenes during a performance. Occasionally a newspaper reporter has been taken back in order to get some necessary information for a notice; but I do not even like them to go behind the scenes until the performance is over. What the girls do outside of the theatre is none of my affair. But we pay them to give us three hours of their time, and we want them to do it.

Perhaps you wonder *what* we pay them. Only a few years ago, a good chorus girl received $25 a week in New York, and $35 a week on the road. But we pay them now $50 a week in New York and $60 on the road. In addition, of course, we pay their traveling expenses. Their costumes are furnished them, too—and at an appalling cost. I have just received a bill for seven costumes which averaged five hundred dollars apiece! And these, mind you, were not for principals but for chorus girls.

I think that this opportunity to wear beautiful clothes is one thing that attracts girls to our companies. Even with pretty girls, fine feathers do help usually to make fine birds, and they realize this. Most of the girls in shows like ours are prettier on the stage than off, because of the wonderful costumes. But some of them are prettier just as themselves, in their own simple frocks and without any make-up at all. So I suppose they would be called by outsiders really our prettiest girls.

26. Motor Sports

No single factor had a greater effect on American culture from 1900 to 1916 than the mechanized vehicle. Automobiles and motorcycles revolutionized patterns of living, working, and playing. They altered the way people perceived the environment, and changed man's very image of himself and his progress. Initially, at least, motor transport did not threaten but rather enhanced the efficacy of the individual. Early motoring was a challenge and adventure—a new frontier on which to prove modern man's prowess. Here a pioneering motorcyclist gives historical and psychological import to the delights of a drive up California's Mount Hamilton.

Up Mount Hamilton on a Motor Cycle
WALTER H. BURR

Modern invention is rapidly depriving mythical and legendary stories of their interest by making it possible for present-day men to easily surpass the wildest feats known to the heroes of old. The speed element is not a factor peculiarly incident to our present civilization. The slowness of natural methods of locomotion has been recognized by every age and condition, along with the possibility of increasing the rapidity of travel. Impressed with this fact, the ancients gave to their deity the attributes of fleetness, and whether it was Hermes who flew about under the sunny Grecian skies, or Mercury who carried the divine messages for the Roman

Walter H. Burr, "Up Mount Hamilton on a Motor Cycle," *Overland Monthly*, 40 (Dec., 1902), 556–561.

favorites—or by whatever name the god of speed was known, he had a necessary existence in the heathen mind. When the fable writer found that he must remove Bellerephon over a great distance in a very short space of time, he invented Pegasus, the winged horse, and seated upon this fleet animal the brave youth made his way on his long and perilous journey in an incredibly short time.

Primitive legends are prophetic of future realizations. Given in the human mind the admiration for speed, recent developments in motor vehicles need not be considered other than a natural sequence. Nearest to fulfilling the prophecies of mythology in giving speed to the individual traveler, and transporting him to inaccessible heights, is the motor bicycle. Mounted on this steed he consigns to oblivion the ancient worthies who were noted for their swift and perilous journeys. Pheidippides is behind in the race; Paul Revere has scarcely more than mounted; and Sheridan is still twenty miles away—when the motor wheel arrives.

Along with others, I inherited the speed craze, and although a novice with the motor wheel, the opportunity to ride one to Lick Observatory on the summit of Mount Hamilton, was much to my liking. Zest and interest were added to the prospective trip when those familiar with the conditions urged that it was impossible of accomplishment. The machine used was a California product, chosen because of its special adaptability for such a test. Contrary to the general impression, the motor wheel is a simple device, and the only requirement in running it successfully is an ordinary store of common sense. The entire weight of the wheel used was about seventy-five pounds, with the one-and-one-quarter horse power engine, the gasoline tank and the carbureter all inside the diamond frame. Fill your tank with gasoline, start the mixture in the carbureter, see that your machine is in proper condition—and you are ready to go. Mount, start the wheel with a couple of revolutions of the pedals, press the switch plug, and fly away at a speed of from five to twenty-five miles an hour at your own discretion.

The fifty mile trip from San Francisco to San Jose was a mere pleasure jaunt. To one accustomed to work his passage on an ordinary wheel it is like being transported to the seventh heaven to sit quietly astride the machine and be carried over the level and up the grades without putting forth the least effort. Do you wish to hasten by yonder slow-moving scavenger wagon? Throw the power on full force, and soon you are past with scarcely an unpleasant sensation. Soon the beautiful bay to the left attracts the attention, and one has the desire to linger beneath the picturesque trees that border the road on either side, and enjoy the scenery.

Slow down to the rate of five miles an hour, and as you glide along without care or exertion, drink in the beauties of that fairy land that stretches all the way from Millbrae to San Jose. An automobile appears in the distance headed the same way, but the little engine is equal to every emergency, the wheel is soon past it, and ere long the automobile is left out of sight in the rear. A wheelman of the old school, pedaling his life out on every little incline, has a decidedly tired look when the rider astride the more modern article shoots past him and is lost in the distance. The towns along the line fly by in quick succession, one scarcely left behind until another appears. Children and older people open their eyes with wonder as the "no pushee, no pullee" concern goes by, and the dogs that are accustomed to impede the progress of the wheelman miss their calculation, and land in the road to find you a half a mile farther on. Such delight. Such exhilaration. Only he who has experienced it can fully comprehend.

Arrived at San Jose, preparations were made for the steeper ascent. The one who rides a motor-wheel must not overlook the fact that he is managing an engine—for the time being he is occupying the position of an engineer. If you will watch a railroad engineer when his train pulls into a station where it is to lie for a short time, you will see that he is very particular to investigate the condition of his engine, and to make sure that it is prepared for the next run. No less care is necessary with the motor wheel, and the only failure ever experienced is due to this lack of attention on the part of the operator. You could not expect a vehicle of such light weight to go a great distance at such speed, with the regular explosions of the engine taking place inside the diamond and still need no attention. It is well to look to all the bolts and screws, to investigate the battery—in fact, to take a careful survey of the entire machine. This will insure a safe and happy trip without necessitating the profane coloring of the air over some mishap that is the result of carelessness.

After making a first acquaintance with the wheel; after having it carry you several miles, responding continually to your every impulse, one need not be ashamed to confess that he has acquired a genuine love for the little engine. He is apt to find himself personifying the machine, and addressing it as "old girl," "little goo-goo," or by some other name equally significant of good fellowship and affection. Neither does it dampen his ardor or lessen his loyalty when some spectator sneers and tells him he has "motor bugs." The rider experiences in continually greater degree the true man's love for his steed. He loses sight of the fact that it is an inanimate thing, and looks upon it as a faithful companion. It was with such a feeling that I prepared the engine for its run up the mountain-side.

Some idea of the test proposed for the motor wheel can be gained when it is remembered that Lick Observatory is situated at an altitude of 4,443 feet, while San Jose is at an altitude of only 86 feet. The entire elevation of the ascent to be made on a twenty-seven mile ride is 4,357 feet, or an average of more than one hundred and sixty-one feet to the mile. However, an average does not give an adequate idea of the grades to be traversed, as a great deal of the time must be occupied in going down hills which are to be climbed again. In an air line the Observatory is only thirteen miles from San Jose, but as I looked at the mountain in the evening, I felt justified in sending the following postal to a friend:

> Arrived O. K.
> At San Jose.
> All went well—
> We came like Hell.
> In the morning at seven
> I started up toward Heaven.

That start was made under auspicious circumstances, the faithful wheel taking hold as though it knew something of the difficult journey before it, and was determined to show its ability to climb wherever there was a trail. The approach to the mountain is a picturesque drive, on either side of which is a row of tall trees, sometimes forming almost a perfect arch over the road. Further to the right and to the left stretch out the fruit ranches, the pride of Santa Clara County. The busy prune pickers stopped long enough from their work to call out a glad salute and wish a prosperous journey. This road, which is called Alum Rock avenue, appears to be almost on a level, because of the gradual slope of the surrounding land. Having no level with which to compare it, and seeing ahead the steep ascent of the mountain, one does not realize that he is climbing one of the steepest grades on the entire route. The little engine understands the situation, and the slackened speed tells you that you are climbing a hill when you thought you were riding on nearly level ground.

Now is the time for one to study to get the full power out of the engine without in any way impeding the progress of the wheel. This is one of the "tricks of the trade" that sometimes puzzles the novice, and he learns the proper combination just as so many other things are learned—while experimenting he happens onto it. Having once made the discovery, it becomes an instinct, and he cannot explain it to another—each must learn for himself. It is just possible that in climbing an extra little grade the engine may become slightly discouraged. It is not to be blamed, and the fault is probably with the operator. At such a time a round or two with the pedals, with about the pressure one would use in riding over a plank floor, will be duly appreciated and the engine will respond readily in expressing its gratitude.

After a few miles ride the grade becomes still more difficult, on account of the numerous sharp turns encountered. While riding on an apparently straight road, one will suddenly come to a place where he must turn on rather short notice and go in exactly the opposite direction. When the citizens of Santa Clara County laid out this road at an expense of $100,000, it was for the convenience of stage coaches and not for the benefit of motor wheels; otherwise it would have been better had the road made a steeper ascent and turned fewer corners.

On we go, upgrade, making about twelve miles an hour, with scarcely any effort. In a short time the Grand View House is reached. The place is well-named. There stretches out before the traveler a regular panorama, which he is better able to enjoy because he is not worn out from the journey. The mountains roll downward until they blend with the valleys, where the fruit groves extend mile after mile. Farther away can be seen the cities and towns that dot the earth like children's play-houses, while still farther in the distance are the beautiful bay and the great ocean. All these grand sights of nature may be seen while riding along the mountain side.

Soon the road begins to lead downward, and the wheel bounds forward as the engine feels the strain removed, and recognizes that it is about to be granted a rest. This decline leads into Hall's Valley, which must be crossed before continuing the ascent. While the ride down hill is a pleasant diversion, nevertheless one rather regrets that having come thus near to the top he must retrace his way downward, only to climb up on the other side. Yet the valley itself is not without its beauties of rock and tree and cliff, which well repay for the descent. After a brief ride beyond the valley there is another slight downward run to Smith's Creek. Here is the place for refreshments and to take another inventory of the wheel. Everything is in good order after the hard climb, and one's admiration for his engine reaches a high pitch.

From Smith's Creek it is just two miles in a direct line to the Observatory. The great white dome arises out of the ground so near that one is tempted to see if he cannot throw a pebble over it. But let him not congratulate himself that the journey is almost finished, for there are yet before him seven miles of the most circuitous road yet traveled. The engine seemed ready for the attempt, so together we rolled across the bridge and started to "buck the mountain." The road winds in and out like the path of a serpent, and frequently creeps so close to the precipice that one can look over the edge hundreds of feet below, and imagine himself and his wheel lying at the bottom in inverted order. However, no such accident occurred, and the wheel was easily steered, the engine doing its work with little assistance. Nearer and nearer we came to the great white dome that is now silhouetted against the sky, and now hidden entirely from view by a projecting rock. At the foot of an exceptionally steep incline I thought, "Surely the little engine will not make it." Laughing at my doubts she plunged through the dust, and rolled up the grade as though she were enjoying a pleasant pastime. Round and round the topmost peaks we spun, the circuit narrowing down as we reached the summit, until finally we rolled out in front of the great Lick Observatory, having made the last and steepest run of seven miles in half an hour. After surveying the wonders of that noted place, nothing remained but to mount the faithful wheel, turn her loose, and guide her back down the mountain on the road home.

No doubt the wild deer that still haunt the fastnesses of the country adjacent to Mount Hamilton witnessed with some surprise the invasion of their realm when the great telescope and its accompanying machinery were hauled slowly up the mountain side and placed upon the very summit. Since then they have been accustomed to watch from a distance the toiling mountain teams and the slow stage coach laboriously wending their way upward, until the sight has become a familiar one. What must be their astonishment as they see this new invention gliding with ease over a road which others have found so difficult, proving that wherever a wagon has gone a motor-cycle can go.

27. The Sport of Scandal

The preferred recreation of millions of Americans in the early twentieth century consisted of reading about the lives and loves of the very rich. Vicarious participation in sensuous escapades was a way of answering the call of the wild in matters of morality and yet avoiding personal risk. As the covert sensuality of the Victorian Age came increasingly into the open, magazines began to publish ever more daring "love stories" or "true stories." But there was nothing like the real thing. The most widely followed scandal of the period broke on the night of June 25, 1906 when Harry Thaw, millionaire playboy, shot and killed Stanford White, renowned architect and social lion. According to Thaw, White had seduced the alluring model and show girl Evelyn Nesbit, before she became Mrs. Thaw. The sensational trial resulting after the shooting placed the love triangle under a public microscope. After the sessions, Harry Thaw was judged criminally insane and spent most of the rest of his life in an institution. In the absence of other forms of mass communication, the public learned about the Thaw-White affair entirely through newspaper accounts.

THAW MURDERS STANFORD WHITE

SHOOTS HIM ON THE MADISON SQUARE GARDEN ROOF

ABOUT EVELYN NESBIT

"HE RUINED MY WIFE," WITNESS SAYS HE SAID

AUDIENCE IN A PANIC

CHAIRS AND TABLES ARE OVERTURNED IN A WILD SCRAMBLE FOR THE EXITS

The New York Times, June 26, 1906, February 8, 1907.

Harry Kendall Thaw, of Pittsburgh, husband of Florence Evelyn Nesbit, former actress and artist's model, shot and killed Stanford White, the architect, on the roof of Madison Square Garden at 11:05 o'clock last night, just as the first performance of the musical comedy "Mamselle Champagne" was drawing to a close. Thaw, who is a brother of the Countess of Yarmouth and a member of a well known and wealthy family, left his seat near the stage, passed between a number of tables, and, in full view of the players and of scores of persons, shot White through the head. Mr. White was the designer of the building on the roof of which he was killed. He it was who put Miss Nesbit, now Mrs. Thaw, on the stage.

Thaw, who was in evening clothes, had evidently been waiting for Mr. White's appearance. The latter entered the Garden at 10:53 and took a seat at a table five rows from the stage. He rested his chin in his right hand and seemed lost in contemplation.

Thaw had a pistol concealed under his coat. His face was deathly white. According to A. L. Belstone, who sat near, White must have seen Thaw approaching. But he made no move. Thaw placed the pistol almost against the head of the sitting man and fired three shots in quick succession.

BODY FELL TO THE FLOOR

White's elbow slid from the table, the table crashed over, sending a glass clinking along with the heavier sound. The body then tumbled from the chair.

On the stage one of the characters was singing a song entitled "I Could Love a Million Girls." The refrain seemed to freeze upon his lips. There was dead silence for a second, and then Thaw lifted his pistol over his head, the barrel hanging downward, as if to show the audience that he was not going to harm anyone else.

With a firm stride Thaw started for the exit, holding his pistol as if anxious to have someone take it from his hand.

Then came the realization on the part of the audience that the farce had closed with a tragedy. A woman jumped to her feet and screamed. Many persons followed her example, and there was wild excitement.

L. Lawrence, the manager of the show jumped on a table and above the uproar commanded the show to go on.

"Go on playing!" he shouted. "Bring on that chorus!"

GIRLS TOO TERRIFIED TO SING

The musicians made a feeble effort at gathering their wits and playing the chorus music, but the girls who romped on the stage were paralyzed with horror, and it was impossible to bring the performance to an orderly close.

Then the manager shouted for quiet, and he informed the audience that a serious accident had happened, and begged the people to move out of the place quietly.

In the meantime Thaw had reached the entrance to the elevators. On duty there was Fireman Paul Broodin. He took the pistol from Thaw's hand, but did not attempt to arrest him. Policeman Debes of the Tenderloin Station appeared and seized his arm.

"He deserved it," Thaw said to the policeman. "He ruined my life and then deserted the girl." Another witness said the word was "wife" instead of "life."

A WOMAN KISSED THAW

Just as the policeman started into the elevator with Thaw a woman described as dark-haired and short of stature reached up to him and kissed him on the cheek. This woman some witnesses declare was Mrs. Thaw.

The crowd was then scrambling wildly for the elevators and stairs. The employees of the Garden who knew Thaw, and nearly all of them did, as he visited the place often, did not seem greatly surprised at the tragedy. When Thaw entered the Garden in the early part of the show he seemed greatly agitated. He strolled from one part of the place to another, and finally took a seat in a little niche near the stage.

He was half hidden from the audience but could see anyone who might enter. It is believed that he knew just where White would sit, and had picked out this place in order to get at him without interference.

Henry Rogers of 222 Henry Street was seated at the table next to the one at which White was sitting when he was killed. He says that Thaw fired when the muzzle of his pistol was only a few inches from White's temple.

Another witness said that after firing three shots and looking at White as if to be sure that he was stone dead, Thaw uttered a curse and added:

"You'll never go out with that woman again."

A WOMAN SAT NEAR WHITE

At another table adjoining that at which White was killed sat a woman dressed in white. It was believed for a time that she was a companion of White's, and it was reported that she leaned over and kissed the face of the dead man, but this could not be verified, and it is positive that White was alone when he entered the Garden.

Some one in the audience hurried to the fallen man to see if assistance was needed. A great pool of blood had quickly formed on the floor. The tables had been pulled back and in the bright glare of thousands of electric lights it was quickly seen that White was beyond any earthly help.

A number of the actors and actresses left the stage, and away from the calcium and the footlights their painted faces showed strangely in the group of employees and friends of Thaw and the dead man which formed as the last of the audience left.

THOUGHT IT A STAGE TRICK

Two of them said that the reason the fright of the audience was not worse when the shots rang out was that just before the tragedy a dialogue concerning a burlesque duel had been carried on by two of the characters, and many people thought that the old trick of playing in the audience had been tried again.

As the lights of the Garden were dimmed, the body of White was straightened out, the arms brought to the sides, and the legs together. A sheet was obtained in one of the dressing rooms, and this was stretched over it.

While all of this was going on, Policeman Debes and his prisoner had reached the street entrance. Thaw never once lost his composure. His linen and his evening suit showed no signs of ruffling. Only the paleness of his face showed that anything had happened to excite him.

STANFORD WHITE'S CAREER

Designed Many of the Finest
Buildings in This Country

Stanford White was born in this city [New York] on Nov. 9, 1853. He was the son of Richard Grant White and Alexina B. Mease. His father was well known as a critic, journalist, and essayist, and for more than twenty years served as Chief of the United States Revenue Marine Bureau for the District of New York. His mother was a daughter of Charles Bruton Mease of this city. . . . Stanford White was educated in the private schools of New York and by tutors, and received the degree of A.M. from New York College in 1883.

He began the study of architecture in the office of Charles T. Grabrill and Henry H. Richardson. . . . He was the architect of the Villard house, on Madison Avenue, now the property of Whitelaw Reid; of the Madison Square Garden, the Century and Metropolitan clubhouses, the Washington Arch, on Washington Square; the New York University, the University of Virginia, and many private residences throughout the country. . . .

A work by which he will always be remembered, and which is considered by many of his friends as the best specimen of his genius, is the Marble House, which he built at Newport for Mrs. William K. Vanderbilt. Its construction marked the zenith of his fame. He received carte blanche as to material and decoration. His bust now stands on a pedestal in the hall as a recognition of the success he achieved. . . .

Mr. and Mrs. White have not been living together recently, and while the husband nominally retained his home at their house at Gramercy Park and Lexington Avenue, he spent but little of his time there.

Madison Square Garden, designed by him, and where he met his death, was known as his "pleasure house." When the Garden was nearing completion he stipulated that he should have a suite of apartments in the tall tower. He had had it ever since.

For a busy man, who worked hard and achieved notable things, he gave up a great deal of time to the pleasures of friendship and sociability. He had a very large acquaintance among actors and singers, lawyers and doctors and society folk. To them all he was known as "Stan."

He was never happier than in the suite of apartments in Madison Square Garden, directly above the spot where he was killed. He was the supreme master and promoter of all the fun hatched there. It was an attractive place for suppers after the play or the horse show, and invitations to a function there were always highly prized.

WHO HARRY THAW IS

*The Life of the Pittsburgh Man Who Wed
Miss Nesbit*

Harry Kendall Thaw and Evelyn Florence Nesbit were married on April 4, 1905, in the parsonage of the Third Presbyterian Church in Pittsburgh. The marriage followed a reconciliation of Thaw with his family from whom he had been estranged for some time on Miss Nesbit's account.

Thaw is about 36 years of age, and is the son of the late William Thaw, who was Vice President of the Pennsylvania Railroad lines west of Pittsburgh. He was a graduate of the Western University of Pennsylvania. While in Pittsburgh he made his home with his mother at Lyndhurst, on Beechwood Boulevard in the east end of that city. After he was graduated from college and attained his majority, Thaw lived very little in Pittsburgh, most of his time being spent in Europe.

His marriage came as the culmination of a romance with Miss Nesbit, which extended over three years or back to the time when she appeared on the stage here as one of the "Floradora" sextet girls. It continued through various stages here and in Europe, until in October, 1904, the pair returned to this country from abroad and went to the Hotel Cumberland.

There Mr. Thaw refused to register Miss Nesbit as his wife, and they were asked to give up the rooms in the hotel. This stirred up a scandal. Thaw and his former chorus girl went from one hotel to another, finally going west to attend the St. Louis Exposition.

Several times during their journey they denied that they were married. Both dropped out of sight until just before the marriage, when the report came from Pittsburgh that they had been summoned there by Mrs. William Thaw, the young man's mother, who had some time before declared that her son would not be given his income of $80,000 a year unless he gave up Miss Nesbit.

Miss Nesbit, or Mrs. Thaw, was born in Pittsburgh, but did not know Thaw while she lived there. She came to this city about five years ago to earn her living. Before she became an actress she was one of the best known artists' models here. She first appeared in "The Wild Rose," as a show girl, but it was only for a short time. Her connection in a similar capacity in "The Girl from Dixie" was even more brief. She appeared for a time in "Floradora," and it was then that she met Thaw.

Miss Nesbit was one of a party, of which Thaw was also a member, that went abroad in the Spring of 1904. It was known then that they were often in each other's company. The gossip about them, however, did not become general, until dispatches told of Thaw's arrest for speeding an automobile in Switzerland in company with his "wife."

Not long after that a story became current that they had been married abroad, and that Thaw's family was so annoyed at the reports that he could hope for no further advances from his father's estate until the provisions of the elder Thaw's will made it mandatory to turn over to him the $5,000,000 which was his share of the $40,000,000 left by his father when he died.

The story of the marriage was indignantly denied soon afterward by Thaw and Miss Nesbit when they returned to this country in October, 1904.

Few men in recent years have been so persistently in the public eye, on account of escapades, as Harry Thaw. There were two things in which he remained firm—his objection to the marriage of his sister Alice to the Earl of Yarmouth, with whom he had previously had a bitter quarrel, and his devotion to Miss Nesbit.

In spite of the fact that his mother, who controlled his income of $80,000 a year, had previously cut down his allowance to $2,500 on account of his affair with the former model and chorus girl, Thaw remained fixed in his purpose to marry her and finally won his mother's consent to the match.

It was said in Pittsburgh some time ago by members of the Thaw family that his mother had spent over $1,000,000 in her efforts to prevent an undesirable match. It was no secret that his family earnestly desired a union that would bring another coronet into the family.

Before he met Miss Nesbit, Thaw gave a dinner in Paris to a score of famous beauties of Europe, at which he was the only man present. The banquet was one of the most elaborate affairs ever given there, and it was said to have cost no less than $50,000.

[The following account of and excerpt from testimony at Thaw's trial appeared in *The New York Times* for February 8, 1907.]

EVELYN THAW TELLS HER STORY
Accuses Stanford White of Causing Her Fall
CONFESSED IT TO THAW
LAYS BARE HER LIFE IN COURT
TO SAVE HUSBAND
HE SOBS AS HE LISTENS
SHE WILL TELL MORE TO-DAY—
THEN CROSS-EXAMINATION—
LETTERS OF THAW'S
LOVE READ

Dressed as a schoolgirl might have been dressed by her mother, Mrs. Evelyn Nesbit Thaw yesterday told the jury which is trying her husband in the Criminal Branch of the Supreme Court for the murder of Stanford White the whole story of her life, and her relations with White.

There were women in the courtroom. The story caused them to bow their heads and hide their faces and the prisoner to veil his haggard features in his hands and weep. Yet it must be said that the former chorus girl and artists' model told the story with a calmness which was little short of astounding. At no time did her voice become inaudible. At no time did her own face seek the shelter of her hands. At times her voice quivered, and it seemed as if the tears would well up in her eyes and course down her cheeks. But no tears came.

Her husband sobbed, and his agony had no hint of theatrical effect about it. He drew a handkerchief from his pocket when he could stand the story no longer, and his heavy shoulders bent over the table. His face was hidden, but the broad shoulders twitched. Those near him could hear great gulping sounds as he fought to master his emotion.

CALM AS SHE TESTIFIED

Yet, telling of her own degradation, the woman whose beauty has cost the life of one man and put at peril the life of the man who married her despite her past never once lost control of herself. Dressed as a child, she comported herself as a woman of many years in the ways of the world. Never once did she lapse into the fluency of everyday conversational language. It was always, "I do not remember" or "I cannot recall." In her long narration there was never a "don't" and never a "can't" or any other of the little signs which usually betoken spontaneity.

Delphin M. Delmas conducted the examination. His voice was, as ever, soft and kindly. But every word he said in leading Mrs. Thaw onward with her narration was distinct. He got the story in evidence on the ground that she had related the facts to Thaw when he asked her to marry him in Paris. She spent an entire night, the witness said, in telling the story to Thaw as a reason why she thought he should not marry her. He was there in the apartments of her mother and herself in a Paris hotel when daybreak came, and he was sobbing bitterly.

"He wanted every detail," said Mrs. Thaw, "and I told him everything. He would sit and sob or walk up and down the room as I told him."

HER ADVENT IN NEW YORK

There was an unconscious touch of pathos in one statement the witness made as she told of the beginning of her career when she started from the studio life to the life of the footlights.

Mrs. Thaw was telling how a girl friend of the chorus had arranged for her to go to the studio of Mr. White.

"I asked her to have the cab sent by the Waldorf," she said, "so that we could stop there for a moment. I had never seen the Waldorf and wanted to see it. But she did not have the cab go that way."

Again and again District Attorney Jerome stopped the narrative and asked if the rules of evidence were not being stretched by the defense.

"You told all this to Harry K. Thaw that night in Paris?" Mr. Delmas would ask, and the witness invariably replied, "Yes." This disposed of every objection by the District Attorney.

HER MEETING WITH WHITE

Mrs. Thaw said that when she began posing in New York and had established an income and a reputation as a model one of the Sunday newspapers sent a reporter to her. The reporter wrote a story and printed her picture in the paper. After that came many other reporters, and soon her picture was in all the papers. Then came a representative of a theatrical firm, and, as she put it, she saw a chance to double the money she was making.

"What did you do with this money?" asked Mr. Delmas.

"I gave it to Mamma," she replied.

SHE MEETS STANFORD WHITE

Her entrance into the chorus of "Floradora" led to the acquaintance-ship of other girls of the chorus. When she was asked to join a party at Stanford White's studio in the tower of the Madison Square Garden she replied that it would be wrong for her to go. One girl in the chorus was seemingly more anxious than any other to have her meet Mr. White. She was told that he belonged to one of the best families in New York. Finally she went with this girl and drank her first glass of champagne. . . .

INCIDENT OF A VELVET SWING

On the first visit to White's studio, Evelyn said, she and her girl friend had what she called "fun with a swing" in this apartment. The swing in question was of velvet. When the girls were in it the men swung them high toward the ceiling. Their toes struck the crisp paper covering of a great Japanese fan swung from the ceiling, ripping the fan to tatters.

Later Mr. White sent her a message to meet him in a photographer's studio. She was to have some pictures taken. She posed as a Japanese girl. When she went to the dressing room to put on her street garb again he came to the door and asked if she did not need some help. She told him, "No." . . .

COURT SILENT AS SHE SPEAKS

She described her feelings. . . .

Thaw was sobbing, his shoulders heaving up and down, the pale face which has stood the keen gaze of hundreds for two weeks must have been terribly distorted behind the white handkerchief. The courtroom was so quiet that a shriek or an outburst of hysterical laughter, the dropping of a book, or the shuffling of feet, anything to distract the mind for a moment, would have been hailed joyously.

Mr. Delmas stood at the railing in front of the bench, calm and placid of countenance. The habit he has of nervously twirling his glasses in his right hand, to relieve his own feelings, was not indulged in. He appeared complete master of the situation, and the situation appeared to be that upon which the life of Thaw hung.

In the silence even the sobs of Thaw had ceased. Outside the snow carpet on the streets deadened all sounds of traffic that might have crept through tiny crevices between the windows and the heavy stone walls of the court. It seemed as if everyone in the room had ceased to breathe.

The women in the courtroom bowed their heads over the backs of the chairs in front of them. The men continued to lean forward to catch every word.

No blush colored the smooth, oval countenance of the witness. But when she opened her lips they trembled. . . .

MOTHER LEAVES HER IN WHITE'S CARE

Q. [Delphin Delmas]—Very well, then. Proceed with your narrative. What else did you tell him about the events?

A. [Evelyn Nesbit Thaw]—Then Mr. White came to call on my mother several times, and asked if she wanted to go to Pittsburgh to visit her friends there, and she said no, that she could not go and visit there and leave me alone in New York, and he said, "No, that is perfectly right," and then he came again and saw mother several times while I was there, and I remember hearing him tell that it was not impossible for her to go and visit Pittsburgh, if I was left with him. He said she might go and visit in Pittsburgh and leave me in New York in perfect safety, and he would take good care of me, and he made me promise I would not go out with anybody but him.

Mr. Delmas.—Proceed.

WITNESS.—And Mamma told me he was a very grand man, and afterward she went to Pittsburgh and I remember he gave her the money to go. Then Mamma went to Pittsburgh, and the next day, I think, after she left Mr. White sent a carriage for me at 10 o'clock in the morning, and told me that I was to come to the studio and have some photographs taken. So at 10 o'clock I got ready, went downstairs, and got in the carriage and went to his studio in East Twenty-second Street.

Q.—I am requested, Madam, by the Assistant District Attorney to ask you to fix the date of that occurrence as near as you remember it?

A.—I think it was in September.

Q.—Of what year?

A.—1901.

Q.—The other occurrences that you have spoken of were also in 1901, and commenced, if I understood you, in August?

A.—Yes.

VISIT TO WHITE'S STUDIO

Q.—Very well. Then you went to his studio?

A.—Yes.

Q.—On East ———?

A.—On East Twenty-second Street.

Q.—Describe, if you please, what you said, or related to Mr. Thaw about the occurrences that took place at that studio, if you said anything on the subject?

A.—I told him that the door opened by itself, and that I had gone up several flights of stairs and there were no curtains in the windows, and the house looked like nobody lived there from the outside. Then when I got upstairs there was a man, a photographer that I knew, a photographer that I had posed for.

Q.—You need not mention his name unless it is called for.

A.—He was there and there was another man.

Q.—There were then this photographer, you told Mr. Thaw, and another person whose name you have given the District Attorney?

A.—Yes.

Q.—Now then did you describe or relate to Mr. Thaw what took place in that photograph studio?

A.—I said they showed me a dressing room, and I put on a very gorgeous kimono, and they went out and I put on this Japanese kimono, and Mr. White said it came from Hongkong, and I posed for a long time.

Q.—Did you describe to Mr. Thaw the general appearance of those garments?

A.—I did.

Q.—Kindly state what you said to him on the subject?

A.—Well, he had seen the photographs of me taken at that time.

Mr. DELMAS.—Very well. Proceed.

Witness.—And then I told him that this man took the photographs, that I had known him before, and had posed before, and the other man that carried the plates for the photographer, and then I got very tired. I posed a long, long time, and Mr. White said that the photographer could go and the other man could go, and asked the other man to send him some food.

Q.—I am asked if Mr. White was there when you first came in?

A.—Yes.

Q.—Well, then, there was Mr. White, there was the photographer that you had mentioned, and—

A.—Yes.

Q.—And there was also some other person?

A.—Yes.

Q.—And they were all three together there up to the time you are arriving at?

A.—Yes.

Q.—And Mr. White told the photographer and the other gentleman to go?

A.—He told the photographer he could go, and the other man I think was sent to get some food.

Q.—Some food?

A.—Yes. And then I went into the dressing room and shut the door and put on my dress. Mr. White came and knocked at the door and asked if I needed any help, and I said no. Then when I got dressed I came out again, and there was some food in the studio. We sat down and ate, and Mr. White wouldn't let me have but one glass of champagne, and then he put me in a carriage and sent me back to the hotel.

Q.—When you say we, you mean yourself, Mr. White and this other gentleman?

A.—No; he had gone away.

Q.—You two had been left there alone?

A.—Yes.

Q.—Very well, proceed. You then went back in a carriage to your home, to your hotel?

A.—Yes.

Q.—Your mother was absent, as I understand you?

A.—Yes, in Pittsburgh.

INVITED TO A PARTY; ONLY WHITE THERE

Q.—Proceed then.

A.—Then the next night after that I received a note from Mr. White at the theatre asking me to come to a party, and he would send a carriage for me, the carriage would be waiting. So after the theatre I got into the carriage and was taken down to the Twenty-fourth Street studio, and when I got there the door opened and I came out and went upstairs, and Mr. White was there, but no one else was there, and I asked him if the same people would be there who were at the other party.

And he said: "What do you think, they have turned us down."

And I said: "Oh, it's too bad. Then we won't have a party."

He said: "They have turned us down and probably have gone off somewhere else and forgotten all about us."

And I said: "Had I better go home?" and he said: "No, we will sit down and have some food, anyhow, in spite of them"; that I must be hungry.

So he sat down at the table and I took off my hat and coat. We sat down at the table and ate this food. Then I remember Mr. White going away for a while and coming back again.

So after the supper when I got up from the table he told me that I hadn't seen all of his place; that they had three floors, and that there were some very beautiful things in all the different rooms, and he would take me around and show them to me.

So we went up another flight of stairs, not the one I had gone up before, but a little tiny backstairs, and came into a strange room that I hadn't seen before, and there was a piano in this room, paintings on the wall, and very interesting cabinets all about, and we looked at this room for some time, and I sat down at the piano and played something.

DRANK GLASS OF WINE: LOST SENSES

Mr. White asked me to come to see the backroom; and he went through some curtains, and the backroom was a bedroom, and I sat down at this table, a tiny little table—there was a bottle of champagne, a small bottle, and one glass. Mr. White picked up the bottle and poured the glass full of champagne. I paid no attention to him, because I was looking at a picture over the mantel, a very beautiful one that attracted my attention, and asked him who painted it, and he told me. Then he told me he had decorated this room himself, showed me all the different things about. It was very small.

Then he came to me and told me to finish my champagne. I said I didn't care much for it. He insisted that I drink this glass of champagne, which I did, and I don't know whether it was a minute or two minutes after, but a pounding began in my ears, a something and pounding; then the whole room seemed to go around; everything got very black.

(Witness hesitates.)

Mr. DELMAS.—I do not desire to distress you any more than is necessary in this matter, but it is absolutely essential that you should go on with your testimony.

Then the witness continued in detail. She told of awaking later, to find herself in a bed surrounded by mirrors. She screamed, and Stanford White asked her to please keep quiet. She screamed more than ever and he went out of the room. Then she went home and sat up all night.

She repeated the conversation she had with White the next day. He praised her beauty and her youth, told her how he liked girls, and said he would do a great many things for her. . . .

28. Refinements in Advertising Technique

The writers of advertisements often prove the best students of American culture; their professional success depends on how accurately they can sense current values and tastes. Automobile advertising in the first two decades of the twentieth century utilized a number of different ploys. Some ads merely extolled the virtues of the car itself; the Oldsmobile simply "goes." More sophisticated sales pitches linked the product to deeply rooted national ideals. The Simplex was even compared as a cultural product to the Milan Cathedral. Increasing emphasis came to be placed on what a particular car revealed about the man who owned and drove it. For the advertisers, "conspicuous consumption"—the linking of status to possessions—became a vital reality.

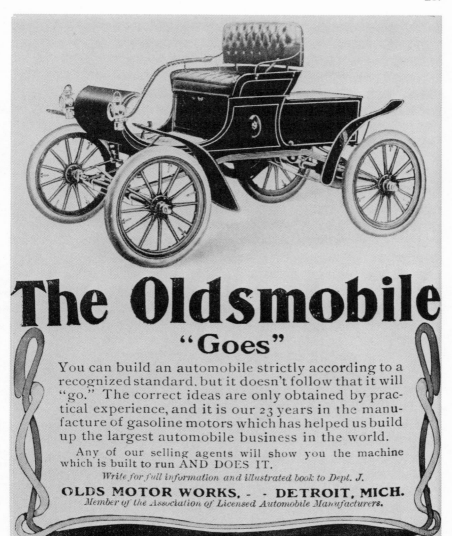

The Oldsmobile
"Goes"

You can build an automobile strictly according to a recognized standard, but it doesn't follow that it will "go." The correct ideas are only obtained by practical experience, and it is our 23 years in the manufacture of gasoline motors which has helped us build up the largest automobile business in the world.

Any of our selling agents will show you the machine which is built to run AND DOES IT.

Write for full information and illustrated book to Dept. J.

OLDS MOTOR WORKS, - - DETROIT, MICH.
Member of the Association of Licensed Automobile Manufacturers.

1. SIMPLY PERFORMANCE: *"The Oldsmobile 'Goes'"* (1903).

2. THE SUBURBAN ROUTINE: *"Maxwell 'Mascotte'"* (1912).

LOZIER motor cars are built for
people who measure cost in *comfort,
style, safety, power* and *dependability.*

The superlative degree of these five qualities
describes the Lozier—the only car in America
that has commanded a price of $5000 or more
for eight consecutive years—a car that is legiti-
mately high-priced.

Everywhere the Lozier commands the attention
and respect of people whose position and training have made them competent judges of a
motor car.

The woman who uses a Lozier may go anywhere—to the fashion shops, to the opera, to
society's most exclusive play-grounds at home or
abroad—with complacent assurance that her
car is correct in every detail of design and
appointment.

| Touring Cars
Five Models
$5000 | **LOZIER**
2405 Mack Ave., Detroit | Limousines
Landaulets
$6500 |

3. THE COST OF RESPECTABILITY: *"Lozier"* (*1912*).

290

"60-Six" Seven-Passenger Touring—$6000

THE EVOLUTION OF THE PEERLESS

THE most obvious characteristic of the Peerless is its irreproach-able beauty—its grace of line and its perfection of finish. Yet the beauty of the Peerless is but a subordinate aim of its makers.

Safety is the first essential, comfort is the second; and not until these imperative qualities have been achieved in the highest possible degree is there any deliberate attention to appearances.

The beauty of the Peerless therefore has this significance: It is the final expression of that type of absolutely faithful construction that insists on fundamentals first—and by so doing evolves naturally into the beauty of form that results from correct design, the best materials, deliberate manu-facture and thorough maturity of every detail.

THREE SIX-CYLINDER MODELS

"38-Six," "48-Six," "60-Six." Scientific heat treatment of steel parts; electric starting and lighting; irreversible steering gear; long stroke motors; seven distinctive body types, at $4300 to $7200.

The Peerless Motor Car Company
Cleveland, Ohio

Makers also of Peerless Trucks

Peerless

ALL THAT THE NAME IMPLIES

4. BEAUTY AS A FUNCTION: *"The Evolution of the Peerless"* (1913).

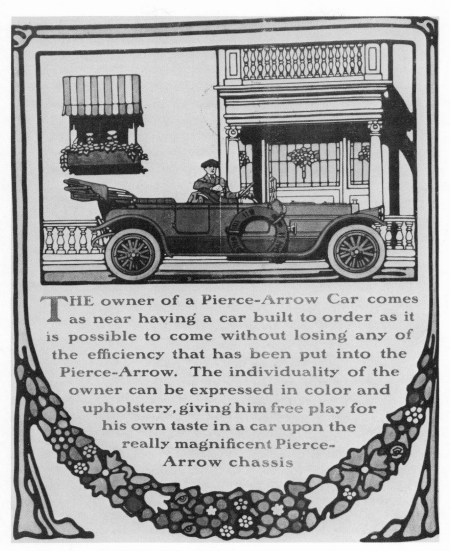

THE owner of a Pierce-Arrow Car comes as near having a car built to order as it is possible to come without losing any of the efficiency that has been put into the Pierce-Arrow. The individuality of the owner can be expressed in color and upholstery, giving him free play for his own taste in a car upon the really magnificent Pierce-Arrow chassis

5. SELF-EXPRESSION THROUGH CONSUMPTION:
"The Owner of a Pierce-Arrow" (1913).

6. PRACTICALITY: *"The New Studebaker"* (1916).

When the Milanese began their cathedral in 1386, no one asked, "How much for the money?" The cathedral was four hundred years building; but the Vision was achieved!

That willingness to take infinite pains is what made the blown glass of Venice, the silk rugs of Persia, the shawls of India, the embroidered screens of Japan.

It is what makes the Crane Model Simplex.

"Neither snow, nor rain, nor heat, nor gloom of night stays these carriers from the swift completion of their appointed rounds." —Herodotus.

SIMPLEX

CRANE Model Simplex Cars are not merely manufactured. Mature engineering knowledge—studied refinement of design—the best materials—the most accurate tools—to all these there is added a wealth of slow and patient finishing, the loving toil of skilled craftsmanship making each detail perfect, comparable to nothing in American automobile construction.

The result is a new measure of silence, sweetness, easy riding and instant control; an indescribable sense of confidence in the car, and of freedom in its marvellous reserve force. To ride in the Crane Model Simplex is to discard all your former ideals of motoring luxury.

Six cylinders; one hundred horse-power. Crane patented spring suspension. Direct drive on fourth. Every chassis given 500-mile road test. Each body built specially for the buyer, like the furnishings of the home.

Every Crane Model Simplex is guaranteed for life while it remains in the hands of the original purchaser.

Chassis, $5,000. Body priced according to cost.

SIMPLEX AUTOMOBILE COMPANY, Inc.
New Brunswick, N. J.

"Genius—the infinite capacity for taking pains."

7. AUTO AS ART: *"Simplex"* (1916).

29. Why They Play Ball

Anthropologists and social psychologists have taught us to realize the cultural significances of various kinds of play and sports. Recreation, it appears, may be an idle pastime, but it is also a symbolic expression of a people's values. In the case of baseball, which blossomed into prominence in the period under consideration, the relationship is particularly clear.

Baseball and the National Life
ADDINGTON H. BRUCE

On July 20, 1858, there was played the first recorded game of baseball to which an admission fee was charged. The opposing teams were made up of carefully selected players representing New York and Brooklyn; the scene of the game was the old Fashion Race Course on Long Island; and some fifteen hundred people paid $750 to see New York win by four runs.

October 16, 1912, or little more than fifty years later, another New York team, playing in Boston, lost by a single run the last of a series of inter-league games for the title of "World's Champions." The newspapers of the country reported the game in the most minute detail, and incidentally announced that the eight games of the series had been attended by more than 250,000 persons, whose admission fees aggregated $490,833, or an average in excess of 30,000 spectators and average receipts of about

Addington H. Bruce, "Baseball and the National Life," *Outlook,* 104 (May, 1913), 104–107.

$60,000 per game. Than these contrasting figures nothing could exhibit more impressively the tremendous growth in popularity of baseball in the comparatively short interval between the earliest and the latest championship game.

When, in the late summer of last year, the Boston "Red Sox" returned from a Western tour which virtually assured to them the championship of the American League, it has been estimated that nearly 100,000 people assembled in the streets of Boston to give them a welcome home. And later, when they played the New York "Giants" in the "World's Series," the course of every game was followed with the most eager attention not alone by the thousands in grand stand and "bleachers," but by many, many thousands more standing in compact masses before the bulletin boards of city newspapers, or in little groups at the telegraph offices of remote and isolated villages. So widespread, in fact, was the interest that the day after the deciding game the newspapers were able to print this astonishing item of news from Washington:

> Unprecedented procedure was permitted today in the Supreme Court of the United States, when the Justices, sitting on the bench hearing the Government's argument in the "bath-tub trust" case, received bulletins, inning by inning, of the "World's Championship" baseball game in Boston. The progress of the playing was closely watched by the members of the highest court in the land, especially by Associate Justice Day, who had requested the baseball bulletins during the luncheon recess from 2 to 2:30 P.M. The little slips giving the progress of the play went to him not only during the luncheon recess, but when the Court resumed its sitting. They were passed along the bench from Justice to Justice.

Veritably baseball is something more than the great American game—it is an American institution having a significant place in the life of the people, and consequently worthy of close and careful analysis.

Fully to grasp its significance, however, it is necessary to study it, in the first place, as merely a game, and seek to determine wherein lie its peculiar qualities of fascination. As a game, as something that is "playable," it of course must serve the ordinary ends of play. These, according to the best authorities on the physiology and psychology of play, are threefold: the expenditure of surplus nervous energy in a way that will not be harmful to the organism, but, on the contrary, will give needed exercise to growing muscles; the development of traits and abilities that will afterwards aid the player in the serious business of life; and the attainment of mental rest through pleasurable occupation.

Until recently it has been customary to emphasize one or another of these purposes and motives as affording the sole reason for play. But scientists are beginning to appreciate that all of them may be operant in determining the action of the play impulse, one motive being influential in one instance, the second in another, the third in yet another, or all three in combination. As between the three, though, the preparation motive would seem to be uppermost, at all events in the play of childhood and youth, children instinctively favoring those games which, although they are completely unconscious of the fact, tend most strongly to form and establish the characteristics that will be most serviceable to them in later years. Or, as stated by Professor Karl Groos, the first to dwell on this aspect of play:

"Play is the agency employed to develop crude powers and prepare them for life's uses, and from the biological standpoint we can say: From the moment when the intellectual development of a species becomes more useful in the 'struggle for existence' than the most perfect instinct, will natural selection favor those individuals in whom the less elaborated faculties have more chance of being worked out by practice under the protection of parents—that is to say, those individuals that play."

Now, in all civilized countries of the modern world, and especially in countries of advanced economic development and of a form of government like that of the United States, success and progress depend chiefly on the presence of certain personal characteristics. Physical fitness, courage, honesty, patience, the spirit of initiative combined with due respect for lawful authority, soundness and quickness of judgment, self-confidence, self-control, cheeriness, fair-mindedness, and appreciation of the importance of social solidarity, of "team play"—these are traits requisite as never before for success in the life of an individual and of a nation. They are traits developed to some extent by all outdoor games played by groups of competitors. But it is safe to say that no other game—not even excepting football—develops them as does baseball.

One need attend only a few games, whether played by untrained school-boys or by the most expert professionals, to appreciate the great value of baseball as a developmental agent. Habits of sobriety and self-control are established in the players if only from the necessity of keeping in good condition in order to acquit one's self creditably and hold a place on the team. Patience, dogged persistence, the pluck that refuses to acknowledge either weariness or defeat, are essential to the mastery of the fine points of batting, fielding, or pitching—a mastery which in turn brings with it a feeling of self-confidence that eventually will go far in helping its possessor to achieve success off as well as on the "diamond."

It takes courage of a high order to play infield positions, as, for example, they ought to be played when "stolen bases" are imminent; and, for that matter, it takes courage to "steal" them when the runner knows that he is likely to be "blocked off" by some courageous infielder of the type of the two Wagners of "Pirate" and "Red Sox" fame.

So, too, courage, and plenty of it, is needed at the bat—courage not simply to face the swiftly moving ball, but to "crowd" the "plate" so as to handicap the pitcher in his efforts to perform successfully and expeditiously the work of elimination. I well remember, in connection with the "World's Series" of 1911, the boldness in this respect displayed by the New York player Snodgrass, when batting against the pitching of the mighty Bender. Time after time Snodgrass stood so close to the "plate" as to draw vehement protests from his opponent, with whom, as an American League partisan, I heartily sympathized. But at the same time I could not withhold some slight measure of admiration for the courage of the batsman, typical of the spirit which, pervading the whole team, had no small share in winning for the "Giants" the National League honors in 1911 and again last year.

As an agent in the development of the "team spirit" baseball is no less notable. The term "sacrifice hit" eloquently expresses one phase of the game which must leave on all playing it an indelible impression of the importance in all affairs of life of unselfish co-operation. The extent, indeed, to which baseball tends to inculcate the lesson of subordination of self for the common good is well shown by a little story I heard not long ago regarding two professional baseball players. One was the short-stop, the other the second baseman, of a "major" league team, and consequently they were required by the duties of their positions to work more closely together than any other members of the team except the pitcher and catcher. One day, the story goes, they had a quarrel so bitter that for the remainder of the season they did not address a word to each other when off the "diamond." But, once the umpire had cried "Play ball!" their antagonism was temporarily dropped, and they fought the common foe in as complete accord as though they had been the best of friends. Surely a game that can develop such a social consciousness—and conscience— is a game of which any nation may be proud, and to which it may well feel indebted.

And, besides aiding powerfully in physical and moral development, baseball is also a splendid mind-builder. The ability to think, and to think quickly, is fostered by the duties of its every position as well as by the complicated problems that are constantly arising in its swiftly changing course of events. Time and again games have been won, or the way has been cleared to victory, by the quickness of a player or a manager in appreciating the possibilities of a critical situation and planning a definite plan of campaign to meet the emergency. It was thus, to give a single illustration, with the final game of last year's "World's Series."

That game was won by the "Red Sox" by the score of three runs to two, an extra inning being necessary, as the score stood one to one in the ninth. The newspapers next day gave unenviable prominence to two New York fielders, to whose errors in the tenth inning the loss of the game was ascribed. Actually the turning-point came in the seventh inning, when New York led by one run to none for Boston.

From the start of the game Mathewson, the premier pitcher of the National League, had been disposing of the "Red Sox" batsmen with all his old-time skill. Bedient, his young rival, had been doing almost equally well, although New York had earned a run off him in the third inning. In Boston's half of the seventh, with two men out and a man on first base, the manager of the "Red Sox"—who also, as it happened, was the man then on first base—made the move that undoubtedly saved the game for his team. It was Bedient's turn to bat, but instead Manager Stahl sent to the "plate" a utility outfielder, Henriksen, who until that moment had not once been at bat in the series. Mathewson, utterly in the dark as to his weaknesses as a batsman, tried him with a variety of pitches. One proved so much to his liking that he drove it past third base for a hit that brought in the tying run. Stahl's judgment, plus Henriksen's ability to "make good," had turned impending defeat into possible victory.

So incessant and so varied are the demands made on the ball-player's intelligence that any one who really knows the game will be inclined to indorse unreservedly the published declaration of that most successful baseball-player and most successful business man, Mr. Albert G. Spalding:

"I never struck anything in business that did not seem a simple matter when compared with complications I have faced on the baseball field. A young man playing baseball gets into the habit of quick thinking in most adverse circumstances and under the most merciless criticism in the world—the criticism from the 'bleachers.' If that doesn't train him, nothing can. Baseball in youth has the effect in later years of making him think and act a little quicker than the other fellow."

To-day this is even more the case than in the days when Mr. Spalding led his Boston and Chicago teams to victory, for with the passage of time the technique of the game has been improved to an extent that makes it more of a developmental agent than it was even ten years ago. Lacking the strength, skill, and experience of the professional player, the school-boy whose efforts are confined to the "diamond" of the vacant lot or public park plays the game under precisely the same rules as the professional, and with no less zest and earnestness, and profits correspondingly. To be sure, in playing it he does not dream for an instant that he is thereby helping to prepare himself for the important struggles of maturity. He plays it merely because he finds it "good fun"—merely because, in its variety and rapidity of action, in the comparative ease with which its fundamental principles may be learned, and in its essentially co-operative yet competitive character, it affords an intensely pleasurable occupation. It is, in truth, a game which makes an irresistible appeal to the instincts of youth precisely because it so admirably meets the principal objects of play—mental rest through enjoyment, exercise for the muscles, the healthy expenditure of surplus nervous energy, and practice and preparation for life's work.

This, of course, does not explain its popularity with the non-playing American public of mature years, a popularity which seems to many the more surprising and reprehensible in view of the fact that to-day, when baseball games are drawing larger crowds than in all the previous history of the sport, the Nation is burdened to an appalling extent by economic and social evils. But in reality this phenomenon is neither so unusual nor so ominous as alarmists would have us believe. "Give us games!" was the cry of the Roman populace in time of disaster many centuries ago, and it has since been unconsciously echoed by many another people under the stress of some great crisis.

Baseball itself, it is worth noting, was a product of the period of anti-slavery agitation that preceded the crisis of the Civil War, having been invented in 1839, two years after the murder of the abolitionist Elijah P. Lovejoy, and one year after the burning of Pennsylvania Hall, in Philadelphia, by a mob of pro-slavery sympathizers; and its first rise into favor as a public spectacle was but a year or so before North and South met in their epochal conflict.

What this means is simply an instinctive resort to sport as a method of gaining momentary relief from the strain of an intolerable burden, and at the same time finding a harmless outlet for pent-up emotions which, unless thus gaining expression, might discharge themselves in a dangerous way. It also means, there is reason to believe, a continuance of the play impulse as an aid in the rational and efficient conduct of life. It is no mere coincidence that the great sport-loving peoples of the world—the Americans, the English, the Canadians, and the Australians—have been pre-eminent in the art of achieving progress by peaceful and orderly reform. There have been times, as in the case of the Civil War, when the issues involved have been such as to make absolutely necessary the arbitrament of arms. But evolution, not revolution, has been the rule in the development of these nations—these nations which above all others respond to the impulse to play.

Baseball, then, from the spectator's standpoint, is to be regarded as a means of catharsis, or, perhaps better, as a safety-valve. And it performs this service the more readily because of the appeal it makes to the basic instincts, with resultant removal of the inhibitions that ordinarily cause tenseness and restraint. For exactly the same reason it has a democratizing value no less important to the welfare of society than is its value as a developmental and tension-relieving agent. The spectator at a ball game is no longer a statesman, lawyer, broker, doctor, merchant, or artisan, but just a plain every-day man, with a heart full of fraternity and good will to all his fellow-men—except perhaps the umpire. The oftener he sits in grand stand or "bleachers," the broader, kindlier, better man and citizen he must tend to become.

Finally, it is to be observed that the mere watching of a game of baseball, as of football, lacrosse, hockey, or any other game of swift action, has a certain beneficial physical effect. It is a psychological commonplace that pleasurable emotions, especially if they find expression in laughter, shouts, cheers, and other muscle-expanding noises, have a tonic value to the whole bodily system. So that it is quite possible to get exercise vicariously, as it were; and the more stimulating the spectacle that excites feelings of happiness and enjoyment, the greater will be the resultant good. Most decidedly baseball is a game well designed to render this excellent service.

Like every virile, vigorous game, it has its defects. But its qualities far outweigh its shortcomings, and it must be accounted a happy day for America when the first players met on the first "diamond" laid out on American soil. The little red school-house has long been extolled as a prime factor in the Republic's progress. I for one am firmly convinced that the lessons taught in it would have lacked much of their potency had it not been for the reinforcement they received from the lessons learned on the baseball field near by. Long may Uncle Sam play ball!

30. The Gospel of Production

In the first two decades of the twentieth century Henry Ford and his Model T skyrocketed into leadership of the automobile industry. Ford also became an industrial deity, admired around the world as the personification of the new productive philosophy. His initiation of the assembly line and the five dollar minimum daily wage were epoch-making, but no less important in a society partially uneasy about growth and change was his justification of the entire industrial enterprise. In the statement below Ford gives the ideals that guided his years of greatest achievement.

My Life and Work
HENRY FORD

We have only started on our development of our country—we have not as yet, with all our talk of wonderful progress, done more than scratch the surface. The progress has been wonderful enough—but when we compare what we have done with what there is to do, then our past accomplishments are as nothing. When we consider that more power is used merely in ploughing the soil than is used in all the industrial establishments of the country put together, an inkling comes of how much opportunity there is ahead. And now, with so many countries of the world in ferment and with so much unrest everywhere, is an excellent time to suggest something of the things that may be done—in the light of what has been done.

Henry Ford, *My Life and Work* (New York, Doubleday, 1923), 1–19.

When one speaks of increasing power, machinery, and industry there comes up a picture of a cold, metallic sort of world in which great factories will drive away the trees, the flowers, the birds, and the green fields. And that then we shall have a world composed of metal machines and human machines. With all of that I do not agree. I think that unless we better understand the mechanical portion of life, we cannot have the time to enjoy the trees, and the birds, and the flowers, and the green fields.

I think that we have already done too much toward banishing the pleasant things from life by thinking that there is some opposition between living and providing the means of living. We waste so much time and energy that we have little left over in which to enjoy ourselves. Power and machinery, money and goods, are useful only as they set us free to live. They are but means to an end. For instance, I do not consider the machines which bear my name simply as machines. If that was all there was to it I would do something else. I take them as concrete evidence of the working out of a theory of business which I hope is something more than a theory of business—a theory that looks toward making this world a better place in which to live. The fact that the commercial success of the Ford Motor Company has been most unusual is important only because it serves to demonstrate, in a way which no one can fail to understand, that the theory to date is right. Considered solely in this light I can criticize the prevailing system of industry and the organization of money and society from the standpoint of one who has not been beaten by them.

As things are now organized, I could, were I thinking only selfishly, ask for no change. If I merely want money the present system is all right; it gives money in plenty to me. But I am thinking of service. The present system does not permit of the best service because it encourages every kind of waste—it keeps many men from getting the full return from service. And it is going nowhere. It is all a matter of better planning and adjustment.

I have no quarrel with the general attitude of scoffing at new ideas. It is better to be skeptical of all new ideas and to insist upon being shown rather than to rush around in a continuous brainstorm after every new idea. Skepticism, if by that we mean cautiousness, is the balance wheel of civilization. Most of the present acute troubles of the world arise out of taking on new ideas without first carefully investigating to discover if they are good ideas. An idea is not necessarily good because it is old, or necessarily bad because it is new, but if an old idea works, then the weight of the evidence is all in its favour. Ideas are of themselves extraordinarily valuable, but an idea is just an idea. Almost any one can think up an idea. The thing that counts is developing it into a practical product.

I am now most interested in fully demonstrating that the ideas we have put into practice are capable of the largest application—that they have nothing peculiarly to do with motor cars or tractors but form something in the nature of a universal code. I am quite certain that it is the natural code and I want to demonstrate it so thoroughly that it will be accepted, not as a new idea, but as a natural code.

The natural thing to do is to work—to recognize that prosperity and happiness can be obtained only through honest effort. Human ills flow largely from attempting to escape from this natural course. I have no suggestion which goes beyond accepting in its fullest this principle of nature. I take it for granted that we must work. All that we have done comes as the result of a certain insistence that since we must work it is better to work intelligently and forehandedly; that the better we do our work the better off we shall be. All of which I conceive to be merely elemental common sense.

I am not a reformer. I think there is entirely too much attempt at reforming in the world and that we pay too much attention to reformers. We have two kinds of reformers. Both are nuisances. The man who calls himself a reformer wants to smash things. He is the sort of man who would tear up a whole shirt because the collar button did not fit the buttonhole. It would never occur to him to enlarge the buttonhole. This sort of reformer never under any circumstances knows what he is doing. Experience and reform do not go together. A reformer cannot keep his zeal at white heat in the presence of a fact. He must discard all facts.

Since 1914 a great many persons have received brand-new intellectual outfits. Many are beginning to think for the first time. They opened their eyes and realized that they were in the world. Then, with a thrill of independence, they realized that they could look at the world critically. They did so and found it faulty. The intoxication of assuming the masterful position of a critic of the social system—which it is every man's right to assume—is unbalancing at first. The very young critic is very much unbalanced. He is strongly in favour of wiping out the old order and starting a new one. They actually managed to start a new world in Russia. It is there that the work of the world makers can best be studied. We learn from Russia that it is the minority and not the majority who determine destructive action. We learn also that while men may decree social laws in conflict with natural laws, Nature vetoes those laws more ruthlessly than did the Czars. Nature has vetoed the whole Soviet Republic. For it sought to deny Nature. It denied above all else the right to the fruits of labour. Some people say, "Russia will have to go to work," but that does not describe the case. The fact is that poor Russia is at work, but her work counts for nothing. It is not free work. In the United States a workman works eight hours a day; in Russia, he works twelve to four-teen. In the United States, if a workman wishes to lay off a day or a week, and is able to afford it, there is nothing to prevent him. In Russia, under Sovietism, the workman goes to work whether he wants to or not. The freedom of the citizen has disappeared in the discipline of a prison-like monotony in which all are treated alike. That is slavery. Freedom is the right to work a decent length of time and to get a decent living for doing so; to be able to arrange the little personal details of one's own life. It is the aggregate of these and many other items of freedom which makes up the great idealistic Freedom. The minor forms of Freedom lubricate the everyday life of all of us.

Russia could not get along without intelligence and experience. As soon as she began to run her factories by committees, they went to rack and ruin; there was more debate than production. As soon as they threw out the skilled man, thousands of tons of precious materials were spoiled. The fanatics talked the people into starvation. The Soviets are now offering the engineers, the administrators, the foremen and superintendents, whom at first they drove out, large sums of money if only they will come back. Bolshevism is now crying for the brains and experience which it yesterday treated so ruthlessly. All that "reform" did to Russia was to block production.

There is in this country a sinister element that desires to creep in between the men who work with their hands and the men who think and plan for the men who work with their hands. The same influence that drove the brains, experience, and ability out of Russia is busily engaged in raising prejudice here. We must not suffer the stranger, the destroyer, the hater of happy humanity, to divide our people. In unity is American strength—and freedom.

On the other hand, we have a different kind of reformer who never calls himself one. He is singularly like the radical reformer. The radical has had no experience and does not want it. The other class of reformer has had plenty of experience but it does him no good. I refer to the reac-tionary—who will be surprised to find himself put in exactly the same class as the Bolshevist. He wants to go back to some previous condition, not because it was the best condition, but because he thinks he knows about that condition.

The one crowd wants to smash up the whole world in order to make a better one. The other holds the world as so good that it might well be let stand as it is—and decay. The second notion arises as does the first—out of not using the eyes to see with. It is perfectly possible to smash this world, but it is not possible to build a new one. It is possible to prevent the world from going forward, but it is not possible then to prevent it from going back—from decaying. It is foolish to expect that, if everything be overturned, everyone will thereby get three meals a day. Or, should everything be petrified, that thereby six per cent interest may be paid. The trouble is that reformers and reactionaries alike get away from the realities—from the primary functions.

One of the counsels of caution is to be very certain that we do not mistake a reactionary turn for a return of common sense. We have passed through a period of fireworks of every description, and the making of a great many idealistic maps of progress. We did not get anywhere. It was a convention, not a march. Lovely things were said, but when we got home we found the furnace out. Reactionaries have frequently taken advantage of the recoil from such a period, and they have promised "the good old times"—which usually means the bad old abuses—and because they are perfectly void of vision they are sometimes regarded as "practical men." Their return to power is often hailed as the return of common sense.

The primary functions are agriculture, manufacture, and transportation. Community life is impossible without them. They hold the world together. Raising things, making things, and carrying things are as primitive as human need and yet as modern as anything can be. They are of the essence of physical life. When they cease, community life ceases. Things do get out of shape in this present world under the present system, but we may hope for a betterment if the foundations stand sure. The great delusion is that one may change the foundation—usurp the part of destiny in the social process. The foundations of society are the men and means to *grow* things, to *make* things, and to *carry* things. As long as agriculture, manufacture, and transportation survive, the world can survive any economic or social change. As we serve our jobs we serve the world.

There is plenty of work to do. Business is merely work. Speculation in things already produced—that is not business. It is just more or less respectable graft. But it cannot be legislated out of existence. Laws can do very little. Law never does anything constructive. It can never be more than a policeman, and so it is a waste of time to look to our state capitals or to Washington to do that which law was not designed to do. As long as we look to legislation to cure poverty or to abolish special privilege we are going to see poverty spread and special privilege grow. We have had enough of looking to Washington and we have had enough of legislators—not so much, however, in this as in other countries— promising laws to do that which laws cannot do.

When you get a whole country—as did ours—thinking that Washington is a sort of heaven and behind its clouds dwell omniscience and omnipotence, you are educating that country into a dependent state of mind which augurs ill for the future. Our help does not come from Washington, but from ourselves; our help may, however, go to Washington as a sort of central distribution point where all our efforts are coördinated for the general good. We may help the Government; the Government cannot help us.

The slogan of "less government in business and more business in government" is a very good one, not mainly on account of business or government, but on account of the people. Business is not the reason why the United States was founded. The Declaration of Independence is not a business charter, nor is the Constitution of the United States a commercial schedule. The United States—its land, people, government, and business—are but methods by which the life of the people is made worth while. The Government is a servant and never should be anything but a servant. The moment the people become adjuncts to government, then the law of retribution begins to work, for such a relation is unnatural, immoral, and inhuman. We cannot live without business and we cannot live without government. Business and government are necessary as servants, like water and grain; as masters they overturn the natural order.

The welfare of the country is squarely up to us as individuals. That is where it should be and that is where it is safest. Governments can promise something for nothing but they cannot deliver. They can juggle the currencies as they did in Europe (and as bankers the world over do, as long as they can get the benefit of the juggling) with a patter of solemn nonsense. But it is work and work alone that can continue to deliver the goods—and that, down in his heart, is what every man knows.

There is little chance of an intelligent people, such as ours, ruining the fundamental processes of economic life. Most men know they cannot get something for nothing. Most men feel—even if they do not know

—that money is not wealth. The ordinary theories which promise every-thing to everybody, and demand nothing from anybody, are promptly denied by the instincts of the ordinary man, even when he does not find reasons against them. He *knows* they are wrong. That is enough. The pres-ent order, always clumsy, often stupid, and in many ways imperfect, has this advantage over any other—it works. Doubtless our order will merge by degrees into another, and the new one will also work—but not so much by reason of what it is as by reason of what men will bring into it. The reason why Bolshevism did not work, and cannot work, is not economic. It does not matter whether industry is privately managed or socially con-trolled; it does not matter whether you call the workers' share "wages" or "dividends"; it does not matter whether you regimentalize the people as to food, clothing, and shelter, or whether you allow them to eat, dress, and live as they like. Those are mere matters of detail. The incapacity of the Bolshevist leaders is indicated by the fuss they made over such details. Bolshevism failed because it was both unnatural and immoral. Our system stands. Is it wrong? Of course it is wrong, at a thousand points! Is it clumsy?—of course it is clumsy. By all right and reason it ought to break down. But it does not—because it is instinct with certain economic and moral fundamentals.

The economic fundamental is labour. Labour is the human element which makes the fruitful seasons of the earth useful to men. It is men's labour that makes the harvest what it is. That is the economic funda-mental: every one of us is working with material which we did not and could not create, but which was presented to us by Nature.

The moral fundamental is man's right in his labour. This is variously stated. It is sometimes called "the right of property." It is sometimes masked in the command, "Thou shalt not steal." It is the other man's right in his property that makes stealing a crime. When a man has earned his bread, he has a right to that bread. If another steals it, he does more than steal bread; he invades a sacred human right.

If we cannot produce we cannot have—but some say if we produce it is only for the capitalists. Capitalists who become such because they provide better means of production are of the foundation of society. They have really nothing of their own. They merely manage property for the benefit of others. Capitalists who become such through trading in money are a temporarily necessary evil. They may not be evil at all if their money goes to production. If their money goes to complicating distribu-tion—to raising barriers between the producer and the consumer—then they are evil capitalists and they will pass away when money is better adjusted to work; and money will become better adjusted to work when it is fully realized that through work and work alone may health, wealth, and happiness inevitably be secured.

There is no reason why a man who is willing to work should not be able to work and to receive the full value, of his work. There is equally no reason why a man who can but will not work should not receive the full value of his services to the community. He should most certainly be permitted to take away from the community an equivalent of what he contributes to it. If he contributes nothing he should take away nothing. He should have the freedom of starvation. We are not getting anywhere when we insist that every man ought to have more than he deserves to have—just because some do get more than they deserve to have.

There can be no greater absurdity and no greater disservice to humanity in general than to insist that all men are equal. Most certainly all men are not equal, and any democratic conception which strives to make men equal is only an effort to block progress. Men cannot be of equal service. The men of larger ability are less numerous than the men of smaller ability; it is possible for a mass of the smaller men to pull the larger ones down—but in so doing they pull themselves down. It is the larger men who give the leadership to the community and enable the smaller men to live with less effort.

The conception of democracy which names a levelling-down of ability makes for waste. No two things in nature are alike. We build our cars absolutely interchangeable. All parts are as nearly alike as chemical analysis, the finest machinery, and the finest workmanship can make them. No fitting of any kind is required, and it would certainly seem that two Fords standing side by side, looking exactly alike and made so exactly alike that any part could be taken out of one and put into the other, would be alike. But they are not. They will have different road habits. We have men who have driven hundreds, and in some cases thousands, of Fords and they say that no two ever act precisely the same —that, if they should drive a new car for an hour or even less and then the car were mixed with a bunch of other new ones, also each driven for a single hour and under the same conditions, that although they could not recognize the car they had been driving merely by looking at it, they could do so by driving it. . . .

The producer depends for his prosperity upon serving the people. He may get by for a while serving himself, but if he does, it will be purely accidental, and when the people wake up to the fact that they are not being served, the end of that producer is in sight. During the boom period the larger effort of production was to serve itself and hence, the moment the people woke up, many producers went to smash. They said that they had entered into a "period of depression." Really they had not. They were simply trying to pit nonsense against sense—which is something that cannot successfully be done. Being greedy for money is the surest way not to get it, but when one serves for the sake of service—for the satisfaction of doing that which one believes to be right—then money abundantly takes care of itself.

Money comes naturally as the result of service. And it is absolutely necessary to have money. But we do not want to forget that the end of money is not ease but the opportunity to perform more service. In my mind nothing is more abhorrent than a life of ease. None of us has any right to ease. There is no place in civilization for the idler. Any scheme looking to abolishing money is only making affairs more complex, for we must have a measure. That our present system of money is a satisfactory basis for exchange is a matter of grave doubt. That is a question which I shall talk of in a subsequent chapter. The gist of my objection to the present monetary system is that it tends to become a thing of itself and to block instead of facilitate production.

My effort is in the direction of simplicity. People in general have so little and it costs so much to buy even the barest necessities (let alone that share of the luxuries to which I think everyone is entitled) because nearly everything that we make is much more complex than it needs to be. Our clothing, our food, our household furnishings—all could be much simpler than they now are and at the same time be better looking. Things in past ages were made in certain ways and makers since then have just followed.

I do not mean that we should adopt freak styles. There is no necessity for that. Clothing need not be a bag with a hole cut in it. That might be easy to make but it would be inconvenient to wear. A blanket does not require much tailoring, but none of us could get much work done if we went around Indian-fashion in blankets. Real simplicity means that which gives the very best service and is the most convenient in use. The trouble with drastic reforms is they always insist that a man be made over in order to use certain designed articles. I think that dress reform for women —which seems to mean ugly clothes—must always originate with plain women who want to make everyone else look plain. That is not the right process. Start with an article that suits and then study to find some way of eliminating the entirely useless parts. This applies to everything—a shoe, a dress, a house, a piece of machinery, a railroad, a steamship, an airplane.

As we cut out useless parts and simplify necessary ones we also cut down the cost of making. This is simple logic, but oddly enough the ordinary process starts with a cheapening of the manufacturing instead of with a simplifying of the article. The start ought to be with the article. First we ought to find whether it is as well made as it should be—does it give the best possible service? Then—are the materials the best or merely the most expensive? Then—can its complexity and weight be cut down? And so on.

There is no more sense in having extra weight in an article than there is in the cockade on a coachman's hat. In fact, there is not as much. For the cockade may help the coachman to identify his hat while the extra weight means only a waste of strength. I cannot imagine where the delusion that weight means strength came from. It is all well enough in a pile-driver, but why move a heavy weight if we are not going to hit anything with it? In transportation why put extra weight in a machine? Why not add it to the load that the machine is designed to carry? Fat men cannot run as fast as thin men but we build most of our vehicles as though dead-weight fat increased speed! A deal of poverty grows out of the carriage of excess weight.

Some day we shall discover how further to eliminate weight. Take wood, for example. For certain purposes wood is now the best substance we know, but wood is extremely wasteful. The wood in a Ford car contains thirty pounds of water. There must be some way of doing better than that. There must be some method by which we can gain the same strength and elasticity without having to lug useless weight. And so through a thousand processes.

The farmer makes too complex an affair out of his daily work. I believe that the average farmer puts to a really useful purpose only about 5 per cent of the energy that he spends. If any one ever equipped a factory in the style, say, the average farm is fitted out, the place would be cluttered with men. The worst factory in Europe is hardly as bad as the average farm barn. Power is utilized to the least possible degree. Not only is everything done by hand, but seldom is a thought given to logical arrangement. A farmer doing his chores will walk up and down a rickety ladder a dozen times. He will carry water for years instead of putting in a few lengths of pipe. His whole idea, when there is extra work to do, is to hire extra men. He thinks of putting money into improvements as an expense. Farm products at their lowest prices are dearer than they ought to be. Farm profits at their highest are lower than they ought to be. It is waste motion—waste effort—that makes farm prices high and profits low.

On my own farm at Dearborn we do everything by machinery. We have eliminated a great number of wastes, but we have not as yet touched on real economy. We have not yet been able to put in five or ten years of intense night-and-day study to discover what really ought to be done. We have left more undone than we have done. Yet at no time—no matter what the value of crops—have we failed to turn a first-class profit. We are not farmers—we are industrialists on the farm. The moment the farmer considers himself as an industrialist, with a horror of waste either in material or in men, then we are going to have farm products so low-priced that all will have enough to eat, and the profits will be so satisfactory that farming will be considered as among the least hazardous and most profitable of occupations.

Lack of knowledge of what is going on and lack of knowledge of what the job really is and the best way of doing it are the reasons why farming is thought not to pay. Nothing could pay the way farming is conducted. The farmer follows luck and his forefathers. He does not know how economically to produce, and he does not know how to market. A manufacturer who knew how neither to produce nor to market would not long stay in business. That the farmer can stay on shows how wonderfully profitable farming can be.

The way to attain low-priced, high-volume production in the factory or on the farm—and low-priced, high-volume production means plenty for everyone—is quite simple. The trouble is that the general tendency is to complicate very simple affairs. Take, for an instance, an "improvement."

When we talk about improvements usually we have in mind some change in a product. An "improved" product is one that has been changed. That is not my idea. I do not believe in starting to make [changes] until I have discovered the best possible thing. This, of course, does not mean that a product should never be changed, but I think that it will be found more economical in the end not even to try to produce an article until you have fully satisfied yourself that utility, design, and material are the best. If your researches do not give you that confidence, then keep right on searching until you find confidence. The place to start manufacturing is with the article. The factory, the organization, the selling, and the financial plans will shape themselves to the article. You will have a cutting edge on your business chisel and in the end you will save time. Rushing into manufacturing without being certain of the product is the unrecognized cause of many business failures. People seem to think that the big thing is the factory or the store or the financial backing or the management. The big thing is the product, and any hurry in getting into fabrication before designs are completed is just so much waste time. I spent twelve years before I had a Model T—which is what is known to-day as the Ford car—that suited me. We did not attempt to go into real production until we had a real product. That product has not been essentially changed.

We are constantly experimenting with new ideas. If you travel the roads in the neighbourhood of Dearborn you can find all sorts of models of Ford cars. They are experimental cars—they are not new models. I do not believe in letting any good idea get by me, but I will not quickly decide whether an idea is good or bad. If an idea seems good or seems even to have possibilities, I believe in doing whatever is necessary to test out the idea from every angle. But testing out the idea is something very different from making a change in the car. Where most manufacturers find themselves quicker to make a change in the product than in the method of manufacturing—we follow exactly the opposite course.

Our big changes have been in methods of manufacturing. They never stand still. I believe that there is hardly a single operation in the making of our car that is the same as when we made our first car of the present model. That is why we make them so cheaply. The few changes that have been made in the car have been in the direction of convenience in use or where we found that a change in design might give added strength. The materials in the car change as we learn more and more about materials. Also we do not want to be held up in production or have the expense of production increased by any possible shortage in a particular material, so we have for most parts worked out substitute materials. Vanadium steel, for instance, is our principal steel. With it we can get the greatest strength with the least weight, but it would not be good business to let our whole future depend upon being able to get vanadium steel. We have worked out a substitute. All our steels are special, but for every one of them we have at least one, and sometimes several, fully proved and tested substitutes. And so on through all of our materials and likewise with our parts. In the beginning we made very few of our parts and none of our motors. Now we make all our motors and most of our parts because we find it cheaper to do so. But also we aim to make some of every part so that we cannot be caught in any market emergency or be crippled by some outside manufacturer being unable to fill his orders. The prices on glass were run up outrageously high during the war; we are among the largest users of glass in the country. Now we are putting up our own glass factory. If we had devoted all of this energy to making changes in the product we should be nowhere; but by not changing the product we are able to give our energy to the improvement of the making.

The principal part of a chisel is the cutting edge. If there is a single principle on which our business rests it is that. It makes no difference how finely made a chisel is or what splendid steel it has in it or how well it is forged—if it has no cutting edge it is not a chisel. It is just a piece of metal. All of which being translated means that it is what a thing does—not what it is supposed to do—that matters. What is the use of putting a tremendous force behind a blunt chisel if a light blow on a sharp chisel will do the work? The chisel is there to cut, not to be hammered. The hammering is only incidental to the job. So if we want to work why not concentrate on the work and do it in the quickest possible fashion? The cutting edge of merchandising is the point where the product touches the consumer. An unsatisfactory product is one that has a dull cutting edge. A lot of waste effort is needed to put it through. The cutting edge of a factory is the man and the machine on the job. If the man is not right the machine cannot be; if the machine is not right the man cannot be. For any one to be required to use more force than is absolutely necessary for the job in hand is waste.

The essence of my idea then is that waste and greed block the delivery of true service. Both waste and greed are unnecessary. Waste is due largely to not understanding what one does, or being careless in the doing of it. Greed is merely a species of nearsightedness. I have striven toward manufacturing with a minimum of waste, both of materials and of human effort, and then toward distribution at a minimum of profit, depending for the total profit upon the volume of distribution. In the process of manufacturing I want to distribute the maximum of wage— that is, the maximum of buying power. Since also this makes for a minimum cost and we sell at a minimum profit, we can distribute a product in consonance with buying power. Thus everyone who is connected with us—either as a manager, worker, or purchaser—is the better for our existence.

31. Patterns of Work and Play

Mass production revolutionized working conditions. Automobiles came off the assembly line in an endless, impersonal succession, but workmen did not "make" them in the traditional sense. On the line one simply placed a screw, gave it a few turns, and passed the partially finished object on down the row. Garment workers sometimes had the satisfaction of turning out completed products, but they never faced their customers or received comment on their wares. In the context of increasingly depersonalized work, recreation, even the spectator variety, acquired special significance as a means of asserting, or applauding, individual competence. Theodore Roosevelt responded to the call of the wild by donning a buckskin hunting suit and pursuing big game. For women, like Boston socialite Eleanora Sears, tennis offered an avenue for demonstrating skill and mastery. The Sierra Club and other outing groups sponsored trips into wilderness areas for both sexes. For most Americans, however, a combination of wilderness and civilization was considered optimum. The national parks and their comfortable inns, which enjoyed a great vogue after 1916, satisfied popular taste for the partly wild.

1. THE ASSEMBLY LINE: *The Ford Motor Company plant at Highland Park, Michigan (1914).*

2. ON THE LINE: *Magneto "feeder" assembly line, Ford Motor Company, Highland Park, Michigan (1914).*

3. THE SWEATSHOP: *New York garment factory (about 1912).*

4. THE MODERN PIONEER:
A young Theodore Roosevelt in the Dakotas.

5. A NEW WOMAN: *Eleanora Sears belts a forehand.*

6. WILDERNESS RECREATION: *The Sierra Club's Tenth Annual Outing on the trail (1911).*

7. NATURE AND CIVILIZATION: *Cars outside the National Park Inn at Mt. Ranier (about 1916).*

32. Men and Machines

Popular or folk culture is often most readily glimpsed in a people's songs and legends. After the turn of the century the theme of mechanization figured in many such. One of the popular tales concerned John Henry and allegedly originated in 1873 when the Chesapeake and Ohio Railroad put through the Big Bend Tunnel in West Virginia. One day a new steam drill was brought onto the job, prompting a challenge from the champion hammer driller—a giant Black. By 1910 the outcome of the contest had become part of the workingman's culture (white as well as black) throughout the country.

On April 30, 1900, on the run from Chicago to New Orleans a crack passenger train of the Illinois Central piled into the rear of a freight near Vaughan, Mississippi. The engineer, one John Luther Jones, ordered his firemen to jump and stayed with his hurtling train. He was found dead, one hand on the whistle cord and the other on the air brake. A Black railroad worker's song about the incident was rewritten by whites and became a hit on the 1909 vaudeville circuit.

The deaths by machine of John Henry and Casey Jones underscored the plight of man in the machine age. Needed was a triumphant retaliation, a way of reasserting the importance of the individual. One result was the popularity after 1910 of the Paul Bunyan legends. Here was a giant who could outwork any machine. The Bunyan tales were collected from the oral tradition of lumberman and initially published in 1914 and 1916.

John Henry

John Henry was a li'l baby, uh-huh.*
Sittin' on his mama's knee, oh, yeah,*
Said: "De Big Bend Tunnel on de C. & O. road
Gonna cause de death of me,
Lawd, Lawd, gonna cause de death of me."

John Henry, he had a woman,
Her name was Mary Magdalene,
She would go to de tunnel and sing for John,
Jes' to hear John Henry's hammer ring,
Lawd, Lawd, jes' to hear John Henry's hammer ring.

John Henry had a li'l woman,
Her name was Lucy Ann,
John Henry took sick an' had to go to bed,
Lucy Ann drove steel like a man,
Lawd, Lawd, Lucy Ann drove steel like a man.

Cap'n says to John Henry,
"Gonna bring me a steam drill 'round,
Gonna take dat steam drill out on de job,
Gonna whop dat steel on down,
Lawd, Lawd, gonna whop dat steel on down."

John Henry tol' his cap'n,
Lightnin' was in his eye:
"Cap'n, bet yo' las' red cent on me,
Fo' I'll beat it to de bottom, or I'll die,
Lawd, Lawd, I'll beat it to de bottom or I'll die."

Sun shine hot an' burnin',
Wer'n't no breeze a-tall,
Sweat ran down like water down a hill,

* The syllables "uh-huh" and "oh, yeah" are to be repeated in each stanza.
They are grunts which might accompany physical effort, indicating that the
song was meant to be sung while working. [Ed.]

"John Henry" in John A. Lomax and Alan Lomax, *American Ballads and
Folk Songs* (New York, Macmillan, 1934), 5–9.

Dat day John Henry let his hammer fall,
Lawd, Lawd, dat day John Henry let his hammer fall.

John Henry went to de tunnel,
An' dey put him in de lead to drive;
De rock so tall an' John Henry so small,
Dat he lied down his hammer an' he cried,
Lawd, Lawd, dat he lied down his hammer an' he cried.

John Henry started on de right hand,
De steam drill started on de lef'—
"Before I'd let dis steam drill beat me down,
I'd hammer my fool self to death,
Lawd, Lawd, I'd hammer my fool self to death."

White man tol' John Henry,
"Nigger, damn yo' soul,
You might beat dis steam an' drill of mine,
When de rocks in dis mountain turn to gol',
Lawd, Lawd, when de rocks in dis mountain turn to gol'."

John Henry said to his shaker,
"Nigger, why don' you sing?
I'm throwin' twelve poun's from my hips on down,
Jes' listen to de col' steel ring,
Lawd, Lawd, jes' listen to de col' steel ring."

Oh, de captain said to John Henry,
"I b'lieve this mountain's sinkin' in."
John Henry said to his captain, oh my!
"Ain' nothin' but my hammer suckin' win',
Lawd, Lawd, ain' nothin' but my hammer suckin' win'."

John Henry tol' his shaker,
"Shaker, you better pray,
For, if I miss dis six-foot steel,
Tomorrow'll be yo' buryin' day,
Lawd, Lawd, tomorrow'll be yo' buryin' day."

John Henry tol' his captain,
"Looka yonder what I see—
Yo' drill's done broke an' yo' hole's done choke,
An' you cain' drive steel like me,
Lawd, Lawd, an' you cain' drive steel like me."

De man dat invented de steam drill,
Thought he was mighty fine.
John Henry drove his fifteen feet,
An' de steam drill only made nine,
Lawd, Lawd, an' de steam drill only made nine.

De hammer dat John Henry swung,
It weighed over nine pound;
He broke a rib in his lef'-han' side,
An' his intrels fell on de groun',
Lawd, Lawd, an' his intrels fell on de groun'.

John Henry was hammerin' on de mountain,
An' his hammer was strikin' fire,
He drove so hard till he broke his pore heart,
An' he lied down his hammer an' he died,
Lawd, Lawd, he lied down his hammer an' he died.

All de womens in de Wes',
When dey heared of John Henry's death,
Stood in de rain, flagged de eas'-boun' train,
Goin' where John Henry fell dead,
Lawd, Lawd, goin' where John Henry fell dead.

John Henry's lil mother,
She was all dressed in red,
She jumped in bed, covered up her head,
Said she didn' know her son was dead,
Lawd, Lawd, didn' know her son was dead.

John Henry had a pretty lil woman,
An' de dress she wo' was blue,
An' de las' words she said to him:
"John Henry, I've been true to you,
Lawd, Lawd, John Henry, I've been true to you."

"Oh, who's gonna shoe yo' lil feetses,
An' who's gonna glub yo' han's,
An' who's gonna kiss yo' rosy, rosy lips,
An' who's gonna be yo' man,
Lawd, Lawd, an' who's gonna be yo' man?"

"Oh, my mama's gonna shoe my lil feetses,
An' my papa's gonna glub my lil han's,

An' my sister's gonna kiss my rosy, rosy lips,
An' I don' need no man,
Lawd, Lawd, an' I don' need no man."

Dey took John Henry to de graveyard,
An' dey buried him in de san',
An' every locomotive come roarin' by,
Says, "Dere lays a steel-drivin' man,
Lawd, Lawd, dere lays a steel-drivin' man."

Casey Jones

Some folks say Casey Jones can't run,
Stop and listen what Casey done,
He left Memphis at a quarter to nine,
Made Newport News 'fore dinner time,
'Fore dinner time, 'fore dinner time,
Made Newport News 'fore dinner time.

Casey Jones, before he died,
Fixed the blinds so the bums couldn' ride.
"If they ride, gotta ride the rod,
Trust their life in the hands of God.
In the hands of God, the hands of God,
Trust their life in the hands of God."

There was a woman named Alice Fly,
Said, "I'm gonna ride with Mister Casey or die,
I ain't good lookin' but I takes my time,
I'm a ramblin' woman with a ramblin' mind,
With a ramblin' mind," etc.

Early one mornin', 'bout four o'clock,
Told his fireman, "Get the boiler hot,
All I need's a little water and coal,

"Casey Jones" in Alan Lomax, ed., The Penguin Book of American Folk Songs (Baltimore, Penguin Books, 1964), 127.

Peep out my window, see the drivers roll,
See the drivers roll," *etc.*

He looked at his watch and his watch was slow,
He looked at the water and the water was low.
But the people all knew by the engine's moan,
That the man at the throttle was Casey Jones,
Was Casey Jones, *etc.*

When he come within a mile of the place,
Old Number Four stared him right in the face.
Told his fireman, "Just keep your seat and ride,
It's a double track road, running side by side,
Runnin' side by side," *etc.*

You ought to been there to see the sight,
Screamin' an' cryin', both coloured and white,
And I was a witness for the fact,
They flagged Mister Casey, but he never looked back,
But he never looked back, *etc.*

"Mama, mama, have you heard the news,
Pape got killed on the C. B. and Qs"
"Quit cryin' children, and don't do that,
You've got another papa on the same durn track,
On the same durn track," *etc.*

Paul Bunyan and His Big Blue Ox

Babe, the big blue ox constituted Paul Bunyan's assets and liabilities. History disagrees as to when, where and how Paul first acquired this bovine locomotive but his subsequent record is reliably established. Babe could pull anything that had two ends to it.

* The Cincinnati, Burlington, and Quincy Railroad.

W. B. Laughead, ed., *Paul Bunyan and His Big Blue Ox* (Westwood, Calif., Red River Lumber Co., 1940), 7, 14, 15, 28, 29, 36.

Babe was seven axehandles wide between the eyes according to some authorities; others equally dependable say forty-two axehandles and a plug of tobacco. Like other historical contradictions this comes from using different standards. Seven of Paul's axehandles were equal to a little more than forty-two of the ordinary kind.

When cost sheets were figured on Babe, Johnny Inkslinger found that upkeep and overhead were expensive but the charges for operation and depreciation were low and the efficiency was very high. How else could Paul have hauled logs to the landing a whole section (640 acres) at a time? He also used Babe to pull the kinks out of the crooked logging roads and it was on a job of this kind that Babe pulled a chain of three-inch links out into a straight bar.

They could never keep Babe more than one night at a camp for he would eat in one day all the feed one crew could tote to camp in a year. For a snack between meals he would eat fifty bales of hay, wire and all and six men with picaroons were kept busy picking the wire out of his teeth. Babe was a great pet and very docile as a general thing but he seemed to have a sense of humor and frequently got into mischief. He would sneak up behind a drive and drink all the water out of the river, leaving the logs high and dry. It was impossible to build an ox-sling big enough to hoist Babe off the ground for shoeing, but after they logged off Dakota there was room for Babe to lie down for this operation.

Once in a while Babe would run away and be gone all day roaming all over the Northwestern country. His tracks were so far apart that it was impossible to follow him and so deep that a man falling into one could only be hauled out with difficulty and a long rope. Once a settler and his wife and baby fell into one of these tracks and the son got out when he was fifty-seven years old and reported the accident. These tracks, today form the thousands of lakes in the "Land of the Sky-Blue Water."

When Paul invented logging he had to invent all the tools and figure out all his own methods. There were no precedents. At the start his outfit consisted of Babe and his big axe.

No two logging jobs can be handled exactly the same way so Paul adapted his operations to local conditions. In the mountains he used Babe to pull the kinks out of the crooked logging roads; on the Big Onion he began the system of hauling a section of land at a time to the landings and in North Dakota he used the Seven Axemen.

At that time marking logs was not thought of, Paul had no need for identification when there were no logs but his own. About the time he started the Atlantic Ocean drive others had come into the industry and although their combined cut was insignificant compared to Paul's, there was danger of confusion, and Paul had most to lose.

At first Paul marked his logs by pinching a piece out of each log. When his cut grew so large that the markings had to be detailed to the crews, the "scalp" on each log was put on with an axe, for even in those days not every man could nip out the chunk with his fingers.

The Grindstone was invented by Paul the winter he logged off North Dakota. Before that Paul's axemen had to sharpen their axes by rolling rocks down hill and running along side of them. When they got to "Big Dick" as the lumberjacks called Dakota, hills and rocks were so hard to find that Paul rigged up the revolving rock.

This was much appreciated by the Seven Axemen as it enabled them to grind an axe in a week, but the grindstone was not much of a hit with the Little Chore Boy whose job it was to turn it. The first stone was so big that working at full speed, every time it turned around once it was payday.

The Little Chore Boy led a strenuous life. He was only a kid and like all youngsters putting in their first winter in the woods, he was put over the jumps by the old-timers. His regular work was heavy enough, splitting all the wood for the camp, carrying water and packing lunch to the men, but his hazers sent him on all kinds of wild goose errands to all parts of the works, looking for a "left-handed peavy" or a "bundle of cross-hauls."

He had to take a lot of good natured roughneck wit about his size for he only weighed 800 pounds and a couple of surcingles made a belt for him. What he lacked in size he made up in grit and the men secretly respected his gameness. They said he might make a pretty good man if he ever got any growth, and considered it a necessary education to give him a lot of extra chores.

Often in the evening, after his day's work and long hours put in turning the grindstone and keeping up fires in the camp stoves—that required four cords of wood apiece to kindle a fire, he could be found with one of Big Ole's small 600-pound anvils in his lap pegging up shoes with railroad spikes.

It was a long time before they solved the problem of turning logging sleds around in the road. When a sled returned from the landing and put on a load they had to wait until Paul came along to pick up the four horses and the load and head them the other way. Judson M. Goss says he worked for Paul the winter he invented the round turn.

All of Paul's inventions were successful except when he decided to run three ten-hour shifts a day and installed the Aurora Borealis. After a number of trials the plan was abandoned because the lights were not dependable.

It is no picnic to tackle the wilderness and turn the very forest itself into a commercial commodity delivered at the market. A logger needs plenty of brains and back bone.

Paul Bunyan had his setbacks the same as every logger only his were worse. Being a pioneer he had to invent all his stuff as he went along. Many a time his plans were upset by the mistakes of some swivel-headed strawboss or incompetent foreman. The winter of the blue snow, Shot Gunderson had charge in the Big Tadpole River country. He landed all of his logs in a lake and in the spring when ready to drive he boomed the logs three times around the lake before he discovered there was no outlet to it. High hills surrounded the lake and the drivable stream was ten miles away. Apparently the logs were a total loss.

Then Paul came on the job himself and got busy. Calling in Sourdough Sam, the cook who made everything but coffee out of sourdough, he ordered him to mix enough sourdough to fill the big watertank. Hitching Babe to the tank he hauled it over and dumped it into the lake. When it "riz," as Sam said, a mighty lava-like stream poured forth and carried the logs over the hills to the river. There is a landlocked lake in Northern Minnesota that is called "Sourdough Lake" to this day.

Chris Crosshaul was a careless cuss. He took a big drive down the Mississippi for Paul and when the logs were delivered in the New Orleans boom it was found that he had driven the wrong logs. The owners looked at the barkmarks and refused to accept them. It was up to Paul to drive them back upstream.

No one but Paul Bunyan would ever tackle a job like that. To drive logs upstream is impossible, but if you think a little thing like an impossibility could stop him, you don't know Paul Bunyan. He simply fed Babe a good big salt ration and drove him to the upper Mississippi to drink. Babe drank the river dry and sucked all the water upstream. The logs came up river faster than they went down.

Big Ole was the Blacksmith at Paul's headquarters camp on the Big Onion. Ole had a cranky disposition but he was a skilled workman. No job in iron or steel was too big or too difficult for him. One of the cooks used to make doughnuts and have Ole punch the holes. He made the griddle on which Big Joe cast his pancakes and the dinner horn that blew down ten acres of pine. Ole was the only man who could shoe Babe or Benny. Every time he made a set of shoes for Babe they had to open up another Minnesota iron mine. Ole once carried a pair of these shoes a mile and sunk knee deep into solid rock at every step. Babe cast a shoe while making a hard pull one day, and it was hurled for a mile and tore down forty acres of pine and injured eight Swedes that were swamping out skidways. Ole was also a mechanic and built the Downcutter, a rig like a mowing machine that cut down a swath of trees 500 feet wide.

In the early days, whenever Paul Bunyan was broke between logging seasons, he travelled around like other lumberjacks doing any kind of pioneering work he could find. He showed up in Washington about the time The Puget Construction Co. was building Puget Sound and Billy Puget was making records moving dirt with droves of dirt throwing badgers. Paul and Billy got into an argument over who had shovelled the most. Paul got mad and said he'd show Billy Puget and started to throw dirt back again. Before Billy stopped him he had piled up the San Juan Islands.

When Paul Bunyan took up efficiency engineering he went at the job with all his customary thoroughness. He did not fool around clocking the crew with a stop watch, counting motions and deducting the ones used for borrowing chews, going for drinks, dodging the boss and preparing for quitting time. He decided to cut out labor altogether.

"What's the use," said Paul, "of all this sawing, swamping, skidding, decking, grading and icing roads, loading, hauling and landing? The object of the game is to get the trees to the landing, aint it? Well, why not do it and get it off your mind?"

So he hitched Babe to a section of land and snaked in the whole 640 acres at one drag. At the landing the trees were cut off just like shearing a sheep and the denuded section hauled back to its original place. This simplified matters and made the work a lot easier. Six trips a day, six days a week just cleaned up a township for section 37 was never hauled back to the woods on Saturday night but was left on the landing to wash away in the early spring when the drive went out.

Documentary evidence of the truth of this is offered by the United States government surveys. Look at any map that shows the land subdivisions and you will never find a township with more than thirty-six sections.

Selected Bibliography

Baur, John I. H. *Revolution and Tradition in Modern American Art.* Cambridge, Mass., Harvard University Press, 1951.

Bourke, Paul Francis. "Culture and the Status of Politics, 1909–1917: Studies in the Social Criticism of Herbert Croly, Walter Lippmann, Randolph Bourne, and Van Wyck Brooks." Ph.D. dissertation. Madison, University of Wisconsin, 1967.

Brooks, Van Wyck. *The Confident Years: 1885–1915.* New York, Dutton, 1952.

Brown, Milton W. *American Painting from the Armory Show to the Depression.* Princeton, Princeton University Press, 1955.

——. *The Story of the Armory Show.* Greenwich, Conn., New York Graphic Society, 1963.

Cady, Edwin H. " 'The Strenuous Life' as a Theme in American Cultural History," in Ray B. Browne, Donald M. Winkelman, and Allen Hayman, eds., *New Voices in American Studies.* West Lafayette, Indiana, Purdue University Studies, 1966. Pp. 59–66.

Dolmetsch, Carl R. *The Smart Set: A History and Anthology.* New York, Dial Press, 1966.

Dulles, Foster Rhea. *A History of Recreation.* New York, Appleton, Century, and Crofts, 1965. 2nd ed.

Ewen, David. *Panorama of American Popular Music.* Englewood Cliffs, N.J., Prentice-Hall, 1957.

Ginger, Ray. *Age of Excess: The United States from 1877 to 1914.* New York, Macmillan, 1965.

Goodrich, Lloyd. *John Sloan.* New York, Macmillan, 1952.

Hays, Samuel P. *Conservation and the Gospel of Efficiency: The Progressive Conservation Movement, 1890–1920.* Cambridge, Mass., Harvard University Press, 1959.

Hoffman, Frederick J., Charles Allen, and Carolyn F. Ulrich. *The Little Magazines*. Princeton, N.J., Princeton University Press, 1946.

Jones, Howard Mumford. *The Bright Medusa*. Urbana, University of Illinois Press, 1952.

Kouwenhoven, John A. *The Arts in Modern American Civilization*. New York, W. W. Norton & Co., Inc., 1967. Norton ed.

Larkin, Oliver W. *Art and Life in America*. New York, Holt, Rinehart and Winston, 1960. Rev. ed.

Lerner, Max. *America as a Civilization*. New York, Simon & Schuster, 1957.

Lord, Walter. *The Good Years: From 1900 to the First World War*. New York, Harper, 1960.

Macgowan, Kenneth. *Behind the Screen: The History and Techniques of the Motion Picture*. New York, Delacorte Press, 1965.

Manson, Grant C. *Frank Lloyd Wright*. New York, Reinhold, 1958.

May, Henry F. *The End of American Innocence: A Study of the First Years of Our Own Time, 1912–1917*. New York, Alfred Knopf, 1959.

McGovern, James R. "David Graham Phillips and the Virility Impulse of Progressives," *New England Quarterly*, Vol. 39, September, 1966, pp. 334–355.

Morgan, Charles H. *George Bellows: Painter of America*. New York, Regnal, 1965.

Morris, Lloyd R. *Not So Long Ago*. New York, Random House, 1949.

——. *Postscript to Yesterday: America, the Last Fifty Years*. New York, Random House, 1947.

Morrison, Hugh S. *Louis Sullivan: Prophet of Modern Architecture*. New York, W. W. Norton & Co., Inc., 1963. Norton ed.

Nash, Roderick. "The American Cult of the Primitive," *American Quarterly*, Vol. 18, Fall, 1966, pp. 517–537.

——. *Wilderness and the American Mind*. New Haven, Yale University Press, 1967.

Rae, John B. *The Early American Automobile: A Brief History*. Chicago, University of Chicago Press, 1965.

Sacks, Claire. "The *Seven Arts* Critics: A Study of Cultural Nationalism in America, 1910–1930." Ph.D. dissertation. Madison, University of Wisconsin, 1955.

Seldes, Gilbert. *The Seven Lively Arts*. New York, Sagamore Press, 1957. Rev. ed.

Sullivan, Mark. *Our Times: The United States, 1900–1925*. Vols. I–V. New York, Charles Scribner's Sons, 1926–1935.

Time-Life Books. *This Fabulous Century: Sixty Years of American Life,* Vol. I: 1900–1910, Vol. II: 1910–1920. New York, 1969.

Wagenknecht, Edward. *The Movies in the Age of Innocence.* Norman, University of Oklahoma Press, 1962.

White, Morton G. *Social Thought in America: The Revolt Against Formalism.* Boston, Beacon Press, 1957. Rev. ed.

Wiebe, Robert H. *The Search for Order, 1877–1920.* New York, Hill and Wang, 1967.